Performing Media Activism in the Digital Age

Neil Alperstein

Performing Media Activism in the Digital Age

palgrave
macmillan

Neil Alperstein
Communication Department
Loyola University Maryland
Baltimore, MD, USA

ISBN 978-3-030-73803-7   ISBN 978-3-030-73804-4 (eBook)
https://doi.org/10.1007/978-3-030-73804-4

This Palgrave Macmillan imprint is published by the registered company Springer Nature Switzerland AG.
The registered company address is: Gewerbestrasse 11, 6330 Cham, Switzerland

Preface

"Power concedes nothing without a demand. It never did and it never will."
Frederick Douglass (1857)

There has been a surge in social and political movements in the last few years, the likes of which we have not seen before, in some cases leading to the toppling of government leaders in Sudan, Algeria, Puerto Rico, Iraq, Lebanon, Bolivia, Chile, Hong Kong, and India. In the United States social movements have emerged in support of a long list of issues including police brutality and racial justice, immigration justice, gun control, women's rights, climate change, LGBTQ rights, and protests against the then president Donald Trump's policies and practices. In 2021 the world faces a confluence of pandemic and protest. Many of us thought that protests would be different in the time of COVID-19. After all, who would go into the streets and risk exposure to the virus? It was anticipated that conventional forms of protest would move online, but in practice that didn't happen or at least not to the extent that many people thought. Yes, the fact that many people were confined to their homes meant they were likely spending more time on the internet and in that engaged in social media. The more time people spend on social media, the likelihood of raising their awareness of injustices. Social media helped to create hot button issues, and beyond expressing their thoughts and feelings on social media platforms, people despite the risk of catching the COVID-19 virus still took to the streets, and movements brought forth a more diverse audience that extended beyond the borders of United States to see activism, both online and in-person, on racial injustice and police brutality in many parts of the world.

The 2019 brutal killing of George Floyd by a Minneapolis police officer was recorded on a bystander's mobile phone and broadcast across the planet through social media as well as mainstream news media, which led, undaunted by the COVID-19 virus, to in-person protestors some donning masks, some not, raising their voices to shout Black Lives Matter throughout much of the world. While social action requires activism and vigorous efforts both online and in-person in order to create social change, what we would like to see, long term, is structural change and that requires advocacy. Ultimately, as social movements progress through stages of development, the central idea is to transform ideas, sometimes radical, into pragmatic solutions.

Thinking back to the seminal moment in 2011 when social media fueled the Arab Spring, first in Tunisia and shortly thereafter in Egypt, many people thought that the use of digital media platforms would transform the world and ordinary people could command the world's attention through the use of their digital devices. But we know that despite great hope the Arab Spring has sadly turned to the Arab Winter. While social media did not turn out to be a panacea for social causes regarding political or racial injustice, economic inequality, climate change, and gender bias, digital platforms have become part of the routine practices of social movements. In other words, you can't have a social movement today without the use of digital media platforms, even if the intent is to bring people to the streets. Digital platforms are necessary to get people invested enough in a cause to rise up in protest. Having said that, there will always be the category of slacktivists who are satisfied to press the like button to express their emotions on a social issue. Various digital media platforms are used by individuals on the political right and left who took on the role of emergent leaders but also governments, NGOs, and mainstream news media, as well as fake accounts and bots play an important role in the attempt to nudge people in a particular direction.

This book is about performing activism in the digital age, as the phrase is intended to signify that activism through the use of digital media platforms is a virtual stage of negotiation; and the focus is on a dialectic in which individuals perform complicated rituals on digital media platforms within the complexity of communities, clusters, and niches representing those social networks that are made up of individuals, governments, organizations, and news media engaged in a social or political movement or issue. In that sense, this book is not about media activism but rather about individual and group performance that is mediated through digital platforms. The concept of performing media activism draws from Erving Goffman's theory of performance based on the idea that whenever people interact with one another, they are putting on a performance and that it is an act meant to position one's self within a social network. Social media platforms are an ideal space in which to see performing media activism at work. The approach taken in this book begins with the idea that social media platforms are conflictual space, not the like-minded communities that we might imagine. As such, conflict is inherently dramatic, which leads to the concept of performance. That drama takes many forms from tweets, to selfies, to livestreamed videos that not only declare the poster's position—their self-presentation—on an issue but also place that individual within a community, which may impact their social status or standing within an ideological community, a product of self-interest.

Performing activism is connected to but extends beyond public space and the moment of public gatherings to consider the more extended view of the development of a social or political movement as digital tools provide newer opportunities to advance a cause or issue. The focus of this book is on the users of various digital media platforms as they engage in social movements, civic association, and social justice-related causes and issues. *Performing Media Activism in the Digital Age* breaks new ground by focusing on the performance of communicating. While media, like traditional news outlets, may come to dominate information dissemination regarding a social or political issue, this is not necessarily the case, as special interest groups as well as celebrities along with ordinary individuals can engage on the highest levels within social media platforms like Twitter, Facebook, Reddit, YouTube, and TikTok, hence the idea that activism is performed by mediators on social networks. This book investigates the structure of social movements like #NeverAgain, #ClimateStrike, and #BlackLivesMatter in order to shed light on social networks within which those movements operate.

The book utilizes primary data extracted from social media platforms by applying a social network analysis (SNA) approach to better understand the messages being transmitted, the people, organizations, and media that are pushing their particular agendas, with an eye toward better understanding the ways in which social movements operate in a networked society. What do I mean by a social network analysis approach? A social network, which is a theoretical construct, refers to the social structure of groups and organizations engaged in a social movement and the ties between and among individuals and groups engaged in the movement, what may be referred to as mediators of the social movement. The goal of social network analysis is to identify patterns of organization such as communities, clusters, or niches, as well the SNA approach is interested in locating influence within those structures, which is of particular importance when considering social movements.

Social network analysis represents an interdisciplinary field that encompasses social psychology, sociology, as well as graph theory, which should suggest this book will be of interest to scholars and students in these and related fields. Sociologists have been studying social networks as sociograms dating back to the 1930s, and the term, "social network" itself, has been in use for more than 100 years. In contemporary society, social network analysis represents a paradigm shift as analytical and data visualization tools can be applied in an interdisciplinary manner. Researchers now have the means to access (scape) data through the APIs (application programming interfaces) of various social media platforms. By combining data science and sociology or cultural anthropology, such an approach provides the means to visualize networks of individuals and organizations engaged in a social movement, to see how movements are organized (structured) into communities, clusters, and niches, and to visualize power structures within social movements to see who is influencing a network over extended periods of time. Furthermore, SNA provides the tools to look at sentiment being expressed in the movement, as language is expressed in positive or negative directions on social media platforms. By viewing the interactions of those engaged in social movements, for example, in the form of tweets, Reddit posts, or YouTube comments, and importantly the associated sentiment expressed in those tweets, comments, likes, and similar forms of engagement, readers can see how individuals are interacting with one another in what may be described as connective action. In this way, the focus isn't so much on the means of communicating but the performance of communicating. Indeed, that is the orientation of this book that communication in the digital age is a performance. By investigating social movements through interactivity of those engaged on digital platforms, we can better understand the role that performing activism plays in the digital age.

Chapter 1 serves as an introduction to the theoretical framework of mediated networks, and it serves as a review of some key social movements, including the Torches of Freedom march in 1929 and its use of the "engineering of consent" as historical background. The chapter begins with Blumer's four stages of social movements and extends his work to consider an alternative model. Cyberconflict theory is introduced, and it is explored through the theories of collective and connective action; the latter is of importance as the focus of this chapter is on uses of digital media among those individuals who engage in social movements, what I call mediated social connections. The chapter conceptualizes publics as individuals that come together around an issue, not based merely on demographics, and situational theory provides the underpinning of the complexity of those engaged in a social movement based on their situational orientation toward an issue. Online audiences are diffuse, and participation in a movement is discretionary, as situational theory suggests levels of engagement are variable, operating on a continuum. The concept of mediated social connections, therefore, views digitally based social movements as complex, including individuals connected through strong or weak ties, those operating at the periphery or the center of a movement, and those individuals that form clusters or niches within the larger network.

When conceptualizing a social movement in the digital age, what comes to mind? In other words, what do you imagine such a community would look like? Many of us would immediately think of like-minded people getting together online to consider issues, share information, and bond with others. After all, if you look at a rally like the March for Our Lives, the expectation is that everyone shares the same values when it comes to gun control and related issues. Castells, in his book *Networks of Outrage and Hope*, describes such relationships between digital media and social movements as "networked social movements" which are centralized in ways that newer communication technologies liberate people creating autonomy that regains power and leads to social change. However, when one observes the online interactions of a social movement, perhaps on Twitter, Facebook, or Instagram, one may see a very different picture, as mixed with tweets, retweets, and posts appropriate to the respective platforms that on the surface may seem homophilic, are dissenters, detractors, and those that seek to denigrate the social movement. In other words, the community that we imagined may in reality not be the community that operates in the online environment. Beyond the interactions that may be an expression of sentiment—positive, negative, or neutral—in social networks are those individuals who play various roles as mediators of the online movement, which may include authority figures, but may include influencers who merely by virtue of their large number of followers or even the number of tweets that they post or get retweeted have the potential—even though their connections to the movement may be weak—to influence the network connections. Chapter 2 presents the social network approach (SNA) to social movements in the digital age. The chapter discusses virtual communities including the social structure of networks. In addition, it delves into issues regarding social capital as well as mediators of social movements and the role of strong and weak ties in the network. The chapter introduces network measures and applies them in a case study of the March for Our Lives social movement.

As this book is primarily concerned with performing media activism, the focus of Chap. 3 is on those individuals that serve as mediators in the social network. The chapter goes beyond traditional views of opinion leadership to consider how bonafide celebrities, authority figures, and other media figures serve as influencers who play a key role in drawing attention to an issue or cause in both traditional and digital media. Also considered are those individuals who for various reasons are thrust into the spotlight and take on a role of key mediator who become what may be referred to as microcelebrities. In conceptualizing influence, the chapter considers the concepts of multi-step flow and social capital as related to opinion leadership, more apropos to the digital age. As an exemplar of solo protester and microcelebrity influencer, the case study developed for this chapter centers on Greta Thunberg, a champion of the global Climate Strike movement.

There are different ways to characterize social movements ranging from redemptive to revolutionary. The goals of different movements may seek minimal change or maximum social change for individuals or for society at large. Contentious politics are likely at the base of some social movements as they consider conflictual issues. Chapter 4 explores pockets of resistance in social movements, most likely in the form of anti- or countermovements, like gun control, for instance. It is such social movements that social norms are likely to collide—gun owners and those who see themselves as protectors of the Second Amendment to the US Constitution versus victims of gun violence. Vaccine resistance is a particular area of contentious politics, as myths and conspiracies have swirled around the issue of vaccines long before there was a COVID-19 pandemic. Vaccine hesitancy and resistance plays out on social media platforms where groups, like the Vaccine Resistance Movement on Facebook, play against vaccine advocates. The case study in this chapter takes a look at the Vaxxhappens subreddit with a particular focus on levels of toxic discourse in the posts and comments.

Social justice, the topic in Chap. 5, considers the plight of those people whose human rights and freedoms have been curtailed, who have received inequitable treatment with regard to opportunities and resources and are discriminated against because of their class, gender, race, or sexual orientation. This chapter explores issues of social justice and data activism. For migrant communities and refugees in Europe and elsewhere, border policing, asylum processes, and access to welfare are key issues related to social justice. Datafication plays a role in countries like Bolivia, for example, where a process of "data colonialism" can be seen at work. In response to concerns about the unjust uses, data activism has emerged to fight against the use of human life as a resource. Much of the issue surrounds the use of algorithms and associated machine learning that include inherent biases and data inequities. The case study in this chapter tracks the trending hashtag #GeorgeFloyd as a matter of social injustice and its impact on the Black Lives Matter movement.

Most people do not realize when they engage online as activists that they leave a digital footprint, or as it is sometimes referred to as digital dust, which raises the question taken up in Chap. 6 as to where the boundaries are regarding public safety and privacy. When the government or a corporation harvests an individual's data, they are not necessarily doing so with "informed consent." Therefore, if the US National Security Agency (NSA) collects phone and surveillance data, what are the rights of individuals that want to protest such intrusions? Privacy is treated differently in the US and Europe, where in the latter privacy is conceived of as a right rather than a privilege. Recent GDPR regulations in Europe have begun to require websites to ask for consent, but to date apps are under no such requirement. In other words, there are no overriding ethic governing digital technologies. Nor is there a governing ethic regarding the use of artificial intelligence that over time seems to develop a life of its own without ever knowing, as a result of machine learning, who the original author is of the algorithm. This, too, raises ethical concerns regarding the use of such data by governments and corporations. The chapter extends the topic to consider the ethical role of researchers who are interested in studying social movements who have to gauge the distance between being observers of or participants in a movement. The chapter concludes with a case study of disability rights on digital media with a focus on accessibility and inclusiveness of digital media platforms.

With a focus on the future, Chap. 7 takes a critical look at performing media activism in light of the evolving role technology plays in everyday life in the developed as well as the developing world. The focus of this chapter is on the growing network of platforms that continue to splinter the audience. When nascent platforms emerge, they tend to attract like-minded people and, therefore, create echo chambers where disseminating news and information is void of dissenting views. Beyond the technologies, where younger generations from Millennials to GenZ have lost faith in institutions, it becomes that social movements will in the future take a different form, as institutionalization, the end of the four stages of social movement development, no longer provides a likely outcome. As autonomous individuals replace institutions with self-reliance, significant shifts take place in the stages of social movement development. This means that there will be more social movements, shorter-term social movements, and less "sticky" ideas tied to newer forms of mediated civic engagement. Media in the digital age of social movements provides a platform by which individuals can engage in various ways without commitment and in that without getting their proverbial hands dirty, as social movements become more virtual, posts more performative, the actual event perhaps serving as a spectacle. The distrust of institutions is fueled by the proliferation of technologies that allow operatives to "game" the system, including algorithms that push content to the top of search or the more than 40 million bots operating on Twitter. According to a report by the Ford Foundation, "In fact, 62 percent of all Internet traffic is made up of programs acting on their own to analyze information, find vulnerabilities, or spread messages." If we start from the present state of slacktivism, what can we expect from a future in which my bot is talking to your bot? Of course, not all bots are bad, as they can be a useful means to elevate stories, for example. But bots are just the tip of the proverbial iceberg, as newer forms of AI emerge in the coming years and as societies continue to grapple with issues concerning privacy as they are related to the datafication of society as well as deep fakes where images operate within a hyperreal media environment.

Performing Media Activism in the Digital Age concludes with a description of particular social media analytic tools utilized for research in this book. A description of social network analysis tools, including Gephi, Netlytic, Communalytic, and YouTube Data Tools are provided, along with a discussion of the applicability of each to studying mediated social connections.

As I complete the manuscript for this book, I realize that writing it could go on for the foreseeable future, as social and political issues feel like they are coming fast and furious. There was an insurrection at the US Capitol that threatened to put an end to democratic elections. There were massive protests, at least by Russian standards, over the arrest of Putin political opponent, Alexei Navalny. The #MeToo movement in France took up the issue of incest with a new hashtag, #Metooincest. And farmers in India are protesting new taxes being levied against their crops with celebrities like pop singer Rihanna, climate activist Greta Thunberg, and the vice president of the United States' niece Meena Harris offering their digital support and amplifying the cause to a worldwide audience. I could go on, but I think you get the point: vying for attention is the basis for performing media activism.

Performing media activism in the digital age is ultimately about attention. After all we live in what has been described as an attention economy, so it stands to reason that if an individual or group wants to gain people's attention and perhaps sustain it—no matter how difficult that may be given the proclivities of digital media—one has to perform to a high degree. By performing to a high degree, I'm referring to amplification, perhaps strategic amplification. If you want to perform media activism in the digital age, you have to amp up your performance, based on who can scream the loudest or act in the most outrageous manner. This contention is based on the truism: Those individuals or groups who can gain enough attention on digital platforms and through mainstream media can through strategic amplification accumulate enough power to effect social change. In this instance, social change can mean a lot of things. It may simply refer to heightened awareness about an issue, and it might mean bringing more people into the fold with varying levels of commitment to the cause. And it may mean turning passive participants, what we might call slacktivists, into activists who, well, might perform media activism in their own right in the form of selfies or videos, perhaps more performative than performance. If the attention that an issue gains through performance is the lens through which to understand the events of the moment, then not only do we need to become more discerning in what media content we choose to consume but also we need to be cognizant of what content we are all putting out there in the digital media ecosystem.

Baltimore, MD Neil Alperstein

Acknowledgments

It is an extraordinary time in history to be writing a book about social movements. Who could have anticipated the convergence of a worldwide pandemic and social and political upheaval? Personally I've pretty much been in proverbial lockdown for many months, and it has given me a perch from which to, at a distance, follow the horrors of police brutally in many parts of the world, social injustice, the effects of climate change, among other social, political, environmental, and economic issues put before us. And because my work involves researching how people respond to injustices in many parts of the world, I have observed in some instances how some activists have torn themselves from their own isolation and digital protesting to risk their lives to support the Black Lives Matter movement in-person to name just one example. And midway through 2020, as the pandemic continued to rage, especially in my home country where we lead the world in COVID-19-related deaths, we lost a great leader of the civil rights movement in Congressman John Lewis. By the time 2020 ended, there was an insurrection to overthrow a duly elected US government. All of these issues and events, and more, continue to spur my interest in social and political movements, especially as many take place across digital media platforms or in a more hybrid form. While I may have spent a good deal of time in isolation, this book is the product of thoughtful collaboration. Although I would describe myself as a tinkerer, one cannot learn how to utilize new technologies by YouTube alone, so I am particularly indebted to my colleague Dr. Paola Pascual-Ferra with whom I have collaborated over the past two years on projects utilizing these social network analytic tools used in this book. We have both learned much about this relatively new way of extracting, analyzing, and visualizing data from social media platforms, as historically this has not been the domain of social scientists or humanities scholars. Along with my colleague Paola Pascual-Ferra, an exceptional opportunity arose to work on COVID-19-related digital media research projects with researchers from the Johns Hopkins University Bloomberg School of Public Health, Dr. Daniel Barnett and Dr. Rajiv Rimal. I am eternally indebted to Dr. Elliot King of Loyola University Maryland with whom I founded the University's Emerging Media graduate program. It was in developing curriculum for that program that I created courses in social network analysis (SNA). I am particularly thankful to have worked with my graduate student Tina Jones with whom I coauthored an SNA study of the March for Our Lives social movement. Although I have been awarded emeritus status at the university where I have taught for more than three decades, I continue to reflect on my wonderful colleagues in the Department of Communication at Loyola University. I thank you for all your support. Most important to me is my family, who keep me motivated to continue to seek creative ways to explore our culture and society. For Joshua, Jessica, Gabriel, Spencer, Joey, Teddy, and most specially my wife Nancy, I do this all for you and for the future of a better world. At Palgrave Macmillan, I am thankful to Camille Davies, Editor Cultural, Media, and Communication Studies, with whom I worked on this and my previous book *Celebrity and Mediated Social Connections*. Camille shepherded this book through the review process. And I am thankful to the reviewers of this project, who provided important insights and helped me develop a theoretical framework for the book. This book has benefited greatly from the work of the production team at SPi Content Solutions, SPi Global, and in particular I want to thank Project Manager Mary Amala Divya Suresh and G. Nirmal Kumar of the Palgrave team. While many people forecasted that because of the pandemic social movements would move online, that prediction has not come to fruition. But digital media continue to play an important role in the development of social movements throughout the world. Hopefully, one day soon the effects of the pandemic will subside, but I don't think the use of digital technologies will diminish. To that end, I believe that people will continue to find new and creative ways to perform media activism as they engage in social movements and the causes for which they hold deep beliefs.

Contents

1 **Introduction: Performing in Mediated Networks in the Digital Age** 1
What Is a Social Movement? 2
Blumer's Four Stages of Social Movements 5
Activists and Powerholders 7
New Social Movement Theory 8
Cyberconflict Theory 9
Torches of Freedom 13
Digital Media and New Social Movements 15
Patterns of Action 17
Imagined Communities 21
Participatory Culture 22
The Role of Spectacle 24
Networked Individualism 26
Situational Theory and Publics 29
Toward a Theory of Mediated Networks 32
Conclusion 33

2 **A Social Network Approach to Analyzing Social Movements** 41
Social Movements as Virtual Communities 42
Social Network Approach 45
Limited Access to Social Data 48
Network Structures 48
Online Social Capital 51

Actor Network Theory (ANT) and the Engineering of Mediators in Performing Media Activism 52
Social Network Mediators 53
Strength of Weak Ties 54
Network Characteristics 55
Case Study: #NeverAgain Hashtag—March for Our Lives Movement 57
Conclusion 69

3 Social Influencers, Content Creators, and Network Mediators in Social Movements 75
Context Collapse 76
From Two-Step to Multiple Step Flow 77
The Power of Worker Protest 80
Microcelebrities and Social Movements 82
Mediators and Moderators 84
Performative Activism 84
Up Chain and Down Chain Amplification 85
Case Study: Greta Thunberg/Climate Change 86
Link Analysis 88
Climate Crisis on Facebook 90
Social Network Analysis 96
Conclusion 100

4 Conflict and Contentiousness: Network Connections and Pockets of Resistance in Social Movements 105
Contentious Politics 108
Normative Social Behavior 109
Anti-mask Movement and Normative Social Behavior 111
Performing QAnon 114
Social Amplification: Organic and Strategic 117
Context Collapse in Social Networks 120
Categorizing Social Movements 123
The 3.5 Percent Rule 125
Case Study: Anti-vaccine Communities on Reddit 127
Toxicity Analysis 129
Social Network Analysis 133
Conclusion 137

5 **Exploring Issues of Social Justice and Data Activism: The Personal Cost of Network Connections in the Digital Age** 143
Market Making 144
Algorithms: Just Math 146
Data Inequities 149
Social Glue Versus Social Fragmentation 150
Cloud Protesting 152
Hashtag Activism 154
Platformitization 157
Case Study: Police Brutality and Social Justice 160
George Floyd Part I 160
#George Floyd on Twitter: Part II 165
Conclusion 173

6 **Issues of Social Movement Ethics, Privacy, Accessibility, and Inclusiveness in Mediated Networks** 179
What to Prevent/What to Protect 180
Cloud Ethics 184
Cloud Protesting 185
Social Movement Research: Ethics of Engagement 187
Social Movements and Corporate Responsibility 189
Case Study: Accessibility and Inclusion in Mediated Social Movements 191
Disability Influencers on YouTube 192
Disability Facebook Groups: ADAPT 196
Disability Rights on Twitter 198
Disability Influencers on Twitter 203
Conclusion 206

7 **The Present and Future of Performing Media Activism** 211
Cyberconflict and Performance 212
Changing Media Ecosystem 213
Algorithm Barons 216
Truth vs. Misinformation 217
Youth Culture and Social Movements 219
TikTok Generation 220
Virtual Protesting 222
Influence of Influencers 224

Collective Action to Connective Action to Collective Consciousness 227
Social Network Analysis Techniques and Tools 228
Netlytic (https://netlytic.org/home/) 230
Communalytic (https://communalytic.com) 230
CrowdTangle (https://help.crowdtangle.com/en/articles/4558716-understanding-and-citing-crowdtangle-data) 231
YouTube Data Tools (https://tools.digitalmethods.net/netvizz/youtube/) 231
Gephi (https://gephi.org/) 232
Media Cloud (https://mediacloud.org/) 232
Stanford Cable TV News Analyzer (https://tvnews.stanford.edu/) 232
Google Trends (https://trends.google.com/trends/?geo=US) 233
Google Books nGram Viewer (https://books.google.com/ngrams/info) 233

Index 237

List of Figures

Fig. 1.1	nGram view of key terms	5
Fig. 1.2	Christiansen's four stages of a social movement	6
Fig. 1.3	Four roles of activists	8
Fig. 1.4	Elements of connective and collective action networks. (Bennet & Segerbert, Elements of Connective and Collective Action Networks. op. cit. p. 756)	11
Fig. 1.5	Torches of freedom parade 1929. (Thesocietypages.org. (n.d.). Torches of Freedom Parade in New York, 1929. Retrieved from: https://thesocietypages.org/socimages/2012/02/27/torches-of-freedom-women-and-smoking-propaganda/comment-page-2/)	14
Fig. 1.6	Three tenets of classical liberal ideal	15
Fig. 1.7	Visualization of the Divisive Ferguson social network	19
Fig. 1.8	Three types of audiences	20
Fig. 1.9	Four categories of social media posts from the #NeverAgain movement	28
Fig. 1.10	Four types of issue oriented publics	31
Fig. 2.1	Three characteristics of virtual communities	43
Fig. 2.2	Social network of nodes (circles) and edges (lines). (Social Network Image. Retrieved from: https://www.needpix.com/photo/822467/network-social-social-networks-group.)	46
Fig. 2.3	Six types of social media networks (Pew Research)	50
Fig. 2.4	Sabatini's dimensions of social capital	51
Fig. 2.5	Top ten posters by percentage of posts to the #NeverAgain social network	59
Fig. 2.6	Ten most frequently used terms by those posting to the #NeverAgain social network	60

Fig. 2.7 These are the top ten posters mentioned in other people's tweets or retweets 61
Fig. 2.8 Network map of the name network of who is mentioning whom 66
Fig. 2.9 #NeverAgain chain network of who replies to whom 68
Fig. 3.1 Context Collapse at the intersection of personal, spectacle, and social issue 76
Fig. 3.2 Elihu Katz's dimensions of opinion leadership 78
Fig. 3.3 Qualities of opinion leaders 78
Fig. 3.4 LaBron James Tweeting in the aftermath of James Black Shooting 81
Fig. 3.5 Actress Jane Fonda supporting the climate change movement 86
Fig. 3.6 Number of Greta Thunberg Media Stories 2018–2019 88
Fig. 3.7 Network Map of Media Covering Greta Thunberg (MediaCloud.org) 91
Fig. 3.8 Types of social mediators 92
Fig. 3.9 Greta Thunberg ego network visualization 99
Fig. 4.1 The rise of the term "populism" (Google nGram) 106
Fig. 4.2 Stanford cable TV news analyzer 107
Fig. 4.3 Pro-mask wearing tweet 112
Fig. 4.4 Four reasons for mask resistance 113
Fig. 4.5 QAnon trending conspiracies on YouTube 115
Fig. 4.6 QAnon trending conspiracies on web search 116
Fig. 4.7 Models of frame alignment 118
Fig. 4.8 A simplified model of mediated engagement 119
Fig. 4.9 Aberle's four categories of social movements 124
Fig. 4.10 Vaxxhappens subreddit posts per day 130
Fig. 4.11 Vaxxhappens subreddit word cloud 130
Fig. 4.12 Top ten vaxxhappens subreddit posters 132
Fig. 4.13 Toxicity analysis summary table for r/vaxxhappens subreddit 133
Fig. 4.14 The distribution of toxicity scores for r/vaxxhappens subreddit, showing that the toxicity score for most posts is under 0.3. (*Y* axis: post count; *X* axis: toxicity score) 134
Fig. 4.15 Network visualization of r/vaxxhappens subreddit social network 136
Fig. 5.1 BlackLivesMatter hashtags used over time 155
Fig. 5.2 Social media use in Nigeria. (Statcounter.com. (October 21, 2020). Social Media Use in Nigeria. Retrieved from: https://gs.statcounter.com/social-media-stats/all/nigeria.) 156
Fig. 5.3 Number of George Floyd stories over time 162
Fig. 5.4 Top 10 themes on George Floyd news stories 163
Fig. 5.5 Top ten organizations mentioned in George Floyd news network 163

Fig. 5.6 Top names mentioned in George Floyd news stories 164
Fig. 5.7 Network map of the George Floyd media network 165
Fig. 5.8 Top ten posters on #GeorgeFloyd Twitter social network 166
Fig. 5.9 Most frequently used words in George Floyd network 167
Fig. 5.10 Top ten posters mentioned in George Floyd social network 168
Fig. 5.11 #George Floyd name network visualization 170
Fig. 5.12 #GeorgeFloyd chain network visualization 171
Fig. 6.1 Four ethics questions for social movement researchers 188
Fig. 6.2 YouTube disability influencers network 192
Fig. 6.3 Aspie World comment network map 194
Fig. 6.4 Facebook disability network 196
Fig. 6.5 Disability rights Twitter posts over time 198
Fig. 6.6 Top ten disability rights posters 199
Fig. 6.7 Disability rights Twitter name network 201
Fig. 6.8 Disability rights Twitter chain network 202
Fig. 6.9 Disability influencers posts over time 204
Fig. 6.10 Disability influencers Twitter name network 205
Fig. 6.11 Disability influencers Twitter name network (number of times name is mentioned) 206
Fig. 7.1 Most popular social media networks. (Statistica.com (n.d.). Global Social Media Users 2020. Retrieved from: https://www.statista.com/statistics/272014/global-social-networks-ranked-by-number-of-users/) 215
Fig. 7.2 Animal Crossing Video Game Used to Protest Hong Kong Government 224
Fig. 7.3 Instagram Invite to Virtual BLM Protest 225

List of Tables

Table 2.1	Tweets Expressing Positive Emotions	62
Table 2.2	Tweets expressing negative emotions	63
Table 2.3	Four categories of social media posts	64
Table 3.1	Top 10 media stories online ranked by quantity of inlinks from 2018 to 2020	89
Table 3.2	Top ten media sources online ranked by quantity of inlinks from 2018 to 2020	90
Table 3.3	Type of Mediators and Examples	93
Table 3.4	Top Facebook Pages/Groups: Interactions and Sentiment	95
Table 4.1	European populist movements	108
Table 4.2	Nine categories of anti-social acts from perspective API[a] available for analysis in Communalytic, their definitions and examples	131
Table 4.3	Number and percentage of toxic posts	132
Table 4.4	Pearson correlation analysis among perspective API scores analysis among perspective API scores	135
Table 4.5	Network-level properties and metrics for r/vaxxhappens subreddit	136
Table 6.1	Categories of YouTube video comments	195
Table 6.2	Disability network Facebook groups—total interactions	197

CHAPTER 1

Introduction: Performing in Mediated Networks in the Digital Age

Who would have ever thought that the iconic Flying Toaster Screensaver of the 1990s would have provided the financial fuel to launch a social movement like Moveon.org? But if we look back to 1998, as a result of the sale of the company that created this software, we can also see how the internet was utilized to gain signatures for an online petition to encourage legislators to "move on" from what the organizers referred to as the "Clinton impeachment mess" to deal with more important—as they saw them—issues facing the government.[1] Joan Blades and Wes Boyd, who emailed their petition to friends, learned quickly of the power of the internet as their campaign went viral. It was their very naivety that opened up the possibilities of this relatively new medium to create social change. In the process, Moveon.org, perhaps unwittingly, utilized an engineered approach, something developed many years ago, applying the techniques of marketing communication to a social movement.

Social movements have in the years since Moveon.org become more sophisticated in their use of digital media, as Black Lives Matter and Occupy Wall Street, for example, at their emergent stage of development were captured by videographers and photographers whose images were replicated across various media channels, both mainstream and alternative. These and other social and political movements were founded not only on the streets of Ferguson, Missouri, or New York City's Wall Street, but also on the internet, as memes, whether they be textual, video, or photographic, played a vital role in spreading their respective messages. The

N. Alperstein, *Performing Media Activism in the Digital Age*,
https://doi.org/10.1007/978-3-030-73804-4_1

utilization of digital media platforms represents a key change over the past 20 years in the ways social movements are conducted in the digital age, as movements today differ from those of the past in that they no longer have to solely rely on in-person protests or the mainstream media to get their messages disseminated and build their fanbase.

This chapter serves as an introduction to social movements in the digital age pointing out a number of contemporary movements, and it looks historically at the "engineering of consent" evident in the Torches of Freedom march in 1929. The chapter discusses Blumer's four stages of social movements and presents an alternative model. Cyberconflict theory is extended to consider connective action as the focus of this chapter is on the users who engage in social movements. People come together to form publics around an issue, but they do so based on their own situational orientation. Online communities, sometimes referred to as imagined communities, because their connections may be weak, but that very weakness may serve, according to theory, to strengthen their impact. Online audiences are diffuse, and participation is discretionary, as situational theory suggests levels of engagement are variable, operating on a continuum. The concept of mediated networks introduced in this chapter views digitally based social movements as complex, including individuals connected through strong or weak ties, those operating at the periphery or the center of a movement, and those individuals that engage in clusters or niches within the larger network.

What Is a Social Movement?

A social movement may be defined as an organized or perhaps disorganized opposition to some unjust—economic, political, or social—aspect of society, although Fuchs describes social movements as self-organized. Social movements go beyond mere social trends or the groups that engage in those trends. The question isn't so much about how long a social movement lasts, as movements likely follow a process from emergence to demise, the latter not referring to the end of the movement but the likely endgame of institutionalizing the movement. One way in which a digitally fueled movement, whether it is one based on images or memes or an online petition, differs from a social movement in the pre-internet era is the shift to clicktivism, which merely involves using social media or other digital platforms to support a cause or issue. As well clicktivist campaigns may employ marketing principles for use in creating communication strategies and tactics. But digitally based social movements also may extend to slacktivism, an even more pejorative way of describing passive forms of digital engagement, in which all one has to do is retweet or press the "like" button on Twitter or some other social media platform. Hodson et al., who study online communication technologies, maintain that in the case of environmental activism that slacktivism remains a concern. The researchers note that people may be willing to share information but may not be willing to put forth more of an effort to engage in initiatives. The paradox is that increased knowledge about environmental causes does not increase online engagement. This is a significant issue for those interested in studying the impact of environmental communication.[2] What does lead to increased engagement? Emotive content. Visual content. In other words, what you will read about in this chapter is, in a word, performance.

Clicktivism, slacktivism, and perhaps hacktivism comprise much of the twenty-first-century approach to digital activism; a kind of performative behavior with little effort extended, as one can, for example, protest from the comfort of one's own mobile device. There are critics and supporters on both sides of the clicktivist issue.[3] Emiliano Treré, in his book *Hybrid Media Activism*, describes contemporary activism as a hybrid of both the physical and the digital.[4] He looks at both sides of the proverbial coin through what he refers to as algorithmic power, which acknowledges the role of both authoritarianism and resistance in social movements. Hybrid media activism, he says, is not a panacea or a solution to complex social and political problems. Rather, in the digital age conditions have to align socially, politically, and culturally for change to occur. Treré investigated what he called the grammar of protest in which he describes five binaries of media hybridity: online/offline, old/new, internal/external, corporate/alternative, and human/nonhuman, the latter referring to the use of algorithms and social bots to drive either repression or resistance.[5] Starting in the mid-2000s, Treré studied the Anomalous Way student movement in Italy, the Movement for Peace and Justice and Dignity in Mexico, and later the #YoSoy132 movement also in Mexico, as well as the Five Start (5SM) political movement in Italy. He also studied the 2015 Indignados (5M) political movement in Spain. Although often attributed to digital media as a driver of these movements, Treré maintains that the media landscape is more complex in which mainstream media and social media coexist. Ultimately, he claims that the purpose of digital media is to move people from clicktivists to activists offline. We can see this play out with the Arab Spring movement of 2011 as what may have started in social media resulted in meetings at Egypt's Tahrir Square.

A unique aspect of moveon.org was the way in which the founders, tech entrepreneurs Joan Blades and Wes Boyd utilized the online petition about the Clinton impeachment in 1998 that they emailed to friends. According to the moveon.org website, "they were as surprised as everyone else when it went viral." This may have been the first time, as the website claims, that an online petition went viral; however, Micah White, a co-creator of the Occupy Wall Street movement, in his book *The End of Protest: The New Playbook of Revolution*, offers a critique of the moveon.org approach claiming its clicktivist approach borrows techniques from marketers, which he claims are devoid of substance and authenticity.[6] Such criticism is reminiscent of that attributed to Edward Bernays in the early part of the twentieth century when his public relations campaign on behalf of the United Fruit Company led to the eventual overthrow of the Guatemalan government. White argues that Moveon.org's founders embodied three qualities that enabled them to foster this movement: they were wealthy because of the sale of a company they founded; they were politically quite liberal; and, they were tech savvy.[7] The ability to utilize their marketing and technology skills and having deep pockets became "heralded as the model for twenty-first-century activism."[8]

This book is about performing media activism, as the concept is intended to signify that activism through the use of digital media platforms is a virtual space of negotiation, a dialectic in which users of social networks perform complicated rituals within the complexity of clusters or niches representing those engaged in a social or political movement. Mediated networks are connected to but extend beyond physical space and the moment of public gathering to consider the more extended view of the development of a social or political movement as newer digital tools provide increased opportunity to advance and sustain a cause or issue. The theoretical approach looks beyond the role of mainstream news media within the social movement but rather views media as just one of the mediators within a social network; in other words, the focus is on all of the users of digital platforms engaged at one level or another in social movements. While media, like mainstream news outlets, may come to dominate information giving regarding a social or political issue, this is not necessarily the case, as special interest groups as well as media figures, including celebrities, along with ordinary individuals can engage, perhaps compete for influence on the highest levels within social media platforms like

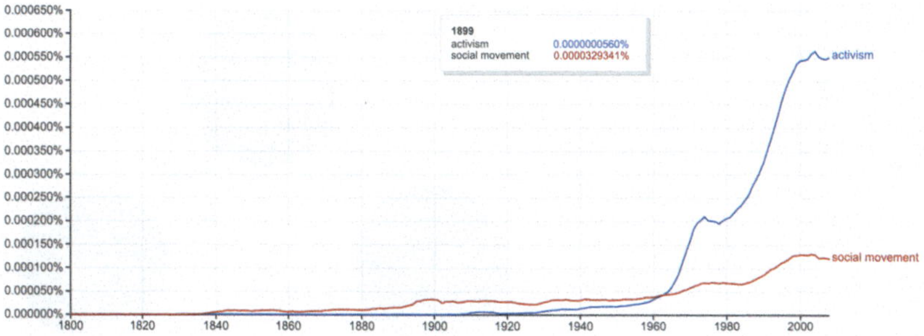

Fig. 1.1 nGram view of key terms

Twitter, Facebook, Instagram, YouTube, and Reddit, hence the idea that activism operates through mediated social connections.

The concept of activism is not new as it began to appear in the 1830s; a year later the term "social movement" began to appear in books (Fig. 1.1).[9] In more recent years, the ratio of the appearance between the two terms is five to one. In other words, activism has taken on greater dominance, especially since the 1960s, which makes sense given the political and social fervor of that era, but the use of the term "activism" really took off as indicated in the chart below in the 1980s.

Could this be due to the emergence of digital technologies that enabled individuals—activists—to participate in social movements in newer ways, perhaps spreading the word through email or chat rooms? Perhaps this period represents the beginning of extending actual or physical presence to the digital or virtual engagement in a social movement.

Blumer's Four Stages of Social Movements

There was a time when people would present themselves physically at a destination of protest perhaps learning about an event through word-of-mouth or coverage in news media. For a movement to emerge, three antecedents are necessary. They include the following: a perceived threat and the opportunity to act, access to resources, and a unifying message. The study of social movements is a well-established field, and scholars have become more aware of the relationship between media and social movements. Sociologist Herbert Blumer described four stages of social movements (Fig. 1.2). The first he referred to as the "social ferment" stage. In

Fig. 1.2 Christiansen's four stages of a social movement

this early stage participants may be agitating in order to gain attention for their cause. In the second stage, known as "popular excitement," the movement becomes more clearly defined and driven by objectives to be achieved by the movement. In the third stage, the movement may build a more formal organization in order to more effectively reach the goals of the movement. And finally, the "institutional stage" suggests that the structure of the movement becomes ingrained in society and operates within a professional structure.[10] More recently scholars have questioned Blumer's evolutionary approach to understanding social movements. De la Porta and Diani maintain that "The direction taken by a social movement, therefore, may be that of moderation, but equally that of radicalization; of greater formalization, but also of progressive destructuration; of greater contact with the surrounding environment, or of sectarian 'implosion.' "[11] A contemporary version of the four stages (Fig. 1.2) is offered by Christiansen, who describes stages of a social movement as emergence, coalescence, bureaucratization, and decline.[12]

The model, first developed by Herbert Blumer, but modified in more recent years, provides a process-orientation of how collective action works and it provides a useful framework for analyzing social movements, both past and present, and understanding their outcomes.

In the emergence stage there is little or no organization to a movement. Rather, a collection of individuals is motivated by widespread discontent or unhappiness about a social or political issue. In the aftermath of the 2018 shooting at Stoneman Douglas High School in Parkland, Florida, while funerals progressed, other student leaders knew "with the clarity of thought that had distinguished them from the beginning, that the headline-industrial complex granted only a very narrow window of attention. Had they waited even a week to start advocating for change, the reporters would have gone home."[13] Activism was borne through social media posts that led to subsequent invitations for student leaders to write op-eds and appear on local and national news programs. But prolonging a movement, especially one initially fueled by tweets based on expressions of frustration regarding legislators' inability to pass gun control laws, needed a stage two, which is the coalescence of forces that led shortly after the February 14 shooting to the March for Our Lives that took place in Washington, DC, and 800 sibling events in other cities and around the world. In the coalescence stage of a social movement, things become more focused as a collective expression of discontent, the March for Our Lives serves as an excellent example. In the third bureaucratization stage, the social movement becomes more organized. In the context of the #NeverAgain hashtag, students organized voter registration drives across the United States, as they lobbied Congress and regional governments to enact anti-gun legislation. In this digital age, it has been said that a typical hashtag campaign will last no longer than three days, sustaining a movement online takes an enormous effort. Decline, the fourth stage, doesn't refer to failure or the end of a movement. Rather, it refers to the institutionalization of a movement as ideas get incorporated into the mainstream. There is an interesting twist to the fourth stage regarding the institutionalization of ideas raising the question whether a movement that moves into the mainstream is still a movement?

Activists and Powerholders

An alternative eight-stage model of social movement development was proposed by social movement theorist Bill Moyer. While Moyer's approach makes reference to the public, as in general public that needs to become aware of the issue, this conceptualization of the public, as will be discussed below, is problematic. What the movement comes down to in Moyer's model is activists versus powerholders. Activists come to a social movement with varying levels of intensity or engagement in the movement: rebels, reformers, citizens, and change agents (Fig. 1.3). Rebels are who

Fig. 1.3 Four roles of activists

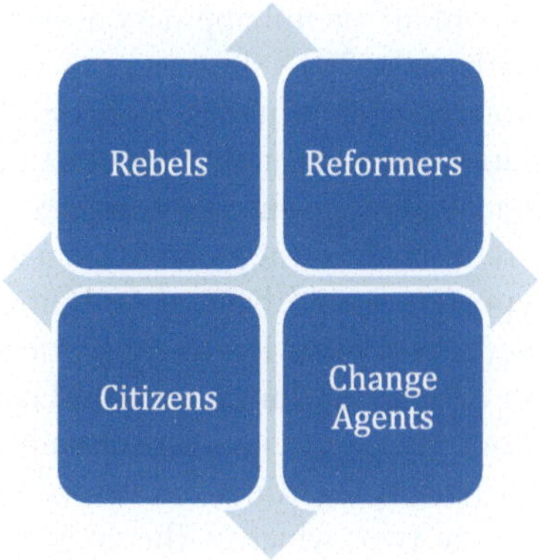

we often think of when we think of activists. This role is closely aligned with the concept of networked individualism as the rebel may represent the "lone voice" at different stages of a social movement. The reformer role takes a less radical approach as these activists maintain their belief in institutions and attempt to work within the system. The third role is that of citizen in which case these activists serve a more centrist role attempting to maintain equilibrium between the fringe and the powerholders. Finally, there are change agents, a key role played by activists, who attempt to educate others and attempt to persuade the public of the efficacy of the movement through grassroots efforts, among other activities. All of these roles may be present in varying stages of a social movement, and they do not always work together in consort toward a common goal.[14]

New Social Movement Theory

Fuchs describes two approaches to social movement theory: the European New Social Movement approach (NSM) and the US resource mobilization approach.[15] The former is concerned with structural conditions and societal changes that are the root causes of social movements. In other words, new social movement theory takes a macro approach. The New Social Movement approach focuses on gender, ethnicity, age, neighborhood, environment, and peace. The idea behind the new social movement approach, as distinguished from political movements, is derived from the sociologist Jürgen Habermas, who suggested a shift away from the proletarian revolutions of classical Marxism toward social and cultural change. In this view new social movements oppose the intrusion of not only the state on the autonomous individual but also the market into social life. The objective of new social movements is to reclaim individuals' rights against the larger system. Therefore, new social movements are not so much about material gain but offer resistance to the intrusion of political institutions as they define personal autonomy.[16] The distinction between old social movements and contemporary ones should not imply that one replaced the other. Rather the basis of the former might have been based on economic struggles but rather than distinguish between old and new, perhaps as Buechler suggests, concepts regarding class, politics, culture—instrumental or expressive—should be combined when viewing new social movements.[17] But Fuchs argues that "NSM theorists oppose economic reductionism and class reductionism: the emergence of SMs cannot be explained solely by economic changes and the position of actors in the production process."[18] Fuchs suggests an approach that emphasizes the self-organization of social movements, in which networks are formed through collective intelligence.

It's important to point out that while sometimes social movements are global, as is the case with #ClimateStrike and #MeToo, other times movements are more national, like the Mouvement des gilets jaunes or regional, as is the case with #NeverAgain. Other movements are local or hyper-local as is the case with the Indivisible movement that was started among family and friends as a countermovement to the Tea Party political movement.[19]

Cyberconflict Theory

In 2006 Athina Karatzogianni developed the theoretical framework for studying conflict in computer-mediated environments. Cyberconflict theory, as it is referred to, borrows from social movement theories, media theory, and conflict theory.[20] Without categorizing actions or events, the framework focuses on two different types of conflict, "each of which is assigned different characteristics and features on the examined cases and events."[21] Karatzogianni describes four phases of digital activism and cyberconflict she maintains began in 1994 that were transformed over the next two decades by significant movements like the Arab Spring, among others.[22] She identifies activists in social movements, those organized within digital networks, primarily as non-state actors, that is those outside of the dominant forces in society, namely government and corporations.

She theorizes cyberconflict as conflict that takes place within computer-mediated environments, namely, by digital activists. From this perspective both digital activism and cyberconflict are not a function or result of technological developments but rather are political effects. But digital activism, conceived within cyberconflict theory, may not account for the diffuse audiences and the types of mediators that engage in a digitally based social movement.

The first phase, Karatzogiani suggests, took place between 1994 and 2001, a period when the new internet provided the optimism that might fuel social, cultural, and political change. The idea was that the internet would provide a free flow of information uncontrolled by hegemonic powers leading to a more democratic society. Of course, the digital divide existed then as it does today, a major criticism of this optimistic period; criticism that extends to the present. The second period from around 2001 to 2007 saw the rise of social media and the impact that those nascent platforms were having on activism. The start of the second decade of the twenty-first century marks the third period with the advent of the widespread use of smartphones in which digital media impacted mainstream politics, including the Obama presidential campaign. And, the fourth era, from 2010 to 2014, characterized by "leaktivists," like WikiLeaks, wherein debates emerged around the role of digital media in surveillance and privacy.[23] Karatzogiani and colleagues maintain that in the digital era social networks have the ability to influence public perceptions of crises, migration, culture, and conflict.[24]

Ioanna Ferra, who utilizes a social network analysis approach in her study of the 2008 Greek economic crisis, combines the three theories that make up cyberconflict theory with yet another, Bennett and Segerberg's theory of connective action.[25] The theory of connective action distinguished by the more familiar collective action or collective intelligence that emerges from collective action is associated with digitally based social movements and the identities of individuals that are engaged in the movement. Connective action is "based on personalized content sharing across media networks."[26] With regard to collective action, the theorists maintain the inclusion of digital media do not change the dynamics of the movement; however, with regard to connective action, those core dynamics do change, which is the basis of mediated networks. Added to the theory of connective action is the concept of collective consciousness. Collective consciousness goes beyond the idea of content sharing to view collective output of that sharing on social media platforms as a neural network.

Ferra's research, employs an extended version of cyberconflict theory, in order to "situate online mediated conflict (sociopolitical and ethnoreligious cyberconflict) in a geosociopolitical and historical context, indicating the dynamic relation between the online media and the offline world."[27] Ferra suggests that the internet serves as a magnifying glass illuminating "conflict, opposition and supporting polarization." The essential question regards what is being magnified as social media become outlets for emotive expression, what has been referred to as the excessive mind or cognitive bloat and the extended or excessive self. The efforts to support or sustain a movement or issue at least as far as social media platforms are concerned may be more like individuals metaphorically shooting arrows into the wind rather than operating in a concerted organized effort. In other words, as social movements may be self-organizing as Fuch maintains, or chaotic and unorganized, so too may the nature of connections be quite varied. Of course, the degree of organization or the lack thereof may relate to the stage of development of the social movement.

Bennett and Segerberg's theory of connective action presents a hybrid model (Fig. 1.4), the cornerstone of which is the sharing economy that emerges through "personalization that leads actions and content to be distributed widely across social networks."[28] These researchers take pains to distinguish connective action as not merely an extension of collective action, but a phenomenon tied to the digital age that is worthy of study on its own merits. The shift from collective (group) to connective (individual) action that Bennett and Segerberg describe coincides with the

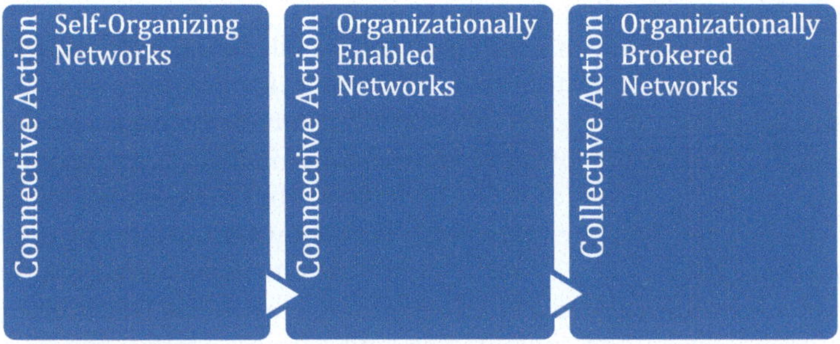

Fig. 1.4 Elements of connective and collective action networks. (Bennet & Segerbert, Elements of Connective and Collective Action Networks. op. cit. p. 756)

advent of flexible social networks based on the strength of weak ties theory.[29] As such individuals can utilize social networks as expressions of personal identity, which means they can shift within or between or transcend groups depending on the situational relevance of the issue. "Whether through texts, tweets, social network sharing, or posting YouTube mashups, the communication process itself often involves further personalization through the spreading of digital connections among friends or trusted others."[30]

I would add that like shooting arrows into the wind, some dissemination of information lacks connection as those individuals are "isolates" floating in the digital ether, on the periphery of a social network. Perhaps those individuals could be referred to as "hangers on" or as "free riders." Bennett and Segerberg contend that digital media are organizing agents; however, I would counter that digital media provide users with platforms through which they may mediate messaging by which I mean that those engaged in a social movement build their connections through sharing of what might be characterized as their "stories" but what is important is the collective nature of that story building into a narrative that supports the movement. In other words, it's not only the action of the individual or the actions of a group; rather focus also needs to be placed on the collective outcome, the narrative produced through the story building that takes place online over time.

Bennett and Segerberg also address the dissolution of public and private space, so that one becomes an extension of the other. This is what is meant by the excessive mind in which cognitions, otherwise held closely by an individual, spill out into the public arena as posts, tweets, retweets, and the like vis-à-vis digital media platforms. This is an important aspect of the sharing economy in which meaning is built through the coproduction as well as the co-distribution, retweeting, for example, acts of personal expression. Are social networks hierarchically organized? Not necessarily, as mediators of social networks may include news media, special interest groups, politicians, and celebrities, but networks also include ordinary people who can engage in the network without authority or public standing, but by virtue of the level of their activity on a platform. Jose′ van Dijck writes about social media platforms as active mediators between users, technologies, and content. Invoking Latour's action-network theory (ANT), van Dijck maintains that a "society rooted in norms of connectivity wields platforms that simultaneously construct and reflect the value of cultivating weak ties and of formalizing informal communication and self-expression—a complex and layered process that is constantly modulated. The emergence of social media platforms is at the heart of a shifting dynamic, where agents of different nature (human and non-human, material and immaterial) and varied size (individuals, groups, collectives, societies) are building a connective space for communication and information."[31]

Torches of Freedom

Stepping back in time for a moment, we can point to the mid-eighteenth century in England as the birth of early social, political, and economic movements. But it was the sophisticated use of psychology taken by Edward Bernays, who many consider the founder of modern public relations, with the launch in the early part of the twentieth century of the Torches of Freedom (see Fig. 1.5) campaign to encourage women to smoke cigarettes. Bernays employed an engineered approach to consent. We normally wouldn't associate women's smoking with a social movement, but in the early part of the twentieth century, smoking was not only seen as immoral, associated with "fallen women," but illegal in some states. The cigarette industry wanted to change the perception of smoking and enlisted the help of Bernays who in 1929 recruited women smokers to march in the Easter Sunday Parade in New York City. Their defiance of social convention was labeled "torches of freedom."

Bernays, who was the nephew of Sigmund Freud, utilized his understanding of psychoanalytic theory to exploit the cigarette as a symbol of personal freedom. Bernays knew there would be media coverage at the event, which made for a photo op that would be carried by many of the nation's news media. Thus, he not only employed a psychological principle to impact perceptions of a social convention, women, and smoking, but utilized a public event covered by the news media to manipulate the situation. The same principles of manipulation are still in force today and may be applied not only to commercial concerns but to social and political movements as well. However, the advent of digital platforms has altered the organization of social movements, but some of the techniques and tactics are still the same.

Writing in the essay "The Engineering of Consent in 1947," Bernays declared that the United States Bill of Rights, particularly the idea of free speech included the corollary, the right to persuasion. He saw this as a function of the expansion of media. "All these media provide open doors

Fig. 1.5 Torches of freedom parade 1929. (Thesocietypages.org. (n.d.). Torches of Freedom Parade in New York, 1929. Retrieved from: https://thesocietypages.org/socimages/2012/02/27/torches-of-freedom-women-and-smoking-propaganda/comment-page-2/)

to the public mind. Any one of us through these media may influence the attitudes and actions of our fellow citizens."[32] Bernays was referring to what we might think of as mainstream media: newspapers, magazines, and radio, but he also included "billboards, handbills, throwaways, and direct mail advertising. Round tables, panels and forums, classrooms and legislative assemblies, and public platforms—any and all media, day after day, spread the word, someone's word."[33]

Bernays position appears rooted in the Classical Liberal ideal (Fig. 1.6) of egoism, intellectualism, atomism.[34] Egoism is based on the idea of self-interest or ego-driven behavior. Intellectualism is based on the idea that people are rational in their decision making, although that concept may be

Fig. 1.6 Three tenets of classical liberal ideal

tempered with the idea that people may be somewhat less predictable. Atomism is based on the Newtonian idea that a society is made up, like an atom, of the sum of its parts. Although that ideal has shifted with the notion that self-interest may be tempered by a certain amount of powerlessness. Bernays advocated an "engineering approach" to communication. By that he meant the knowledge gained through research and the application of scientific principles to commercial interests. He likened the development of a public relations campaign to that of a civil engineer who is planning to build a bridge. Planning is the key word here, as Bernays offered a very systematic approach to campaign development playing off of those ideals, the process of which is still in use today. He was clear about the role of communication in getting sound ideas across to publics whom he felt, based on the soundness of the idea, would become activists. "People translate an idea into action suggested by the idea itself, whether it is ideological, political, or social."[35] But in the end, he said, these things don't happen on their own, hence the idea behind engineering of consent.

Digital Media and New Social Movements

Media activism (distinguished from mediated networks), a particular form of activism according to Bennett, focuses on how activists utilize media and communication strategies to advance various causes.[36] But rather than creating spectacle like Bernays' Torches of Freedom in order to gain the attention of traditional media, in the digital age, activists are in essence the media, spreading messages and connecting in various ways to others engaged in a social movement. In the digital age, the one-way asymmetric model of message dissemination described by public relations theorist

James Grunig no longer works well within a participatory environment, as newer social media platforms provide opportunities for content to spread beyond local geography and perhaps under some circumstances become viral. As such, even in the bureaucratization or institutionalized stages of development, digital media, as new social movements theory suggests, provide the means for more individuals to circumvent the power of corporations, government, organizations, and the news media to more fully engage in social networks where various interests may compete. It is simply not going far enough to even suggest that a two-way symmetric model works efficiently, as operating within the context of "mutual benefit" does not quite fit the pull and tug of competing interests, nor does it reflect the polarization that takes place around many contemporary social movements. In other words, it is not just about an organization, government, or business attempting to reach a single public, activist or otherwise. Rather, publics in the age of digital media, like audiences, are diffuse. Bennet describes the difference between "old-school" activists and media activists. The former, he says, operate through hierarchical organizations, including strong leadership. But in the digital age, we can see that leadership may be shared, less hierarchical, as are available resources, if for no other reason because social media platforms are widely available. We can see the democratization in the shared leadership and connective action of the #NeverAgain movement and in what has come to be known as the Arab Spring in 2011, just to name two.

Schroeder and colleagues studied a million tweets during the Egyptian uprising, a social movement that led to the downfall of then president Hosni Mubarak. When the scholars looked at who was "driving" the conversation, their analysis revealed that two leading news organizations, Al Jazeera Arabic and Al Arabiya, were dominant, that is, they "framed" the conversation. But they also tracked thousands of people who participated in the discussion of their grievances toward the government. Ironically, perhaps, there was a very active Hosni Mubarak parody account that portrayed him as a corrupt leader. The researchers concluded that this fake news account may have added to the negative perception of Mubarak.[37] The authors cite three interrelated causes that are at the root of social movements: "perceived threat and opportunity to act, access to resources, and a unifying message."[38] Because of their spreadability, social media may speed up the development of social movements more so than in the past. The sociologist Todd Gitlin, in his book *The Whole World Is Watching*, refers to the role of media as an agent of change in a "floodlit-society" in which it is difficult for an opposition social movement to define itself and build up an infrastructure outside the dominant culture.[39] Gitlin, writing in the pre-Facebook era, claimed that ordinary people had "no voice in what the media make of what they say or what they do"; however, in today's digital media environment, it is difficult to imagine a social or political movement or issue that is not brightly lit by media.[40] But beyond serving as part of the organizational infrastructure of social movements, we have only begun to understand the mediated social connections of those engaged in today's participatory culture; those who serve as mediators on social networks. Rather than adopting a media-centric approach, an analytical framework based on mediated networks is advanced that considers how audiences engage on social issues through the use of digital media platforms and in that, as was the case with the Arab Spring, such an approach allows us to map onto the social structures that exist within those social networks that make up a movement or rally against or in support of an issue.

Patterns of Action

Erving Goffman's work, especially *The Presentation of Self in Everyday Life*, is noted for his reference to the dramaturgical, that is, theatrical qualities of performance, referencing aspects of different roles individuals play in various walks of life. Although he was writing in 1956, Goffman's approach to performance is relevant in the digital age. Each of us plays multiple offline roles, perhaps as wife or husband, father or daughter, teacher or manager, among many others. But for those engaged in social media, we also play varying roles partially based on the platform, that is to say the role one plays on Twitter may be quite different than the performance one gives on Reddit. And, performances vary, too, based on the level of interest or connection we have to a social network. The tapestry of performance that we weave through everyday life and digital life constitute patterns of action, as Goffman would describe them.[41] His interest is in how a performance works by which he refers to the social connections that form among audience, observers, or co-participants. When it comes to digital media, Goffman's definition of performance can be applied to online identities that we craft by curating content, posting original thoughts and ideas, liking, giving a thumb down, among other patterns of actions. The effort to create an impression or play a role is pretty much a continual effort considering the amount of time people spend on social media. And the strategic effort that people put into managing their online presence, creating and maintaining a persona, must be quite stressful. In the context of an online social movement, social relationships, although virtual and to some degree imaginary, constitute co-participants in the social network. More specifically, when one engages in an online social movement, they are signally to others their ideological or political beliefs. Aligning one's self with a social movement, because it involves others in the network provides the structure to encourage or nudge or reinforce one's belief in a cause.

Both membership and status within a social network are being referred to here and the management of one's social identity that is part of a continual authenticating process. For example, the degree of interest expressed in social media that may be defined as amplification is a demonstration of status, commitment, and in that activism. There is a reciprocal arrangement at work—through your online performances you tag yourself through online statements, sometimes as simple as liking a post. At the same time, in this instance, liking a post positions you within the social network. There is self-reinforcing aspect to this performative process, especially when operating in what may be called an echo chamber where like-minded people perform the same roles, although there is always likely to be contentiousness and disagreement in the online social network. The process of establishing and maintaining membership as well as managing one's shape-shifting identity is part of a collective performance, as others are engaged in performing their roles. In the world of social media news and information as well as ideas spread rapidly and while sometimes mediators help to direct or shape the message, often they lack a unifying voice as in a leaderless social movement.

The cacophony of noise can be characterized as an "infodemic," a term born out of the COVID-19 pandemic by the World Health Organization that they defined as too much information as well as the dissemination of misinformation or disinformation. Digital media may be a gateway to excessive amounts of information, but it is human nature to seek out news and information that supports existing beliefs. In that way, social networks have great potential to become echo chambers. In her study of protests regarding social justice in the shooting of Michael Brown in Ferguson, Missouri, Pierson studied 200,000 tweets. In the image below (Fig. 1.7), you can see the divisiveness in the social network and the silos that are created around the issue of police brutality and social justice.[42] In the context of identity politics, those engaged in the Ferguson social network are

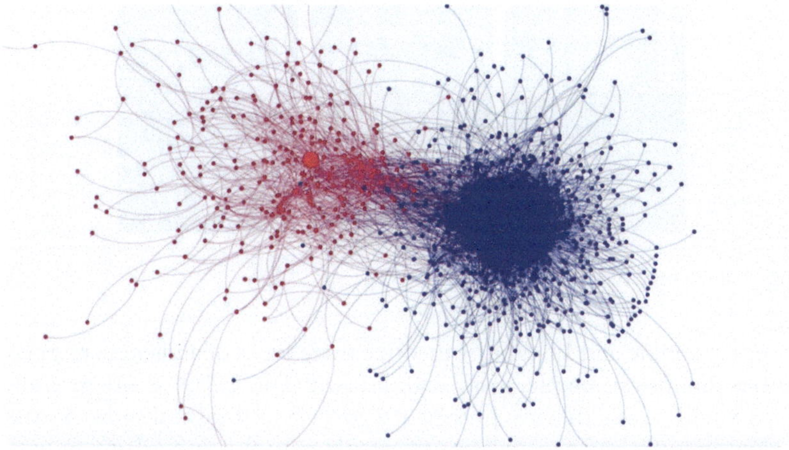

Fig. 1.7 Visualization of the Divisive Ferguson social network

performing to political orientation and race. Perhaps Goffman should have made reference to the presentation of multiple selves, as this is a complex managerial problem for both digital and offline identities. Performance in the context of the presentations of selves constitutes the work we do in the culture and the "work" that is done to us—a sort of reciprocal arrangement.

An interesting aspect of Goffman's dramaturgical application of everyday life actions is what he refers to public versus private behavior as the back (rehearsal) and front (performance) stage. There is a paradox at work here, as a person through their performative act online can never reveal their true or authentic self and their repeated presence on social media suggests they cannot conceal their self. It is the merger of the two on social media—rehearsal and performance and concealing and revealing—that makes up the process associated with the authenticating self. As identity is always in process, so too is authenticity. The interactions between the individual and co-participants in the social network lead to what I refer to as mediated social connections. Digitally based social networks may facilitate social and political movements as those movements are fueled by users. But it is important to point out that algorithms, too, play a role and in fact have been shown to promote racism as well as fuel an "infodemic."[43]

Fig. 1.8 Three types of audiences

Abercrombie and Longhurst theorize three types of audiences relevant to this discussion: simple, mass, and diffused (Fig. 1.8).[44] A simple audience would be one that was present at a concert or theatrical show. A mass audience might refer to millions of people who watch a television program. A diffuse audience, however, is one that is spread out but links through media in a continual manner. In that way, being a part of a diffused audience lacks the special nature of attendance inherent in the other two types of audiences. The everyday use of Twitter would serve as an example of how diffuse audiences operate, as individuals many with weak connections tweet, like, retweet, comment, or do nothing.

As a social interactionist, Goffman is concerned with how a performance works. Therefore, within a social network the diffuse audience may serve by several competing interests at work on a single social or political issue. It is in this way that audiences, or publics as they also may be referred to, interact through digital media. The contentious politics of a social movement are exemplified by cyberconflict, as digital media that have opened up opportunities to create a more participatory culture, connective action. Contemporary life for many people is based on their social connections enabled by social media platforms like Facebook, for example. And such platforms both enable people to feel closer even though they may be physically separated by great distance, but also there is a feeling or sense of anonymity that may cause some people to post some things that they ordinarily would not. In other words, in a world dominated by social media, to a degree, our filters are off. But it is the availability of technology that allows people to always be connected through, for example, their mobile devices. Indeed, many people check into their mobile device hundreds of times a day for fear of missing out (FOMO). One study found that Americans check their phones every 12 minutes and more than

80 times per day.[45] The internet-based diffused audience is one that may be referred to as an imagined community, a concept advanced by Grudz and colleagues, which plays into the always-on ways in which digital media inform social movements in contemporary society.[46]

Imagined Communities

When we picture community in our minds, often we are making reference to the physical proximity of one person to another. This might refer to neighbors or neighborhoods, and it might also refer to the nation-state, especially one based on "print capitalism," a product of industrialization.[47] But the fact of the matter is that in contemporary society people who live in neighborhoods do not necessarily know one another or share the same beliefs or values as their neighbors. In his 1991 book *Imagined Communities*, Benedict Anderson defined nations as imagined political communities.[48] He envisaged nations as communities of equals but with rules or boundaries as to who could join, in this way communities are conceptualized as disaggregated. Some people, like marketers or politicians, try to aggregate people into false constructs like the Black community or LGBTQ community, as if all people who are Black or gay or whatever, hold the same beliefs or values. Itzigsohm and vom Hau described imagined communities in three Latin America countries as contested space based on hegemonic differences between social actors.[49] Even before the advent of social media platforms, scholars began to think about nonlocal ties. And, in the digital age, connection has become more complex as people can communicate without ever meeting. Complexity extends to what may be referred to as "portable communities." Adams and Sardiello cite fans who followed the band the Grateful Dead among such portable communities.[50]

Barry Wellman, who has been studying online communities for more than two decades, maintains that online relationships can be real relationships and that relationships often involve a multitude of interactions both in-person and mediated. Although there are some scholars that deride the intrusion of digital media into everyday life as they believe mediated connections negatively impact community. However, in the digital age physical proximity gives way to a more dynamic vision of community in which physical proximity is mixed with more distant connections. Both may work together as would be the case where Twitter or Facebook are utilized to pass on information about an impending march or protest. In the digital age, we might refer to those who Tweet using #MeToo as members of a hashtag community. Members of such a community, although social network seems more apropos, need not be in close physical proximity to one another in order to share their views or present opposing ideas. The relationships among connections within a social network are not only virtual but hashtag warriors—those who are most active on a social issue—may be asymmetric, meaning even if I follow you, there may be no compelling reason for you to follow me back. And, I have pointed out, there are likely to be detractors operating within the social network as well.

Participatory Culture

The concept of a participatory culture is closely associated with the work of Henry Jenkins. The central idea of participatory culture is that consumers become producers, an idea originated with Jenkins' mentor John Fiske. And the related idea of textual poachers was originated by Michel de Certeau in his book *The Practice of Everyday Life*. In de Certeau's conception, he analogized the audience-producer relationship thusly: Those in power get to place the furniture in the apartment, but the individual living in the apartment can arrange the furniture as they please. Jenkins defined "participatory culture as one:

1. With relatively low barriers to artistic expression and civic engagement
2. With strong support for creating and sharing one's creations with others
3. With some type of informal mentorship whereby what is known by the most experienced is passed along to novices
4. Where members believe that their contributions matter
5. Where members feel some degree of social connection with one another (at the least they care what other people think about what they have created)

Not every member must contribute, but all must believe they are free to contribute when ready and that what they contribute will be appropriately valued."[51] Participatory culture turns consumers into prosumers; in other words, producers of content and meaning. Applied to social movements we can see the dynamics between consumption and production play out as was the case with Occupy Wall Street. The Occupy Wall Street Tumblr blog—We Are the 99 Percent—crowdsourced stories of social and economic hardship representing various sectors of US society. Through such collaborations social justice issues can be moved to the forefront through social media activism. In contrast to Bennett's argument regarding "connective action," from Gerbaudo's perspective the opposite is taking place through the use of digital tools that impact social movements. In other words, connective action turns into or is replaced by collective identities produced through network individualism.[52] Furthermore van Dijck is critical of the user agency ascribed to participatory culture, as he claims it is based on the idea that all users are active participants. Rather, he points out that "social media sites do not turn all users into active participants. In fact, the term user rather than previous terms such as 'audience', 'viewer' or 'customer' conceals the fact that the large majority of users are anything but active participants."[53] But the question remains, how does one define active participants? The range may begin with non-active or passive participants, and it may include lurkers or free riders. At the more extreme end we might find those that are indeed active on the issue. This topic is explored further below with the description of situational theory as it relates to an expanded definition of publics that are defined as groups of people that come together as individuals around an issue; coming together does not imply agreement. Digital media platforms, rather than being intermediaries as we might expect, according to Latour, are mediators. But the question may be raised regarding whether digital media that are doing the mediating, or as I put forth, users are mediating not only the content, but meanings ascribed to that content, and it should not be lost that they are mediating themselves as purveyors of that content. Within digitally based social networks, Isa and Himelboim describe social mediators as "influential key actors who attract more attention in their own clusters (defined by in-degree centrality) and act as a bridge between two clusters (defined by betweenness centrality). This unique position in the network allows them to spread information within their own clusters and to other clusters, which would otherwise be devoid of that information."[54] They describe three types of mediators: elite, non-elite, and core mediators. Elite social mediators might include political leaders, journalists, media outlets, and human rights organizations, while non-elite social mediators might be comprised of ordinary individuals. A third type are core mediators, that may include media networks, or elite mediators as well as non-elites who have a greater vested interest in an issue than others.[55] The goal, therefore, is to move beyond the media platforms themselves to focus on social structures and the connections that form through individuals who engage at whatever level in a social movement.

Interestingly, van Dijck takes issue with the term "connectivity" as it is presently associated with the concept of networks. Networks, he says, are "both infrastructural and social organizations—systems of technologies and people—made up of 'ties' and 'nodes' that render conduits for connectivity." Rather, platforms like Facebook, for example, are "producers of sociality, enabling connections as well as forging them. Platforms are therefore socio-technical and cultural-ideological constructs that are built to create and mediate a new type of social capital: connectivity."[56]

The Role of Spectacle

Consider Greta Thunberg, the teenage Swedish climate change activist who took an unorthodox route in August 2019—literally and figuratively—in order to highlight her beliefs about carbon emissions by sailing across the Atlantic Ocean in order to appear at the United Nations climate summit.[57] Thunberg began her protests by skipping school on Fridays; hence the hashtag campaign #Fridays4Future emerged worldwide as the basis for a global youth movement. For her individual effort, she received both praise and backlash, which ranges from a nomination for the Nobel Peace Prize to a multitude of personal attacks. While the voyage itself, lasting approximately two weeks, took on the image of a spectacle that would rival many major global events, the campaign is sustained on digital platforms including her Facebook page, TED Talk, and Twitter. Douglas Kellner, who sees spectacle as a tool of commercial interests, critically explores the role of spectacle in an internet-economy as a means to "dazzle."[58] While Kellner was referring to the use of spectacle in the commercial realm in order to attract consumer attention, as pointed out earlier in this chapter, the same techniques utilized by Edward Bernays' Torches of Freedom and Moveon.org apply to social movements that in order to participate in the digital space one must mimic the same tactics utilized by commercial enterprises. Although spectacle in and of itself is nothing new, media culture Kellner states it "not only takes up expanding moments of contemporary experience but also provides ever more material for fantasy, dreaming, modeling thought and behavior, and constructing identities."[59] Technospectacles have become a defining feature of globalization. Whether Thunberg's efforts and those of her generation take on the qualities of megaspectacle that are necessary to not only gain attention but to maintain it remains to be seen. However, the use of tactics in social movements gleaned from commercial, political, and other events, including sports, become an amplification device in the digital age. Here, I'm not referring to what might be called an organic spectacle based on some natural phenomenon; rather, what is being referred to here is the manufactured spectacle. Whether it is the visual spectacle of Occupy Wall Street, people literally camping out on the streets, or Thunberg's sail across the Atlantic Ocean, social movements have co-opted techniques gleaned from marketing and media, no different than Bernays' engineering of consent, in order to gain and maintain attention on a social or political issue.

The Arab Spring first emerged in late 2010 as social media was used by Tunisians to organize protests, spread ideologies, and try to push President Zine El Abidine Ben Ali out of power. It was also the use of cellphone cameras depicting the horrible conditions being streamed globally that demanded action.[60] The revolution spread virally online and eventually extended throughout the Middle East, most notably in Egypt, with Esraa Abdel Fattah, an Egyptian democracy activist known as "Facebook Girl" leading the protest. She organized the event in Tahrir Square on January 25 to demand the removal of President Hosni Mubarak but is the first to admit democracy is not easy and "isn't so sure the work is over."[61] The community of activists, started by young Tunisians filmed the protests that arose after 26-year-old Mohamed Bouazizi burned himself alive in his own extreme form of protest after being embarrassed by a police officer. Posting such potent images—spectacles—on social media fanned the flames of outrage and with fellow citizens, who may not have even known Bouazizi, banned together to create a movement. One leader of the Egyptian uprising that toppled the government of Hosni Mubarak, Wael Ghonim, once said, "If you want to liberate a society, all you need is the Internet." In retrospect, however, Ghonim changed his view: "I said those words back in 2011, when a Facebook page I anonymously created helped spark the Egyptian revolution. The Arab Spring revealed social media's greatest potential, but it also exposed its greatest shortcomings. The same tool that united us to topple dictators eventually tore us apart."[62]

While digital media may be useful to impact political change, it can also have deleterious effects creating social issues as was the case of the Rohingya Muslims whose massacre took place in Myanmar in 2017. According to UN investigators, a significant amount of blame was directed toward Facebook where there was much hate expressed toward the Rohingya. "Everything is done through Facebook in Myanmar ... Facebook had helped the impoverished country but had also been used to spread hate speech."[63] On the one hand, a social media post represents an individual's thoughts and beliefs—their state of mind. Such posts are an expression of their agency. As van Dijck suggests, "social media platforms introduce new types of agency in online communities that help shape the technologically inscribed social norms of interaction and communication in the connective sphere, and vice versa, platform owners deploy agency to calibrate technological architecture and interface design, for instance to accommodate advertisers."[64] The end result, however, is not necessarily to the social good.

Networked Individualism

It is through movements and issues like those discussed thus far that we can see how networked individualism in the digital age plays a critical role in the development of a movement. The concept of networked individualism is attributed to Barry Wellman who wrote that people have in the technological age become networked as individuals as opposed to them being a part of or embedded in groups.[65] In social networking parlance, individuals are not networks, but rather represent nodes. In this sense the individual operator is more important than other social units. This is reminiscent of the classical liberal world view regarding atomism, mentioned earlier in this chapter, a derivative of Newton's law that designates the individual as the main component of society. However, as Purcel points out, networked individualism represents a form of "flexible autonomy."[66] As such, networked socialization in the digital age requires the social capital of those with the ability to utilize digital platforms, in particular social media, in order to create and participate in complex social networks, although it is important to point out that social capital in the digital age is unevenly distributed. Networked individualism in the digital age is based on the "collection of links between elements of a unit."[67] A social movement, therefore, is a system of linked individuals with complex connections.

The implications of this alone-together paradox should not be lost regarding the way we think about social movements in the digital age. Marzouki and Oullier state: "the possibility of a leaderless revolution is likely to be (at least partially) explained by the spontaneity, the homogeneity and the synchronicity of the actions of these cyber-activism networks that were catalyzed by social media through the efforts of individual players. This explanation is supported by what has been coined as virtual collective consciousness (VCC), referring to an internal knowledge shared by a plurality of persons. Coupled with 'citizen media' activism, this knowledge emerges as a new form of consciousness via communication tools."[68] Social media are anything but spontaneous, as the performative nature of posting memes or tweets requires forethought and a certain amount of planning, although what appears often comes out unfiltered, a product of the excessive mind, or as P. David Marshall characterizes social media as a presentational culture as opposed to a representational culture. Although writing about celebrities, Marshall's ideas regarding the presentation of self can be applied to anyone engaged in social media, including those individuals engaged in an online social movement. Marshall describes presentation of self in the following manner: the public self, private public self, and transgressive intimate self. The latter relates to the excessive mind in that it includes personal aspects of one's self that perhaps should not have been shared but because of the performative nature of social media aspects of one's self are shared on social media, including strong emotions related to one's position regarding a social, political, or environmental issue.[69] This concept can be applied to the 2019 "Yellow Jacket" movement in France. The movement began as a protest against a gasoline tax that was having an economic impact on people living in the communities beyond Paris as well as a general unhappiness with the economic policies of French President Emmanuel Macron. In this case, Facebook may have unwittingly caused the *gilets jaunes* protest in France. I say unwittingly as in an effort to diminish the presence of fake news on its platform, Facebook privileged memes and vitriol from populist groups that would become the organizing rally of the movement.[70]

At the emergence stage, the Occupy Wall Street movement started in New York City but then spread to 100 other cities in the United States and another 1500 cities globally.[71] The movement was intended to highlight economic inequality, high unemployment rates, corporate corruption, and corporate influence in government.[72] The movement's slogan, "We are the 99%" was a call for participants to bring a tent to literally occupy Wall Street. This was repeated in various memes and a long list of related hashtags, and the protest was highlighted on Facebook and a sub-Reddit as well as a Tumblr blog, as well as a dedicated website.[73] The movement has been described as decentralized, meaning the memes and hashtags are the product of networked individualism, and this may provide support for the idea that digitally based social movements extend beyond collective action to connective action, because as Malcolm Gladwell has written, "social networks make it easier for activists to express themselves, and harder for that expression to have any impact. The instruments of social media are well suited to making the existing social order more efficient. They are not a natural enemy of the status quo… Social networks are effective at increasing participation—by lessening the level of motivation that participation requires."[74] In that way, digitally based social movements may have the opposite of the intended effect by demobilizing the social network. But networked individualism goes beyond the demobilization associated with slacktivism, as shifts in attitudes toward traditional institutions of family, religion, and national pride, all indicate a significant shift, especially among young people under 30 years of age.

Generally speaking, digital media serve two primary functions: information dissemination and direct communication. In an analysis of 100 thousand tweets during the emergence stage of the #NeverAgain hashtag campaign, four types of social media posts were identified (Fig. 1.9).[75] Sharing news and events is an important factor at various stages of a movement because to grow and sustain the movement, it is important that followers are aware of and understand the main or common goal. In the #NeverAgain movement, the core members, also referred to as mediators, served as a conduit of sorts doling out information and updates regarding upcoming events. In the second category, sharing knowledge and support, social media posts encouraged individuals into the movement by offering hope that change is possible.

The final two categories deal more with sharing of opportunities and personal experiences. In this instance, the sharing of personal experiences is indicative of the pervasiveness of gun violence and the breath of its impact across the social network. Sharing personal experiences also reflects the type of network individualism described above.

Along with the #NeverAgain hashtag movement to support gun control, the #Fridays4Future movement serves as a case in point. In her TED Talk, Luisa Neubauer, a climate change activist, states:

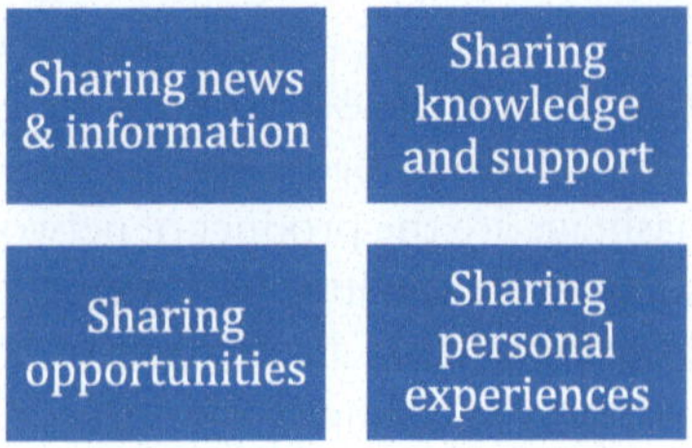

Fig. 1.9 Four categories of social media posts from the #NeverAgain movement

> I was now certain that no one else was going to fix this for us, and if there was just the slightest chance that this could make a difference, it seemed almost foolish not to give it a go. So, I traveled back to Berlin. I found allies who had the same idea at the same time, and together we thought we'd give this "Fridays For Future" thing a go. Obviously, we had no idea what we were getting into. Before our first strike, many of us, including me, had never organized a public demonstration or any kind of protest before. We had no money, no resources and absolutely no idea what climate striking really is. So, we started doing what we were good at: we started texting, texting en masse, night and day, everyone we could reach, organizing our first climate strike via WhatsApp.[76]

Situational Theory and Publics

A term that shows up consistently among activists is an understanding that most people operate within their "zone of convenience." In other words, individuals are encouraged to shed their fatalistic attitudes and passive behaviors in order to rise above mere awareness to become active on an issue. But it is individuals' relationships to a specific issue, problem, or situation that leads to the formation of a public, which Grunig describes as groups of people that come together around an issue—latent, aware, or active. These types of publics relate to situational theory which is centered on three variables: problem recognition, constraint recognition, and level of involvement. Therefore, an apathetic or latent public is one that has yet to realize there is a problem; more specifically they have not yet come to understand that a problem exists that may affect them personally, although their values may be aligned with the issue. Aware publics do recognize a problem exists, in the case of climate change that it is real, but they are constrained in their response to the issue. In such an instance an individual might say, "I know climate change is a real threat, but what can I do about it?" Third, there are active publics, which are people who are aware, and as the name suggests, are active on the issue. They feel a personal involvement and believe they can have a personal impact on the issue. The goal of a social movement, therefore, is to turn latent publics or those who are passive on the issue into publics that are active on the issue. Within all of this, it is important to understand there are also non-publics, individuals that simply are not aware, for whatever reason, of an issue.

The concept of publics does not lend itself to the traditional ways that marketers segment audiences based on demographics or psychographics.

As publics are groups of people that come together as individuals around an issue, they require what may be termed differential responses, which are different from purchase decisions that may be directed toward a specific demographic category. In an applied sense, the global issue of climate change may draw differential responses from various demographic groups, incomes, and ages, among other social attributes, consistent with both cyberconflict theory and the logic of connectivity.

The question therefore regards who is most likely to attend to climate change messages based on the situational relevance of those messages. Publics begin as "disconnected systems of individuals," that see a common problem.[77] We can see this play out within Blumer's four stages of social movements. In particular, at the emergence stage, publics are disaggregated networks that see a common problem. The potential is for them to coalesce into a movement, especially as cognitive schemas are built over time as information seeking and processing grows. In other words, dynamic cognitive schema are based on the ebb and flow of most social issues, which suggests that the number of publics and the intensity of those publics will drive the issue at any particular time. In social networking parlance, such publics become communities which may be in actuality be made up of clusters or niches within a social network.

Grunig sees these variables as either internal or external to the individual, and he suggests by way of explanation that those differences determine the likelihood that an individual will become active on an issue or remain passive.[78] What this theory tells us is that there may be the global issue of climate change that individuals may have and express feelings about but there are more specific issues related to climate for situational reasons individuals or groups may be more or less motivated to become active on, like an impending hurricane, for example that might motivate people who live in low-lying areas to think more about the effects of climate change on their immediate environment (Fig. 1.10). To put it another way, is climate an all issue or single-issue situation to which individuals are expected to respond through activist behaviors? The question for organizers or mediators of social movements is to turn a global issue or even a single issue into a hot button issue. It is the latter to which even passive publics are likely to respond. The opposite might be said for those groups or organizations that oppose an issue—climate change deniers. For example, the broader issue of climate change is a global issue, in this case global not referring to location but a general or generic category. And, it is likely that most people if asked would say that climate is an issue

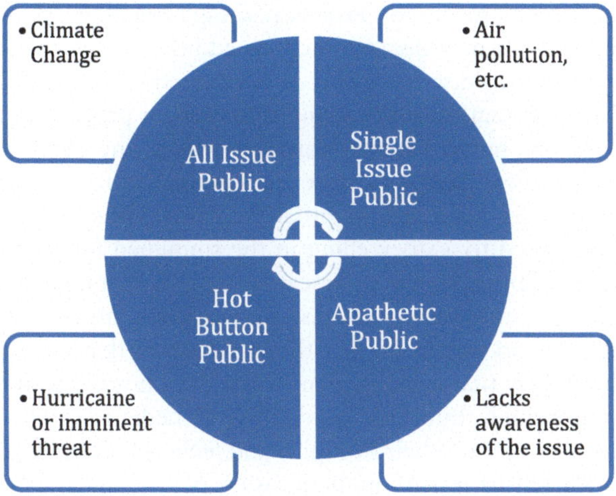

Fig. 1.10 Four types of issue oriented publics

regardless of how they feel or think about it (even climate change deniers think about climate). Air pollution, on the other hand, is a single issue that affects climate, and to that end most people hold attitudes toward air pollution, so a smog filled city, like Mumbai, might motivate people to not only have attitudes toward air pollution but to express cognitions they have formed over time about the issue. Third, a hurricane that impacts millions of people, perhaps one that is located where or near you live, would turn into a hot button issue based on the immediacy or situational relevance of that climate related issue. The question is: how do attitudes toward each of these issue levels impact cognitions or thoughts on these issues?

ZiZi Papacharissi introduced the concept of "affective publics," which she describes as "public formations that are textually rendered into being through emotive expression that spread virally through networked crowds."[79] On digital media this manifests as collaborative storytelling that might be formed through the use of hashtags that form networked publics. In the digital age, this distinction between attitudes and cognitions is important, when we consider the difference between information seeking and information processing behaviors. In the former, individuals seek out information on a given issue. They may read or watch news in mainstream media, read online media, like blog posts, engage in a Reddit subgroup, Facebook group, or Twitter hashtag campaign. Along the way, however, individuals may discover new or additional information on the issue or problem; this discovery process is referred to as information processing. Both information seeking and information processing are building blocks for cognitive schema, through which one stitches together information and ideas from various sources in the formation and reformation of thoughts, feelings, and potential behaviors. On social media, all of this may be reduced to a storytelling in the simplified form of a hashtag, tweet, retweet, or post. However, research suggests that information seeking leads to communication effects, in particular attitude formation, although there is no way to predict the direction of that attitude. Critics of this approach say that looking at attitudes does not tell us much about the ways people think. But if we look at digital media platforms as a place where individuals present their thoughts and feelings, it can be argued that such platforms tell us much about the ways people think. For example, conducting a sentiment analysis of a sub-reddit on climate change can tell us much about how people on that platform feel about the problem or issue as their story of climate emerges through posts and comments and reactions in the form of up or down votes. Similar kinds of analyses, which will be taken up in later chapters of this book, also provide methods to analyze sentiment and toxicity as well as presenting visualizations of social networks that map community structures in the form of clusters and niches that exist around social movements.

Toward a Theory of Mediated Networks

It is perhaps easy to see how the term networks comes up in reference to social movements, as the term implies both the facilitation of various aspects of a movement, like resources for example, and the term also implies the network is a negotiated space in which various meanings are made. Fuchs, describes social movements as self-organized "as the idea of the networked, co-operative, synergetic production of emergent qualities and systems should be employed in order to arrive at a dynamic concept of protest."[80] However, as has been pointed out in this chapter, in a mediated network, there are going to be strong ties as well as weak ties. There will be those in the network that operate on the periphery and those at the center of the movement. There will not likely be a monolithic social structure, but rather clusters both large and small that make up the network. As well, there will be outliers, sometimes referred to as isolates. Digital networks are not just a place for stakeholders, but as situational theory suggests, the level of engagement is variable, operating on a continuum, ranging from not engaged to actively engaged. And finally, mediated networks are not necessarily based on connective action but also are based on collective consciousness that emerges from engagement through social networks. Engagement in social movements at least in terms of collective action is a form of political action; rather, I would conclude that a collective consciousness emerges that is more a form of symbolic expression based on performance, membership, and identity.

Conclusion

This chapter began by looking at the emergence of an early digitally based social movement—moveon.org as one that adopted the properties and processes associated not only with, at the time, new media, but also by utilizing techniques gleaned from marketing. Such an approach isn't new to social movements, as we also looked at an early movement, Torches of Freedom, that utilized principles associated with engineering of consent developed by Edward Bernays, who some refer to as a founder of modern public relations. Social movements are nothing new, predating the Torches of Freedom campaign. What has changed is the shift toward hybrid activism that considers both actual and virtual activism; this became evident with the stages of development of cyberconflict theory. Mediated networks, a manifestation of virtual activism, may take the form of clicktivism or slacktivism as a function of the ebb and flow of engagement on a social issue based on the internal motivations of individuals and external persuasive forces encouraging engagement in social movements and related issues. These actions or forms of engagement are also examples of performance. This chapter frames performance as posts, comments, replies, likes, and videos, all are examples of the dramaturgical responses to social, political, and environmental issues "demonstrated" on digital platforms.

The advent of newer digital media platforms changes the dissemination of news and information by turning consumers into producers of content. Newer digital platforms, in particular social media and social networking sites (SNS), to a degree level the playing field, so to speak. While social media are not really democratic, more voices can be heard and various ideas are proffered, and in the process mediated networks may be formed as the social movement evolves from the emergence stage of disconnected individuals to coalesce into a movement in which active publics are formed with the understanding, however, that not all of those engaged in a hybrid social movement will be active, as the situational relevance of the issue will likely dictate the degree of interest and level of engagement. The chapter considered a number of theories in order to frame the discussion including new social movement theory, cyberconflict, and the theory of connective action, whose cornerstone is the idea of sharing content across networks. The concept of publics provides a way of moving beyond the ways in which marketers conceptualize audiences based on demographics, psychographics, or behavioristics to look at the ways in which people come together around an issue or problem. But the concept of publics is problematized based on the situational relevance of an issue, which may lead to activism on the part of groups of individuals, but others may feel constrained in their ability to do something about an issue or feel fatalistic toward the outcome of a problem. And yet there are others, referred to as latent or non-publics, who don't recognize there is an issue at all. Along the way, individuals develop cognitive schema as they build through information seeking and processing their "database" of knowledge that may lead to attitude formation, reinforcement, and perhaps attitude change. The role of media has been extended in the digital age to not only attract the attention of mainstream media through spectacles but to consider the social networks, including communities, clusters, and niches, that form around an issue vis-à-vis social media. By connecting theories that recognize the connected nature of individuals, as well as their interdependence digital media platforms, we can understand the social structure of networks associated with social movements as they relate to society and culture.

In order to explore the underpinnings of this theoretical framework, a social network analysis approach to social movements is presented in Chap. 2. The chapter examines the structure of social networks, including the analysis of network characteristics that concentrates on the individual, their connective actions, as well as their collective consciousness that manifests as content, curated, or otherwise, and it examines the larger network that comprises a social movement. Contextualization will be emphasized as a means to understand how the online is linked to the offline world, as a product of cyberconflict, connective action, and collective consciousness that can be quantitatively measured and described qualitatively through visual mapping and textual analysis. Specific focus will be on mediators in the network, whether they be elite (media figures), non-elite (ordinary people), or core influencers and the ways in which social movements operating in the digital age are structured through strong and weak ties.

Notes

1. Moveon.org. (n.d.). A Short History of Move On. Retrieved from: https://front.moveon.org/a-short-history/.
2. Hodson, J., Dale, A., & Petersen, B. (2018). The Instagram #climatechange Hashtag Community Does It Impact Social Capital and Community Agency? *The International Journal of Interdisciplinary Environmental Studies*, 12:3/4, pp. 17–35.
3. Regan, C. (January 15, 2015). Social Media 'Clicktivism' Creates More Apathy Than Empathy. Development Education.ie. Retrieved from: https://developmenteducation.ie/feature/social-media-clicktivism-creates-more-apathy-than-empathy/.
4. Treré, E. (2019). *Hybrid Media Activism: Ecologies, Imaginaries, Algorithms.* New York: Routledge.
5. Ibid.
6. White, M. (August 12, 2010). Clicktivism ruins left activism. *The Guardian.* Retrieved from: https://www.theguardian.com/commentisfree/2010/aug/12/clicktivism-ruining-leftist-activism.
7. White M. ibid.
8. White, M. op. cit.
9. Google book nGram Viewer. (n.d.) Activism and Social Movements. Retrieved from: https://books.google.com/ngrams/graph?content=activism%2C+social+movement&year_start=1800&year_end=2000&corpus=15&smoothing=3&share=&direct_url=t1%3B%2Cactivism%3B%2Cc0%3B.t1%3B%2Csocial%20movement%3B%2Cc0#t1%3B%2Cactivism%3B%2Cc0%3B.t1%3B%2Csocial%20movement%3B%2Cc0.
10. Blumer, H. (1969). Collective behavior. In Lee A.M., (Ed.), *Principles of sociology* (3rd Ed.). New York: Barnes and Noble Books.
11. De la Porta, D., & Diani, M. (2006). *Social movements: An introduction* (2nd Ed). Malden MA: Blackwell Publishing.
12. Christiansen, J. (n.d.). Four Stages of Social Movements. Retrieved from: https://www.ebscohost.com/uploads/imported/thisTopic-dbTopic-1248.pdf.
13. Witt, E. (February 9, 2018). How the Survivors of Parkland Began the Never Again Movement. *The New Yorker.* Retrieved from: https://www.newyorker.com/news/news-desk/how-the-survivors-of-parkland-began-the-never-again-movement.
14. Moyer, B. (1990). *Movement Action Plan. The Practical Strategist.* San Francisco: Social Movement Empowerment Project.

15. Fuchs, C. (2006). The Self-Organization of Social Movements. *Systemic Practice and Action Research*, 19:1 (February), pp. 101–137.
16. Melucci, A. (1988). Getting Involved: Identity and Mobilization in Social Movements. In B. Klandermans, H. Kriesi, and S. Tarrow (eds.), *From Structure to Action*. Greenwich, CT: JAI Press, 329–348.
17. Buechler, S. (1995). New Social Movement Theories. *The Sociological Quarterly*, 36:3 (summer), pp. 441–464. Retrieved from: https://www.jstor.org/stable/4120774.
18. Ibid., p. 103.
19. Indivisible.org. (n.d.). Retrieved from: https://indivisible.org/.
20. Karatzogianni, A. (2006). *The Politics of Cyberconflict*. New York: Routledge.
21. Ferra, I. (2020). *Digital Media and the Greek Crisis: Cyberconflicts, Discourses and Networks*. England: Bingley, West Yorkshire.
22. Karatzogianni, A. (2015). *Firebrand Waves of Digital Activism 1994–2014: The Rise and Spread of Hacktivism and Cyberconflict*. Palgrave Macmillan, London.
23. Karatzogianni, A. (2015). Introduction: Four Phases of Digital Activism and Cyberconflict. In: *Firebrand Waves of Digital Activism 1994–2014*. Palgrave Macmillan, London.
24. Karatzogianni, A., Nguyen, D., & E. Serafinelli, Eds. (2016). *The Digital Transformation of the Public Sphere: Conflict, Migration, Crisis and Culture in Digital Networks*. Palgrave Macmillan, London.
25. Bennett, W. L., & Segerberg, A. (2012): The Logic of Connective Action: Digital media and the personalization of contentious politics, *Information, Communication & Society*, 15:5, pp. 739–768. Retrieved from: https://doi.org/10.1080/1369118X.2012.670661.
26. Ibid., p. 739.
27. Ferra, I. (2020), p. 15.
28. Bennet & Segerbert, op. cit. p. 760.
29. Granovetter, M. (1973). The Strength of Weak Ties. *American Journal of Sociology*, 78:6, pp. 1360–1380. Retrieved from: www.jstor.org/stable/2776392.
30. Op. cit. pp. 744–745.
31. van Dijck, J. (2012). Facebook and the engineering of connectivity: A multi-layered approach to social media platforms. *Convergence: The International Journal of Research into New Media Technologies*, 19(2), p. 142.
32. Bernays, E. (1947). The Engineering of Consent. Retrieved from: http://www.fraw.org.uk/data/politics/bernays_1947.pdf.
33. Bernays, E. ibid., p. 113.

34. Rotzell, K., Sandage, C., & Hall, S. (1996). *Advertising in Contemporary Society: Perspectives toward Understanding*. University of Illinois Press.
35. Bernays, E. op. cit. p. 120.
36. Bennett, W.L. (2017). *Media Activism in the Digital Age*. New York: Routledge.
37. Schroeder, R., Everton, S., & Shepherd, R. (2012). Mining Twitter Data from the Arab Spring. 2:4, pp. 56–64. Retrieved from: https://globalecco.org/documents/10180/605826/CTXVol2No4.pdf/8701f69a-ec4a-4f7a-b08d-c8a793e3fc27.
38. Schroeder, R., Everton, S., & Shepherd, R. ibid., p. 57.
39. Gitlin, T. (2003). *The Whole World is Watching*. Calif: University of California Press. Gitlin attributes the phrase "floodlit society" to Walter Adamson.
40. Gitlin, T. ibid., p. 3.
41. Goffman, E. (1956). *The Presentation of Self in Everyday Life*. New York: Doubleday Publishing.
42. Pierson, E. (November 24, 2014). See How Red Tweeters and Blue Tweeters Ignore Each Other on Ferguson. *Quartz.com*. Retrieved from: https://qz.com/302616/see-how-red-tweeters-and-blue-tweeters-ignore-each-other-on-ferguson/.
43. Nobel, S.U. (2018). *Algorithms of Oppression: How Search Engines Reinforce Racism*. New York: New York University Press.
44. Abercrombie, N., & Longhurst, B. (1998). *Audiences: A Sociological Theory of Performance and Imagination*. New York: SAGE Publications Ltd; 1 edition.
45. Studyfinds.com. (2017). No Escape: Average Person Checks Phone Every 12 Minutes—While On Vacation! Retrieved from: https://www.studyfinds.org/no-escape-average-person-checks-phone-every-12-minutes-vacation/.
46. Gruzd, A., Wellman, B., & Takhteyev, Y. (2011). Twitter as Imagined Community. *American Behavioral Scientist*, 55:10, pp. 1294–1318.
47. Itzigsohm, J., & vom Hau, M. (2006). Unfinished Imagined Communities: States, Social Movements, and Nationalism in Latin America. *Theory and Society*, 35:2, pp. 193–212.
48. Anderson, B. (1991) [1983]. *Imagined Communities: Reflections on the Origins and Spread of Nationalism*, 2nd ed. New York: Verso.
49. Itzigsohm, J., & M. vom Hau. op. cit., p. 197.
50. Adams, R., & Sardiello, R. (2000). *Deadhead social science*. Walnut Creek, CA: AltaMira.
51. Jenkins, H. (October 19, 2006). Confronting the Challenges of Participatory Culture: Media Education for the 21st Century (Part One).

Confessions of an Aca-Fan. Retrieved from: http://henryjenkins.org/blog/2006/10/confronting_the_challenges_of.html.

52. Gerbaudo, P. (2017). In Cahiers de doleance 2.0: Crowd-sourced social justice blogs and the emergence of a rhetoric of collection in social media activism, In Pickard, V. & Guobin, Y. (eds). Media Activism in the Digital Age. New York: Routledge.
53. van Dijck, J., p. 147.
54. Isa, D., & Himelboim, I. (2018). A Social Networks Approach to Online Social Movement: Social Mediators and Mediated Content in #FreeAJStaff Twitter Network. *Social Media + Society*. https://doi.org/10.1177/2056305118760807.
55. Ibid., p. 6.
56. Op. cit., p. 150.
57. Sengupta, S. (August 13, 2019). Greta Thunberg Sets Sail for U.N. Climate Talks. *The New York Times*. Retrieved from: https://www.nytimes.com/2019/08/13/climate/greta-thunberg-sailing.html.
58. Kellner, D. (n.d.). Media Culture and the Triumph of Spectacle. Retrieved from: https://pages.gseis.ucla.edu/faculty/kellner/essays/mediaculture-triumphspectacle.pdf.
59. Kellner, D. ibid., p. 1.
60. NPR.org (December 17, 2017). The Arab Spring: A Year of Revolution. NPR.org. Retrieved from: https://www.npr.org/2011/12/17/143897126/the-arab-spring-a-year-of-revolution.
61. NPR.org. ibid.
62. Wael Ghonim, W. (2015). Let's Design Social Media to Create Real Change. *TED.com*. Retrieved from: https://www.ted.com/talks/wael_ghonim_let_s_design_social_media_that_drives_real_change.
63. The Guardian (March 12, 2018). Myanmar: UN blames Facebook for spreading hatred of Rohingya. *The Guardian.com*. Retrieved from: https://www.theguardian.com/technology/2018/mar/13/myanmar-un-blames-facebook-for-spreading-hatred-of-rohingya.
64. van Dijk, J. (2015). Facebook and the engineering of connectivity: A multi-layered approach to social media platforms. *Convergence: The International Journal of Research into New Media Technologies*, 19:2, pp. 141–155. https://doi.org/10.1177/1354856512457548.
65. Wellman, B. (Rainie, Lee) (2012). *Networked: The New Social Operating System*. Cambridge, MA: MIT Press.
66. Purcell, P. (2006). *Networked Neighbourhoods: The Connected Community in Context*. London: Springer-Verlag.
67. van Dijk, J. (2006). *The network society: social aspects of new media*. Thousand Oaks, CA: SAGE, pp. 1–64.

68. Marzouki, Y., & Oullier, O. (December 6, 2017). Revolutionizing Revolutions: Virtual Collective Consciousness and the Arab Spring. *Huffpost.com*. Retrieved from: https://www.huffingtonpost.com/yousri-marzouki/revolutionizing-revolutio_b_1679181.html.
69. Marshall, P.D. (2010). The promotion and presentation of the self: celebrity as marker of presentational media. *Celebrity Studies*, 1:1, pp. 35–48. https://doi.org/10.1080/19392390903519057.
70. Read, M. (December 8, 2018). Did Facebook Cause Riots in France? *Intelligencer.com*. Retrieved from: http://nymag.com/intelligencer/2018/12/did-facebook-cause-the-yellow-vest-riots-in-france.html.
71. O'Brian. M. (n.d.). New forms of Activism in a Network Society. Retrieved from: http://www.michelleobrien.net/wp-content/uploads/2011/10/Presentation_notes_OBrien.pdf.
72. OccupyWallStreet.org. (2001). Retrieved from: http://www.occupywallst.org.
73. Coyle, J. (November 24, 2011). Occupy Wall Street Memes Sprout Up On The Internet. *HuffPost.com*. Retrieved from: https://www.huffpost.com/entry/occupy-wall-street-memes_n_1111848.
74. Gladwell, M. (2010). Small Change: Why the revolution will not be tweeted. *The New Yorker*, October 4, 2010. Retrieved from: http://www.newyorker.com/reporting/2010/10/04/101004fa_fact_gladwell.
75. Alperstein, N., & Jones, T. (Forthcoming, December, 2020). The Online Social Movement of #NeverAgain: How social networks build a sense of membership, influence, support and emotional connection on Twitter. *Journal of Society Media in Society*.
76. Neubauer, L. (July 2019). Why I Became a Climate Activist and Why You Should too. *TED.com*. Retrieved from: https://www.ted.com/talks/luisa_neubauer_why_i_became_a_climate_activist_and_why_you_should_too.
77. Grunig, J. (n.d.). A Situational Theory of Environmental Issues, Publics and Activists. Retrieved from: https://files.eric.ed.gov/fulltext/ED304332.pdf#page=53.
78. Ibid., p. 53.
79. Papacharissi, Z. (2015). Affective Publics and Structures of Storytelling: Sentiment, Events and Mediality. *Information, Communication & Society*, 19:3, pp. 307–324.
80. Fuchs, C. (2006). The Self-Organization of Social Movements. *Systematic practice and Action Research*, 19:1 (February), p. 133. Retrieved from: https://doi.org/10.1007/s11213-005-9006-0.

CHAPTER 2

A Social Network Approach to Analyzing Social Movements

When conceptualizing a social movement in the digital age, what comes to mind? In other words, what do you imagine such a community would look like? Many of us would immediately think of like-minded people getting together online to consider issues, gather and share information, and bond with others. As the saying goes, "birds of a feather flock together." After all, if you look at an offline rally like the March for Our Lives, the expectation is that everyone shares the same values when it comes to gun control and related issues.

Manuel Castells, in his book *Networks of Outrage and Hope*, describes such relationships between digital media and social movements as "networked social movements" that he says are centralized in ways that newer communication technologies liberate people creating autonomy that regains power and leads to social change. However, when one observes the online interactions of a social movement, perhaps on Twitter, Facebook, or Instagram, one may see a very different picture, as mixed with tweets, retweets, memes, and posts or comments appropriate to the respective platforms that on the surface may seem homophilic, are dissenters, detractors, and among them those individuals that seek to denigrate others in the social movement. In other words, the community that we imagined may in reality not be the community that operates in the online environment.

Beyond the interactions that may be an expression of sentiment—positive, negative, or neutral—in social networks are those individuals who

N. Alperstein, *Performing Media Activism in the Digital Age*,
https://doi.org/10.1007/978-3-030-73804-4_2

play various roles as mediators of the online movement, which may be actual leaders of the movement, but may include influencers who merely by virtue of their large number of followers or even the number of tweets that they post or get retweeted have the potential—even though their connections to the movement may be weak—to influence the networked community.

This chapter presents a social network analysis (SNA) approach to social movements in the digital age. The chapter discusses virtual communities, clusters, and niches including the social structure of digitally based networks. In addition, the chapter delves into issues regarding social capital as well as mediator roles within social movements and the role of strong and weak ties in the network. The chapter introduces network measures, like modularity and centrality among others and applies them in a case study of the #NeverAgain hashtag associated with the March for Our Lives.

Social Movements as Virtual Communities

Castell's view of networked social movements is based on his extensive research on social movements in Spain, Brazil, Turkey, Chile, and Mexico in which he optimistically claims that coordinating offline action with online initiatives opens up opportunities for networked social movements to become "super counter powers."[1] Social movements certainly hold the potential to form both offline and online communities. When thinking of community, often we conceptualize communities as people in close proximity to one another; however, digital media have changed things so that social movements have to grapple with the tension between concrete relationships and those we imagine; hence the often-used reference to imagined communities. With regard to digital media's role in social movements, Twitter is an asymmetric platform in which I might follow you, but you don't necessarily have to follow me back, yet we may operate within the broader social network that brings us together perhaps around a social issue and related hashtag. While physical distance seems to be an issue with regard to defining social media users as members of communities, there is growing evidence that engagement in online communities enhances social interaction and that it extends it beyond the social media platform.

Benedict Anderson in his 1983 book *Imagined Communities* writes about developing societies in which leaders were trying to create a common identity among the populace. As most people in the populace never really know one another, he referred to them as imagined communities.

The phrase has been utilized and perhaps romanticized to the extent that it has, according to some scholars, become cliché.[2] Grădinaru describes the virtual community as one that is dynamic, including tensions among the layers of the community based on factors like technology, conversation, and relationship.[3] The author claims "the degree of its imagined side depends on multiple factors, such as the dimension of the community, its age, the clarity of its rules, and its specificity." The composition of the virtual community is another important factor: "the imagined part may be significantly different if this community is entirely online made, if its activities combine online and offline environments and people know each other, or if the virtual community is another form of interaction for a traditional local group constituted before in offline."[4] While the idea that similar values and beliefs undergird the virtual community, it's important to keep in mind that the dissimilarities of beliefs and values among those individuals engaged in a social network, important to its functioning, also create tension within the community. In other words, differences as well as similarities give shape and organization to the virtual community. While Anderson made no reference to social media given that his book was published in 1983, newer conceptualizations like virtual community or virtual settlement may apply to the age of digital media. Although being a member of a virtual community does not imply membership or even a sense of belonging, there are characteristics that are deemed important: interactivity among two or more participants; a common place to meet including but not limited to social media; and the ability to sustain the connection over time (Fig. 2.1).

But these characteristics also need to be considered within the broader sense of community, which includes not just membership (however that

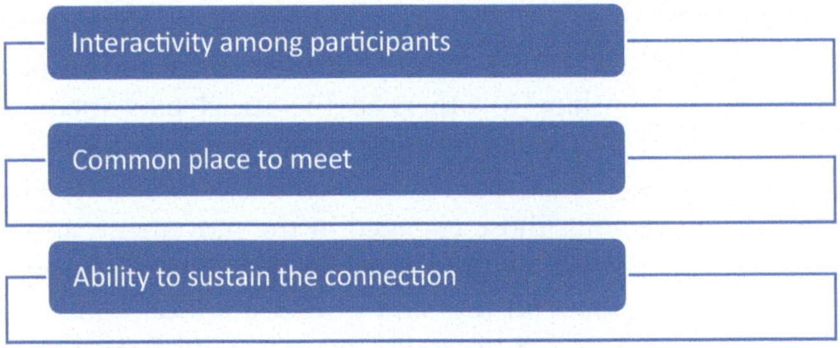

Fig. 2.1 Three characteristics of virtual communities

might be defined) but leadership and in that the ability to influence or make a difference in the community. Additionally, there needs to be a shared sense of needs among a critical mass that some might define as criteria for membership as well as an emotional connection among those engaged in the community.[5] Digitally based virtual communities, therefore, operate on two levels: group or collective, and individual. These levels do not imply polarization in the sense that, as Grădinaru posits, one suggests distance and the other closeness, or one suggests temporary and the other permanent. When addressing values and beliefs at the core of a social movement, reference is made to the work of culture, and culture in the digital age finds its terra firma within the tensions created by the "conversations" that take place in virtual spaces. There is the associated issue of context collapse, a concept associated with the infinite audience of social media. From the perspective of performing media activism, context collapse is the outcome of what may be described metaphorically as shooting arrows into the air and not knowing if or where they might land. Or, to put it another way, communicating via social media is like talking to everyone and no one. In other words, "context collapse is the process of disparate audiences being cojoined into one." Gil-Lopez and colleagues maintain in their study of context collapse that Facebook audiences manage their online self-presentation in ways that are consistent with imagined audience.[6]

Related to the notion of virtual community is the idea of imagined virtual sociability, the foundation of which is the way those engaged in a social movement imagine its structure but also the atmosphere embodied in the interactions and the dynamic quality of the relationships experienced in the virtual community. As Fox states: "the imagined perception of community includes the technology, the content and representation, the history of members, the intertextuality of content, and the communication among users (p. 53)."[7] The imagined part is the basis of the individual's mediated social connection to the movement and in particular their imagined relationships to others in the social movement. In this manner, engagement in a social movement elevates the digital aspect of the experience to the virtual sphere. In a virtual community, gaps exist because of distance among those engaged in the movement, anonymous or semi-anonymous participants, and weak ties that foster the imagination. The imagination is a powerful tool and in that a critical component for making sense of ourselves and the world around us, including the virtual communities in which people engage. Social media are a sense-making mechanism manifest in tweets, memes, videos, follows, likes, posts, comments, direct messaging, and other ways in which we operate within the social networks to which we keep the conversation entre nous; all of them make up the narrative that is an expression of the collective consciousness of the social network.

Social Network Approach

Social movements in the digital age are made complex because of the factors illuminated above including the inclusion of supporters and detractors, physical distance, the amorphous nature of the organization, leaderless perhaps, among other factors. In order to better understand the social structure of a movement, a social network approach is advanced in this book based on graph theory to analyze a network's structure and the relationship among the people engaged in a social movement, what I call performing media activism. Although graph theory is derived from mathematics and usually applied by computer scientists, it is being adopted by social sciences and the humanities to create visualizations of social structures, like social movements. In other words, all of the variables mentioned above, like influence and connection as well as emotion can be measured and the connections among those within the network can be visualized. Such an approach provides a unique approach, combining both interests in social movements and social network analysis. As well, the social network approach provides a means to locate an individual within the network's hierarchy, identifying influencers, for example, and in that to determine how well connected—strong or weak—the individuals are in the network. In order to analyze a social network comprising a virtual community and perhaps the clusters and niches within the community, algorithms are used to analyze the network to better understand, for example, social capital within the network and links between subgroups, as well as the strength of the ties within the network. The social network approach provides a way to look at qualitative variables in the network, like words used, pairs of words, and sentiment—positive, neutral, or negative—in the network. Differentiated from sentiment, the social network approach also provides a method to measure toxicity within a social network. Social network analysis (SNA) provides a way to look at mediator roles in the network, whether they be core, elite, or non-elite mediators, and it provides a way to better understand social influencers who operate within the network, as well as those people who are most active in posting to a particular social medium.

There are several ways of formally defining a network, depending on the branch of mathematics used. Although in graph theory, a social network is conceptualized as a set of vertices, also referred to as nodes, which are the social actors in the network, and the network is connected by a set of edges, represented as lines indicating a social relationship among the nodes (Fig. 2.2). The relationship can be outward, also referred to as out-degree, in which one node communicates to another node in the network. When another node communicates back into the network, it is referred to as in-degree. Relationships may be outward or inward reaching in which case a social network is visualized as a graph, that is, a set of vertices (or nodes, units, points) representing social actors or objects and a set of lines (edges) representing one or more social relations among them.

Fig. 2.2 Social network of nodes (circles) and edges (lines). (Social Network Image. Retrieved from: https://www.needpix.com/photo/822467/network-social-social-networks-group.)

In the digital age, we freely utilize the term "social networks" to describe the myriad ways in which people connect and interact on social media. But the term "social network" has been around much longer than the internet, dating back to the beginning of the twentieth century when sociologists began to apply the term. Lee Rainie and Barry Wellman, authors of the book *Networked* state: "Social scientists have been using the metaphor of 'the social network' for more than a century [well before FB] to connote complex sets of relationships at all scales, from interpersonal to international ... Yet it wasn't until the 1950s that they started using the term systematically & self-consciously to describe patterns of ties that cut across traditional concepts of bounded groups (villages, families) & social categories (gender, ethnicity) that create people as discrete individuals" (pp. 39–40).[8] A social network approach to social movements is, of course, concerned with the social web whether it be blogs, Reddit, LinkedIn, Twitter, Facebook, Instagram, YouTube, and TikTok, among others where people share words and images that are expressive of their cognitions on, well, mostly any subject, including social justice, political, and environmental issues.

A hallmark of the social web is the ability of ordinary people from anywhere to participate in mediated culture through what is referred to as user-generated content (UGC), which can be comprised of tweets, posts, comments, shared links, videos, and other types of content. The ability to perform social media gives way to the idea of participating in a public forum where relationships are, and in that connection is, being conducted in an artificially constructed performative space. In her article "Browsing the Performative: A Search for Sincerity," author Kate Hawkins distinguishes between performance and performative. Performance is something that happens in the present, but is one that can be repeated, like a theatrical play. Performative, however, refers to the act of doing; it does not require an audience in the theatrical sense. The social web, an artificially constructive performative space, continues to evolve since the advent of the Web in 1991. To that extent, the World Wide Web's inventor, Tim Berners-Lee, saw the Web as a place where people could interact—a collaborative medium. It is the content made available on those social platforms from which researchers draw data in order to conduct a social network analysis. However, since 2018 access to data has become problematic.

Limited Access to Social Data

In light of the Cambridge Analytica scandal, on April 4, 2018, Facebook announced restrictions on data access and deprecation of the Instagram API (application programming interface) severely limiting academic access to those platforms.[9] APIs generally are intended for use by programmers who may be building apps within the various social networks, but researchers have also utilized APIs to study online behavior. These restrictions have severely impacted the ability of researchers who use analytic tools like NodeXL, Netlytic, and Netvizz among others that utilize the APIs to collect data. Researchers up until 2018 were able to pretty freely access data from social media platforms like Facebook. However, it was Aleksandr Kogan whose research start-up allegedly collected profile information from 270,000 Facebook users and millions of their friends using a personality test, data that was subsequently utilized by Cambridge Analytica to target political campaigns in the United States and various other countries.[10] Twitter, too, has questioned researchers' access to data, as social media platforms are "making it increasingly difficult and expensive for academics to access tweets to research important questions ranging from how information about diseases like Zika spread to how social movements like Black Lives Matter work to how social media can be used to promote democracy."[11] Bottom line: social network analysis today operates within the limitations imposed by large social media companies.

Network Structures

A social network approach to social movements conceptualizes mediated activism as both a community and clusters or niches in which there are key actors or mediators who fuel the movement with content that may lead to connections within the broader or smaller community. What does it mean to take a social network approach? By looking at the structure of the social network created by actors engaged with the social movement, we can identify clusters and niches of those engaged on a topic or issue who utilize a hashtag or hashtags that represent the issue, as well as identify the mediators of the social movement. Social network analysis allows us to map onto those social structures within the movement and visualize the nature and direction of communication within the movement as an expression of cognitions that reflect unconscious or latent thoughts and feelings that spill out into social media through various ways in which we engage, like tweeting or posting memes. The surface of the network may look like an expression of the collective consciousness of the movement, similar to Durkheim's description of the ways in which certain values, traditions, and beliefs are constant across a society. Structures within a social movement refer to the ways in which individuals connect directly, interconnect among subgroups, or those that don't connect at all, but are still engaged in the larger network. The latter are individuals who, as they tweet, for example, are metaphorically shooting arrows into the air. While those arrows or rather messages may land with the possibility that others will respond, to a great extent those arrows merely fall to the proverbial ground. In the Twittersphere this would manifest as tweets that exist on the periphery of the network, what may be referred to as isolates. In that case such messaging may serve the personal interest of the individual but adds little to the overall conversation and narrative building within the social network. Nevertheless, all those tweets, for example, reflect the expression of the sum total of the collective consciousness—values and beliefs—around the movement and related issues. Collective consciousness needs to be distinguished from community or collective identity in that the former is based on the shared ideas of a society, whereas the latter refers to the shared identity that motivates people to join a group. It is the latter that is necessary for the formation of a social movement but it is the former that is the output of community building.[12]

Although the concept of network structure is not new, as it is derived from classical sociology, using a social network approach, we can see the network as a set of ties and interactions among the actors in the network. Social networks may be comprised of social groups through what might be called a socio-centered approach.[13] An important aspect of studying social networks is to focus on network structure, the network's structural properties, and how structure affects outcomes within social movements. Some movements are, for example, leaderless, others are driven by political leaders or celebrities, and yet others are influenced by media, among other possibilities. An alternative to the socio-centered approach is to view the network from the perspective of the actor or ego-centered approach.[14]

The Pew Research Center developed six network structures from their study of the Twitter networks including the following: polarized crowds, tight crowds, brand clusters, community clusters, broadcast networks, and support networks.[15] As can be seen in Fig. 2.3, some of those network structures are tightly connected while others are loosely connected and yet others are disconnected. The latter might be exemplified by the metaphor

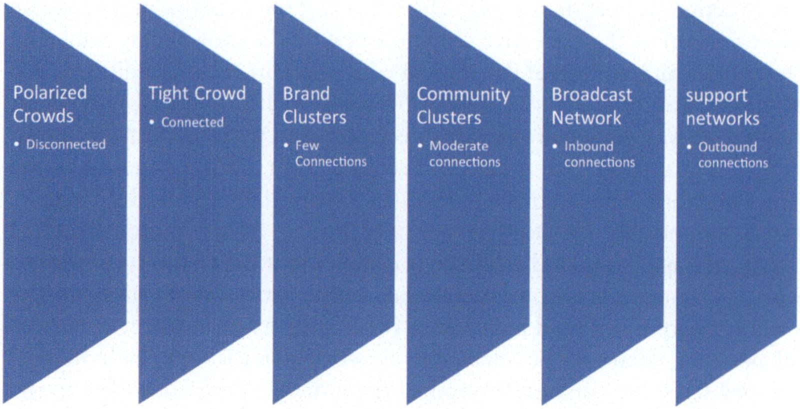

Fig. 2.3 Six types of social media networks (Pew Research)

for tweeting provided above regarding shooting arrows into the air not knowing if or where they might land. It would be expected that the types of structures seen in social movements would be somewhat varied.

An online social movement around gun control, for example, might attract both individuals that are pro-control of guns (supporters of second amendment rights) and those against (supporters of banning assault rifles). In this complex social network, the crowds that make the structure would be polarized and likely disconnected. Those who paid attention to conversations within the social network would likely narrow their focus on topics or issues that were situationally relevant to them, while disregarding messaging offered by the so-called opposition. In other words, a social network in regard to a social movement is neither homogeneous in its composition nor monolithic in its ideas, and therefore the movement may comprise "likers" as well as "haters."

To a greater extent brand and community structures associated with social movements are represented as many small- or medium-size clusters, as opposed to polarized crowds that more likely will be comprised of two divergent groups. In brand communities, individuals may have few connections and therefore many isolated individuals operating within the network. There may be many smaller clusters surrounding the brand. Community clusters are demonstrated by several or many smaller groups, sometimes referred to as niches. As a small group, we would expect to see greater connections among the participants. But as the group grows in size attracting others into the cluster, connections the social network may become weaker. The ties and messaging may be inbound (in-degree), outbound (out-degree), or both (degree).

Online Social Capital

An ancillary component of network structure is the idea of social capital that can be defined as the network of contacts within a social movement and the associated values attached to these networks of contacts that make individuals noticeable and praiseworthy. As Grădinaru points out, social capital is "increasingly important not only for the online cohesion, but also for the mobilization of networks in order to solve offline vital issues (political, humanitarian or social)."[16] Grădinaru points to online protests as an example of the importance of online social capital. The term "social capital" can mean different things, and perhaps the term may best be seen in application, as Sabatini, whose concern is econometrics presents the following five main dimensions of social capital: strong family ties (i.e. bonding social capital), weak informal ties (bridging social capital), voluntary organizations (linking social capital), active political participation, and civic awareness (Fig. 2.4).[17] When considering social capital as the currency of influence within the social network, the actor-centered model provides insights into how influencers moderate the social network.

Fig. 2.4 Sabatini's dimensions of social capital

Actor Network Theory (ANT) and the Engineering of Mediators in Performing Media Activism

We might begin by asking the question: What are the natural connections between performing activism on digital media and being physically present at a rally or protest? In the pre-digital era, we might ask that question differently, but within an environment of performing media activism, we must consider that the stage set by newer communication technologies and the pivotal role they play in the process of political and social change. In this sense, the technology itself is one (nonhuman) of the actants or in this case elements in a network. Human and nonhuman relationships to technology can be described in terms of actor networks in which actants are simply constituent nodes that facilitate a larger functioning of the network. The theory comes from French sociologists Bruno Latour and Michel Callon and British sociologist John Law. The central idea is that nature, technology, and society do not operate alone in a vacuum. Rather than looking at these as dichotomies, social networks need to be understood in the broader context of operating within all three categories. Action associated with activities within a social network need to be viewed as collective activities, a product of relationships among human and nonhuman actors. Action or agency is not a solitary act but rather an "arrangement" among the constellation of actors or entities.[18] Looked at another way, ANT moves beyond the transmission model of communication characterized by sender and receiver to place communication within the cultural confines of the social network that considers communication technology; in other words, the media mediates.

As applied to social movements, we might see anyone who tweets on the hashtag #BlackLivesMatter, for example, as an actant or node within that social network that forms around the hashtag. However, actor network theory falls short of identifying the power structure within the network, as there is no distinction, demographic, for example, between or among the actors. Internet researcher danah boyd posits that digitally based social networks often reflect the larger society in which they operate, for example, in the Egyptian uprising, media like Al Jazeera played a vital role disseminating information. But boyd acknowledges that in recent years with the advent of newer technologies that amplification has grown more complicated in that mainstream media may no longer play their traditional role as gatekeepers of news and information.[19] In other words, we have to account not only for content providers—traditional news media and newer digital platforms—but also the technologies that deliver that content. Such a viewpoint regarding technology's ability to amplify an issue fits squarely within the boundaries of actor network theory. Strategic amplification is a concern of boyd's, for example, a conspiracy theorist's ability to impact digital media platforms, including search engines, through strategic amplification. Strategic amplification includes creating spectacle, a topic addressed in Chap. 1 and revisited in later chapters of this book. But it also includes words and phrases, sometimes in the form of hashtags or polarizing language that can bias a public discussion. The implication for social movements is that they may be subjected to manipulation and data voids. To put it more simply, in any social movement there may be "bad actors." The question for a functioning democracy remains unanswered as mainstream media, technology companies like Google or Facebook, as well as government and ordinary citizens continue to grapple with the complexity of operating in an attention economy.

Social Network Mediators

By applying the concept of mediated social connections—the ways in which our inner thoughts are expressed outward through social media—to digital activism, readers can better understand how social mediators operate to push an agenda and how social movements as they become organized can better utilize dialogic communication within their social network.[20] Understanding the types of mediators or hubs they create can better inform us about the mediated connections between the social movement and its publics or diffused audiences. Social network analysis allows us to look for patterns of interactions among the social actors, whether they be individuals, the media, or organizations. Following Himelboim and colleagues, social mediators may be defined as "the entities that mediate the relations between an organization and its publics through social media and regard mediated public relations as communicative relationships and interactions with key social mediators that influence the relationship between an organization and its publics."[21] Mediators of social networks, who may serve the role of mediator in a social network, can be categorized as elites, non-elites, or core.[22] Celebrities, for example, might qualify as elites in a social network, whereas ordinary people would be categorized as non-elites. Members of the media are considered core mediators, as are people with a highly vested interest in the issue. The role of the mediator, as opposed to a moderator, is to affect the outcome of a social movement.

Strength of Weak Ties

Connections or "ties" made with people in a social network that one does not know personally are referred to as the strength of weak ties, a theory put forth by Mark Granovetter.[23] An example of a strong tie would be someone you know well and with whom you have regular interactions, while weak ties are acquaintances.[24] Paradoxically, Granovetter suggests that it is those weak ties in a social network that sometimes keep the entire relationship strong; hence his strength of weak ties theory. To extend this a bit further, if one exists in a tight social circle of strong ties, there is a chance one could miss information that a weak tie could provide. Because weak ties are on the edges of one's social network, they are gathering information that one may not normally have access to in one's immediate social relationships. Additionally, as there is less dissonance, meaning less significance to the relationship, weak ties gain importance not afforded to strong ties. As the online social network grows, the ties are likely to become weaker. It may be that with regard to conceptualizing publics or audiences within a social network, communication based on weak ties may turn an aware public into an active public.

While Granovetter's theory pre-dates the internet, it can be applied in several more recent events fueled by digital media including the Arab Spring and #NeverAgain social movements. The Arab Spring was first seen in late 2010, early 2011, in which social media was utilized to highlight dissatisfaction with the government of Tunisia. As was highlighted in Chap. 1, social media was used by Tunisians to organize protests, spread ideologies, and try to push President Zine El Abidine Ben Ali out of power. It was also the use of cellphone cameras depicting the horrible conditions being streamed globally that demanded action. This revolution spread virally online and eventually extended throughout the Middle East, most notably in Egypt, with Esraa Abdel Fattah, an Egyptian democracy activist known as "Facebook Girl" leading the movement.[25] The community of harassed, in this case, was started by young Tunisians who filmed the protests that arose after 26-year-old Mohamed Bouazizi burned himself alive in his own form of protest after being embarrassed by a police officer. Posting such potent images on social media fanned the flames of outrage and with fellow citizens, who may not have even known Bouazizi coalesced into a movement, an example of the power of weak ties, to combat the government.

In their study of the #NeverAgain hashtag and March for Our Lives social movement, Alperstein and Jones found all three categories of mediators are represented, including the three Parkland High School students who took on the role of core mediators.[26] However, their study found that the top non-elite account is from @sandrahallstrom, who was responsible for posting over 16 percent of the tweets in the network, an indication this individual is very engaged, although not a core mediator in the movement. When we consider locating the power or direction of amplification of a social issue, it may not be elite or core mediators that are driving the discussion; rather non-elites through their heightened engagement in the network demonstrate their ability to play a role in the discussion and perhaps even help nudge the movement in a particular direction.

Network Characteristics

As can be seen in the case study below, social networks exhibit characteristics that help to understand how communication works between people engaged in the social movement. Centrality is one such measure that indicates how information flows among those engaged in the network. In a highly centralized network, for example, there are a few influencers who drive the conversation or messaging. But in a network of low centralization, many individuals communicate freely but not necessarily to each other. With regard to the social network analysis approach, two measures are of particular importance: degree centralization and betweenness centralization, as these indicate the importance of a person (node) in a network. Before describing these two concepts, the term "degree" needs to be understood as referring to two aspects of communication: in-degree and out-degree. In social network analysis algorithms calculate the messages that are coming into a node, as well as those messages going out to others (nodes). Degree centrality refers to the number of links or ties (edges) a person has to and from others in the network. In other words, the measure calculates how many times someone in the network mentions another person in the network. Betweenness centrality is a measure of influence within the community. Another characteristic of social networks of interest is density, which is a measure of how close participants are in a network. A dense network, which may also be described as a close-knit community, will have many participants communicating with many others. But a less dense network will show fewer connections; however, density measures may give false readings as large networks, merely because of their size, may indicate low density. Takhteyev and colleagues describe yet another characteristic of social networks, reciprocity, which refers to the two-way communication within the network, referred to earlier as in- and out-degree.[27] In this case, low reciprocity means that a few people are dominating a conversation, but measures of high reciprocity indicate an equal chance to engage in the network. Modularity is yet another characteristic that is utilized to identify specific communities or clusters within the social network, individuals that are engaged with one another. I stated earlier in this chapter that social networks are rarely made up only of like-minded people, as networks are more likely to comprise clusters, subgroups, and niches that represent a great deal, little or no intersection or collaboration across the network. To that end, a network may include people who operate on the periphery of the network. As well, there may be clusters made up of dissenters. Because of the nature of social media, the March for Our Lives social movement that seeks to end gun violence will include in the network pro-gun people. And the #ClimateStrike movement includes both people who believe in climate change and those that do not. A high measure of modularity would indicate a closely connected network; however, a low measure might be indicative of several or many clusters that may serve as bridges to other subgroups.

Hashtags are often used in online social networks as a way of organizing areas of interest. When analyzing a twitter network, data may be comprised of hashtags, users, and tweets. The tweets are valuable data that may be utilized to conduct a sentiment analysis to help determine the feelings of those engaged in the social movement and perhaps the direction the movement is leaning. While many hashtag campaigns are ephemeral in nature, some have more lasting power as the social movement moves from the emergence stage and beyond. In order to illustrate how these measures operate, a case study of the #NeverAgain hashtag is presented in the form of a data visualization and analysis of the social network surrounding the hashtag.

Case Study: #NeverAgain Hashtag—March for Our Lives Movement

This case study focuses on the aftermath of the 2018 shootings at Stoneman Douglas High School in Parkland, Florida, and the movement that emerged under the hashtag #NeverAgain that spearheaded March for Our lives. It was 40 days after the shootings at Stoneman Douglas High School in Parkland, Florida, that a group of students mobilized to conduct a nationwide protest to support gun control in the United States.[28] Operating under the banner of March for Our Lives, the emerging movement utilized the hashtag #NeverAgain as a calling card. The Parkland shootings unwittingly thrust several of the students into a "kind of terrible celebrity that only afflicts the very talented or the very unlucky."[29] After the shooting, many Parkland students were motivated by personal fear to champion gun reform; however, several core mediators emerged like Emma Gonzalez, one of the most visually present and vocal leaders of this movement. Isa and Himelboim describe social mediators as "influential key actors who attract more attention in their own clusters (defined by in-degree centrality) and act as a bridge between two clusters (defined by betweenness centrality). This unique position in the network allows them to spread information within their own clusters and to other clusters, which would otherwise be devoid of that information."[30] Gonzalez, whose Twitter handle is @Emma4Change, has twice the Twitter followers as the National Rifle Association (NRA) and uses her platform to inspire others to join the movement, console students across the world who have survived shootings, and call out politicians whom she feels treat her and other student survivors of gun violence with little or no respect. Another core mediator is David Hogg. Some critics of his outspokenness even suggested he wasn't a Parkland student at all; rather a crisis actor placed in front of cameras to "push the left's anti-gun agenda."[31] His detractors were perhaps hoping the negative publicity would discredit him as well as other Parkland students championing the fight for gun reform. This also illustrates how actor network theory actually works in a virtual space in which someone who is proficient at social media may be perceived as fake. Another core mediator is Cameron Kasky, a Parkland survivor who has been front and center on both mainstream media as well as social media. He has appeared with Gonzalez and Hogg on *The Ellen Show*, *The Today Show*, and *Jimmy Kimmel Live*.[32]

The Twitter application programming interface (API; http://apiwiki.twitter.com) was utilized to retrieve tweets associated with the hashtag, #NeverAgain. About 100,000 tweets were collected over the March 24 to March 29, 2018, period during which the live event, March for Our Lives, took place. Of those 100,000 tweets, there were 65,915 unique posters. The Twitter API limits the number of tweets collected to 100,000 per day as a default. There were 70,274 names found in the network with 52,585 ties (self-loops). There were 20,568 posters with ties within the network. With regard to who replies to whom, the chain network, there were 3889 posters with ties and 12,868 ties (self-loops). To process, analyze, and visualize the data, the research relied on Netlytic software (Netlytic.org). The analysis provided a list of top posters to the #NeverAgain hashtag network. Also provided was a list of the most frequently used words and a list of the top posters mentioned within messages. The data provided the basis for a sentiment analysis based on positive and negative terminology used in the Tweets. Sentiment analysis, a helpful way to better understand emotions being expressed in the social network, serves as an indicator of the tone behind a series of words, in this case Tweets. Finally, the data provided the basis for visualizations of both the name and chain networks associated with the #NeverAgain hashtag.

In the case of the #NeverAgain social network, all three mediator categories—elites, non-elites, and core are represented.[33] Three core mediators among the Parkland High School students took on a leadership role. Of interest, however, the top non-elite account is from @sandrahallstrom who was responsible for posting over 16 percent of the tweets (Fig. 2.5). It is worth noting, and as an indication of the reach of the movement, this poster is from Sweden. Although it is difficult to determine whether @sandrahallstrom is a Swedish native or an American living in Sweden, the volume of the tweets makes it clear this individual is very engaged in this movement. This individual follows elite mediators including politicians such as Kamala Harris and Beto O'Rourke, and follows topics related to pop culture and current event notables (at that time) such as Stormy Daniels and attorney Michael Avenatti. And, @sandrahallstrom is a follower and frequently retweets several of the Parkland students, which is indicative of this individual's engagement in the #NeverAgain hashtag movement. Figure 2.5 shows the top ten active members of this community based on the total number of posted messages.

The next most frequent poster was @WomenSaveUSA and this account dates to 2016 under the auspices of the DemocraticCoalition.org that

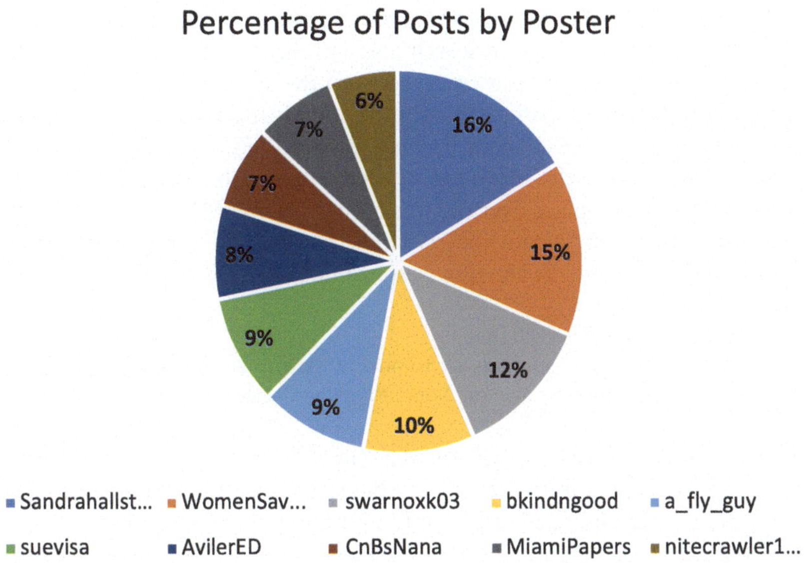

Fig. 2.5 Top ten posters by percentage of posts to the #NeverAgain social network

focuses their communication on political issues. In February 2018 when the Parkland shooting had just happened, the account tweeted on the issue and retweeted several messages from the students and referenced news articles regarding the event. For a period of time their tweets focused on Donald Trump and the Russia investigations that were ongoing at the time. Clearly politically motivated, this organization operates Artists Against Trump, a group of 50 artists and entertainers. The handle on Twitter @WomenSaveUSA is a veiled attempt to distance itself from political party politics, although the topics this organization tweets about are clearly political and directed specifically at Donald Trump.

A core mediator @Miamipapers is an account that represents Miami Secret Papers, an online news blog whose mission is to "shed light on the working conditions in Miami-Dade County." The account has 5000 followers and has posted close to a quarter of a million tweets since 2016 on a variety of political issues. A review of the tweets indicates involvement in gun law reform. Also, much like @WomenSaveUSA, @Miamisecretpapers utilizes most of their posts, retweeting information and news. An analysis of the words most often used in #NeverAgain tweets was conducted as well as an analysis of emotional sentiment—positive or negative—that was evident in the tweets. The research also developed a typology of tweets based on four categories that emerged from the analysis.

In Fig. 2.6, data regarding the most frequently used words in the tweets surrounding the #NeverAgain hashtag is presented. The word "tomorrow," for example, is the second most used word, as the data collection for this case study took place over the weekend when the March for Our Lives was held. The word "tomorrow" is utilized frequently in reference to the future of the movement, like one post exemplified below:

> @MargaretLesh 21 Feb 2018
> Today's #Parkland students are tomorrow's members of Congress. They are our future, and they give me hope. #ParklandStudentsSpeak

The #NeverAgain hashtag, identified as the calling card of the movement shows up frequently in tweets as does the reference to the March for Our Lives events planned nationwide and internationally.

Figure 2.7 lists the top posters mentioned in the movement: Emma Gonzalez (@emma4chage) is the top poster mentioned; the NAACP is a core mediator in the social network; and, so too is the video channel MTV. The NAACP, which already has a significant online following and the younger audiences engaged around the world by MTV, reflect varying

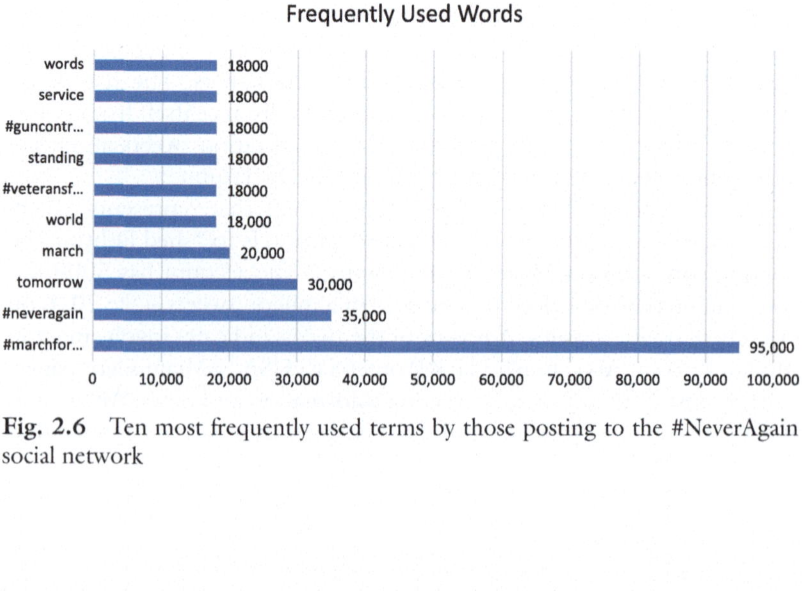

Fig. 2.6 Ten most frequently used terms by those posting to the #NeverAgain social network

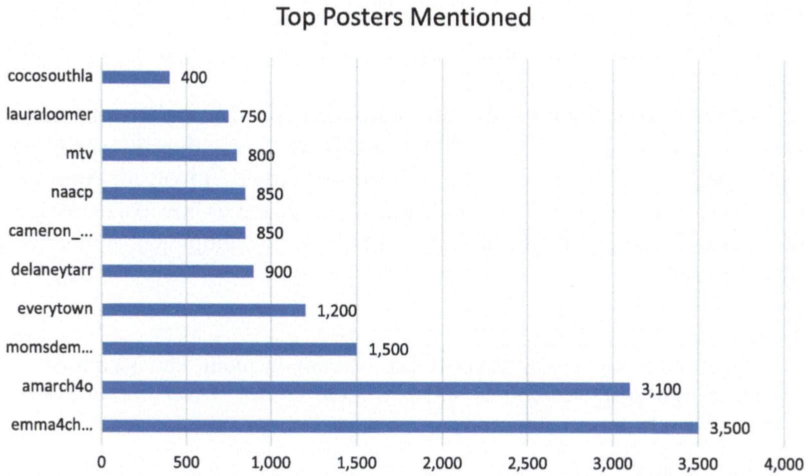

Fig. 2.7 These are the top ten posters mentioned in other people's tweets or retweets

types of relevance on this issue. The following are a sampling of tweets put forth by elite mediators:

> jimmy fallonVerified account @jimmyfallon 24 Mar 2018. Today is @ AMarch4OurLives. I'm partnering with @MTV and @NAACP to sponsor a bus full of smart young young people traveling from NYC to #MarchForOurLives Washington, D.C. today. Thank you for standing up and saying you've had #ENOUGH. See you there.

> Lady Gaga Verified account @ladygaga 23 Mar 2018
> @BTWFoundation & I believe in the power of young people to create a better future. We're so proud to stand with @MTV & @NAACP to support the young people marching for safer schools and communities. I am proud to sponsor a bus, heading from Harlem to DC for #MarchForOurLives

In order to better understand the social network that developed around the #NeverAgain hashtag, a textual analysis of tweets was conducted associated with the ongoing campaign. The analysis looked at both positive and negative sentiment expressed in the tweets identified by the Netlytic algorithm. There were 10,360 tweets expressing positive feelings, and there were 1548 tweets expressing negative feelings. Of the positive tweets, the words proud, good, great, brave, courageous, excited, and happy are predominant (Table 2.1).

A closer look at the data indicates the word "proud" is the word most often used in the positive tweets. The word was utilized as a hashtag to express support for the movement and those directly involved. Another way that the word "proud" was utilized was in regard to how participating in marches made people feel about themselves, as exemplified by the following tweets:

> @LittleAlix 26 Mar 2018
> So proud to support @AMarch4OurLives with my mom, who is a retired teacher, this past weekend at #MarchForOurLivesdc #marchforourlives #MarchForOurLivessigns #proud

> @StacySwann
> 24 Mar 2018
> Marching makes me #hopeful that change is possible. #Proud to see so many reject extremist views around gun control. The mainstream is #sensible.
> #MarchForOurLives
> #NeverAgain
> #Emma4Change

The tweets indicate that the movement not only inspires political action, but it is also making those engaged in the movement feel positive and hopeful about their future. The next most frequently used word is "good." The term, in some instances, is utilized in a way that can apply to different

Table 2.1 Tweets Expressing Positive Emotions

Positive emotions	*Percent (%)*	*Total*
Proud	40	4149
Good	14	1484
Great	9	906
Brave	10	987
Courageous	6	621
Excited	6	580
Happy	8	784

(N = 10,361)

contexts. Below are examples of how "good" was utilized to garner support and attention:

@DaTeOla 24 Feb 2018
You don't argue w/a #pinhead #brainwashed #NRA #Troll. They're. #Psychopaths they don't differenciate btw #Good&Evil or #Happy&Sad for them all the same.
A #Sickbrain like #Potus45 #NeverAgain #MarchForOurLives #EnoughIsEnough #WomensMarch #MomsDemandAction #metoo #BoycottNRA

@cmclpt 24 Mar 2018
The baby boomers in their entitled delusional arrogance call the young "snow flakes" when they seek to raise the standards and challenge the poor behaviour and attitudes of their selfish elders.
Today we see an avalanche of righteous civility from them.
#MarchForOurLives#good

Table 2.2 provides a list of negative words present in the tweets, but they are not always reflective of negative sentiment. For example, a word like "hurt" is the most used negative word in tweets posted by those engaged in the movement. The word "fierce" was used 82 times and was represented in 5 percent of the negative tweets. While the issue that began this movement may be dark, a negatively charged word like "fierce" in a particular context can actually be an expression of admiration and support.

Table 2.2 Tweets expressing negative emotions

Negative emotions	*Percent*	*Total (N)*
Hurt	32	484
Angry	18	283
Bad	7	110
Lazy	5	84
Fierce	5	82
Tired	5	74
Evil	4	68
Ill	3	45
Sore	3	39
Selfish	2	38

N = 1548

Table 2.3 Four categories of social media posts

Category	*Social media post*
Sharing news & events	1. @teamtrace 21 Jun 2018 Parkland survivors brought their voter registration bus tour to Sioux City, Iowa, on Wednesday, where they joined local students for a die-in outside the office of Congressman Steve King, a vocal #MarchforOurives critic. 2. @sandyhook 2 Jun 2018 ICYMI: Earlier this week Parkland students inspired voter registration at 1000 schools https://t.co/sMpWbblJqJ
Sharing knowledge, information & support	1. @nowayjose1947 Can't wait to vote for one of these young people. They will surely make better leaders than the ones destroying our country today. These two are outstanding—#Emma4Change @davidhogg111—but there are hundreds of others who will help save our democracy. 2. @RandiRhodes 27 Mar 2018 Good Morning! Republican Justice John Paul Stevens: Repeal the Second Amendment https://nyti.ms/2Gghke4 #neveragain #emma4change #repealthesecondamendment #enoughisenough #GOPMEANSGUNSOVERPEOPLE
Sharing opportunities	1. @joncoopertweets 24 Nov 2018 The Parkland students who created an international movement to raise awareness for gun violence after a deadly school shooting were awarded the International Children's Peace Prize at a ceremony in South Africa by Archbishop Desmond Tutu. #NeverAgain 2. @FastCompany 1 Jun 2018 The Parkland teens led America beyond thoughts and prayers—and they're just getting started. @DavidHogg111, @JaclynCorin, @Cameron_Kasky, @Emma4Change, and @Al3xW1nd ignited a nationwide movement to take the gun-control debate to Wall Street. http://f-st.co/RxKGSH3 #NeverAgain
Sharing personal experiences	1. @MorningEdition 14 Dec 2018 "Sandy Hook Promise," a non-profit anti-gun violence group formed after the attack, is training students around the nation to spot warning signs in other would–be shooters, and to anonymously report concerns through a mobile app. 2. @sethmoulton 29 May 2018 Last week, following the #SantaFeHighSchool shooting, I walked out of another "moment of silence" on the floor of the House of Representatives because the silence is deafening, our refusal to act is criminally negligent, and yet WE CAN FIX THIS for our kids.

In addition to analyzing sentiment, four broad categories of tweets were identified, including the following: sharing news and events, sharing knowledge and information and support, sharing opportunities, and sharing personal experiences. Table 2.3 categorizes the types of tweets found in the social network. Sharing news and events is an important factor because to grow and sustain the movement, you must make sure the followers are aware of and understand the main goal. As seen in the tweets below individuals who are not the core mediators of the movement are disseminating the information, acting as a conduit of sorts, demonstrating that in Iowa, for example, hundreds of miles from Parkland, other young activists are getting involved. A second category that plays a part in this process is sharing knowledge, information, and support. In order for others to have a desire to join the movement, they want to know that real change is possible. The empathy displayed in sharing information and showing of support may be a way to connect with followers and turn passive publics into active publics. In addition to sharing news, information, and support about the movement, the final two categories deal more with sharing of opportunities and personal experiences. The sharing of personal experiences is indicative of how pervasive the issue of gun violence is and breath of its impact across the social network.

Below are visualizations that illustrate the social network among Twitter users including mentions, retweets, or replies. Metrics for both reciprocity and modularity were utilized to summarize the nature of these interactions. The value for reciprocity, for example, is the ratio of reciprocal interactions, with values closer to 1 indicating that most users are having two-way interactions. The value for modularity is the level of network clustering, with values closer to 1 suggesting that a network consists of many weakly connected users, rather than one coherent, highly connected group.

Figure 2.8 is a visualization of a name network in order to discover social connections among community members. Clusters of the same colors represent "nodes" or groups of users communicating/sharing/reposting a tweet or tweets. The larger the group within a particular color, the more users it represents of those interacting around a post. The lines connecting users represent "ties" between users who may mention another user in a tweet or sharing a tweet with a specific user. A name network examines messages while connecting one person (name) to another if they mention, reply, or repost another person's tweet. In the case of #NeverAgain, the resulting network generated by Netlytic included

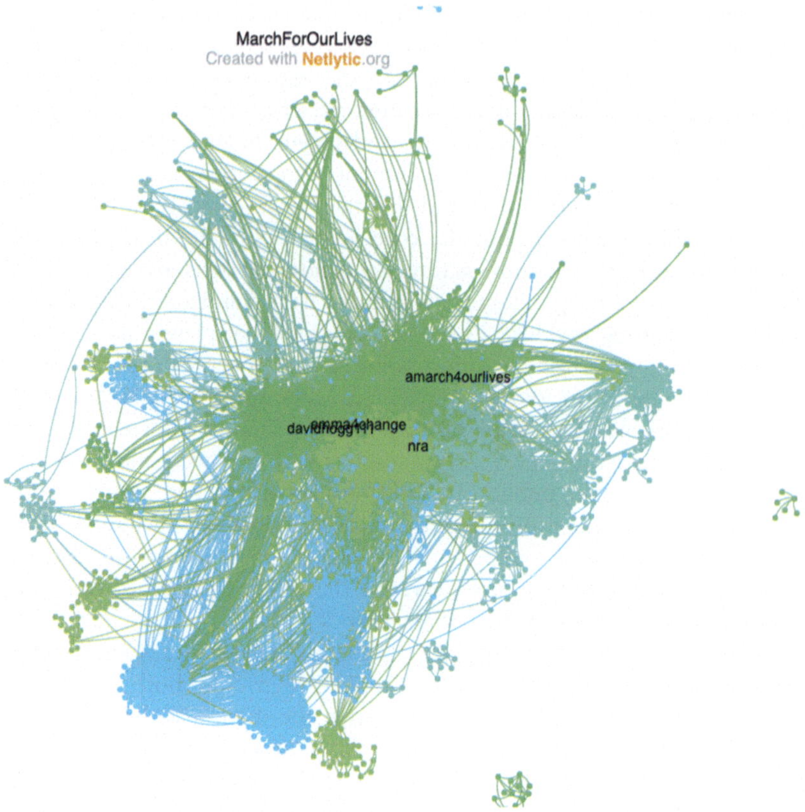

Fig. 2.8 Network map of the name network of who is mentioning whom

20,568 nodes and 52,585 ties (including self-loops). There were 70,274 names found in the network.

Figure 2.8 depicts the clusters within and structure of the social network. In this name network, the colors represent different name clusters built from mining personal names in the messages. The clusters are the subgroups of users who are more interconnected among themselves than with users of other clusters.

In this name network visualization @emmaforchange, the handle for Emma Gonzalas, one of the movement's mediators is prominent along with David Hogg. There is little reciprocity (.0028) in this network signifying there is little back-and-forth communication but more likely a lot of retweeting of messages. Modularity is a measure of the communities within the network. In this case the modularity is relatively high (.0768) indicating there are distinct communities operating within the network, as opposed to a core group of nodes representing the network. To that end, both the National Rifle Association and @realdonaldtrump are represented in different clusters.

Figure 2.9 represents the chain network that reflects who is replying to whom. In this instance, Twitter users engaged indirectly and did not reciprocate communication from one user to another, identified by minimal two-way, back-and-forth conversations; this was reflected by low reciprocity value (Reciprocity: 0.0066). The relatively high modularity value (Modularity: 0.837) indicated that users interacted in small groups or clusters. There are 3889 posters with ties, and the number of ties (including self-loops which are nodes that link back to themselves) is 12,865. The low value associated with reciprocity indicates a lack of reciprocal communication. And, the high modularity value indicates that small clusters are formed in the chain network.

The case study set out to better understand how individuals join together and build social movements with the theoretical understanding that publics form around the situational relevance of a social or political issue. Rather than a community that could be categorized by their fatalism or their belief in responding directly to a social issue, the analysis found clusters that operate within the broader social network in which those engaged represent divergent positions and political orientations. Social media has been often referred to as tribal, referring to the ways in which individuals coalesce around an issue and that clusters within social networks operate as echo chambers reinforcing existing positions on an issue or sentiment toward the issue or movement. However, in this instance, while the balance is in the direction that the movement desires, the broader social network includes other perhaps divergent opinions. In other words, among those within the social network are "likers" as well as "haters." The network is not monolithic in the ways in which we might imagine social networks. There were in fact several clusters that formed; some were in support of the students and the cause and others were groups that formed were ridiculing the students and fighting to keep second amendment rights as they are presently construed. Clusters within the social network coalesced in response to particular posts from the main Parkland advocates (referred to as non-elite mediators) or when certain conversations

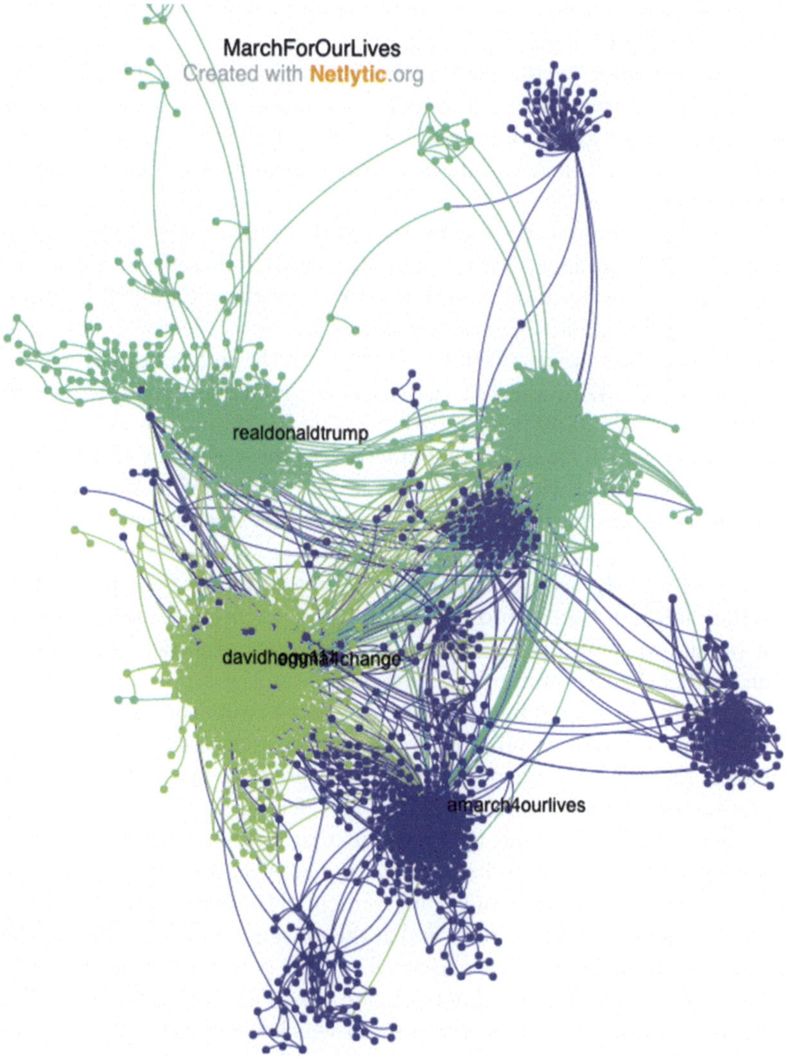

Fig. 2.9 #NeverAgain chain network of who replies to whom

surrounding stricter gun laws became more prevalent in the news. Other mediators fit into the elite and core categories to include celebrities and news media. Engagement in any of these clusters within the network simply requires the willingness to express oneself on social media or to share what someone else is posting.

Social networks, as demonstrated by this analysis of the #NeverAgain hashtag, are made up of clusters and niches through which sentiment is expressed that is reflective of the relevance of the issue to those engaged in the network. Some individuals engage in the network to "rally the troops" so to speak encouraging direct participation, while others use the network to denigrate the students and their supporters. Yet others use the platform to spread news and information or use the network to share their feelings and personal experiences. There were tweets from individuals that were parents of Sandy Hook students (another school shooting) tweeting to parents of Parkland students in solidarity and support. Politicians were tweeting about how the Parkland movement had inspired them to champion change. There were also individuals who thought the Parkland students were disrespectful and acting like spoiled children. The data indicated that tweets were formed around four categories: the sharing of news and events, personal knowledge or beliefs, information and support, opportunities to engage in the movement, and the sharing of personal experiences. When the movement was in the emergence stage, the sharing of news and events was crucial to building the base, meaning that was how people knew to come to rallies and marches and voter registration events. As the movement quickly gained momentum, tweets evolved to extend sharing of information and support. There were many tweets using the hashtag #NeverAgain, #Parkland, and #Enough just to name a few that generated clusters of engaged people showing sympathy and support. As the movement progressed clusters of people formed that were expressions of personal impact by other mass shootings.

Conclusion

In this chapter the social network approach to analysis of social movements was introduced. While the concept of social networks dates back to the early part of the twentieth century, the social network approach to analyzing social networks has its theoretical roots in the work of sociologists like Georg Simmel and Emile Durkheim, both of whom were interested in the relationship between social actors. Today we are able to apply graph theory to both analyze and visualize social structures with particular regard to how relationships unfold on social media platforms in the digital age. The chapter discussed the differences between offline and online communications, the latter being conceptualized as imagined communities based on the work of Bennett Anderson and newer considerations of virtual communities. The chapter identified the structures of social networks by introducing concepts like nodes or vertices to describe those who are engaged in the network as well as the connections, described as edges, between them. Characteristics of social networks as they relate to graph theory were defined in order to better understand influence within the network. Betweenness centrality was one measure that was utilized in order to identify influencers in the network. As influence is important when considering the spread of ideas, a discussion of the strength of weak ties theory was presented as the basis for understanding not only the role of weak ties within the community but also through the introduction of Actor Network Theory (ANT), the chapter explored the expenditure of social capital within the social movement. Finally, a case study regarding the #NeverAgain hashtag was presented in order to illustrate how the social network approach can be applied to a social movement.

Chapter 3 will bring into greater focus the role of influencers and other media figures who play a key role in drawing attention to an issue or cause in both mainstream news and digital platforms. The chapter also considered those people who for various reasons are thrust into the spotlight and take on a role of key mediator who become what may be referred to as micro-celebrities. Chapter 3 considers the multi-step flow as it relates to opinion leadership, a theoretical orientation apropos to the digital age. And, a case study of the #ClimateStrike movement and its key influencer, Greta Thunberg is presented.

Notes

1. Castells, M. (2015). *Networks of Outrage and Hope: Social Movements in the Internet Age*. 2nd edition. Cambridge: Polity Press.
2. Brabazon, T. (2001). How imagined are virtual communities? *Mots pluriels* 18, Retrieved from: http://www.arts.uwa.edu.au/MotsPluriels/MP1801tb2.html.

3. Gradinaru, C. (2016). The Technological Expansion of Sociability: Virtual Communities as Imagined Communities. Academicus International Scientific Journal. 7(14), pp. 181–190.
4. Ibid., p. 189.
5. Gruzd, A., Wellman, B., & Takhteyev, Y. (2011). Imagining Twitter as an Imagined Community. *American Behavioral Scientist.* 55(10), pp. 1294–1318.
6. Gil-Lopez, T., Shen, C, Benefield, G., Palomares, N., Kosinski, M., Stillwell, D. (2018). One Size Fits All: Context Collapse, Self-Presentation Strategies and Language Styles on Facebook, *Journal of Computer-Mediated Communication*, 23:3, (May), pp. 127–145, https://doi.org/10.1093/jcmc/zmy006.
7. Fox, S. (2004). The New Imagined Community: Identifying and Exploring a Bidirectional Continuum Integrating Virtual and Physical Communities through the Community Embodiment Model (CEM). *Journal of Communication Inquiry* 28 (1): 47–62.
8. Rainie, L. & Wellman, B. (2012). Networked: The New Social Operating system: Cambridge, MA: MIT Press.
9. Facebook.com. (April 4, 2018). An Update on Our Plans to Restrict Data Access on Facebook. Retrieved from: https://newsroom.fb.com/news/2018/04/restricting-data-access/.
10. TheConversation.com. (March 30, 2018). How Cambridge Analytica's Facebook targeting model really worked—according to the person who built it. Retrieved from: https://theconversation.com/how-cambridge-analyticas-facebook-targeting-model-really-worked-according-to-the-person-who-built-it-94078.
11. Alaimo, K. (October 16, 2018). Twitter's Misguided Barriers for Researchers. Retrieved from: https://www.bloomberg.com/opinion/articles/2018-10-16/twitter-s-barriers-for-academic-researchers-are-misguided.
12. Buechler, S. (1995). New Social Movement Theories. *The Sociological Quarterly.* 36:3 (summer), p. 446. Retrieved from: https://www.jstor.org/stable/4120774.
13. 6/99A SNA (n.d.). Social Network/Vertex. Retrieved from: https://www.scribd.com/document/369180537/6-99A-SNA.
14. Ibid.
15. Smith, M., Rainie, L., Shneiderman, B. & I. Himelboim. (February 20, 2014). Mapping Twitter Topic Networks: From Polarized Crowds to Community Clusters. Pew Research Center. Retrieved from: https://www.pewinternet.org/2014/02/20/mapping-twitter-topic-networks-from-polarized-crowds-to-community-clusters/.
16. Gradinaru, C. (2016), pp. 186–187.

17. Sabatini, F. (2009). Social capital as social networks: A new framework for measurement and an empirical analysis of its determinants and consequences. *The Journal of Socio-Economics*. 38:3, pp. 429–442.
18. Latour, B. (1999). Pandora's hope: essays on the reality of science studies. Cambridge, MA: Harvard UP. pp. 174–215.
19. boyd, d. (September 14, 2018). Media Manipulation, Strategic Amplification, and Responsible Journalism. Retrieved from: https://points.datasociety.net/media-manipulation-strategic-amplification-and-responsible-journalism-95f4d611f462.
20. Alperstein, N. (2019). Celebrity and Mediated Social Connections: Fans, Friends and Followers in the Digital Age. New York: Palgrave.
21. Himelboim, I., Golan, G., Moon, B. & J. Ryan. (2014) A Social Networks Approach to Public Relations on Twitter: Social Mediators and Mediated Public Relations, *Journal of Public Relations Research*, 26:4, 359–379, DOI: https://doi.org/10.1080/1062726X.2014.908724.
22. Isa, D., & Himelboim, I. (2018). A Social Networks Approach to Online Social Movement: Social Mediators and Mediated Content in #FreeAJStaff Twitter Network. *Social Media + Society*. Retrieved from: https://doi.org/10.1177/2056305118760807.
23. Granovetter, M. (1973). The Strength of Weak Ties. *American Journal of Sociology*. (May) 78:6, pp. 1360–1380. Retrieved from: https://sociology.stanford.edu/sites/default/files/publications/the_strength_of_weak_ties_and_exch_w-gans.pdf.
24. Miller, S. (June 14, 2018). All of The Most Powerful Lines from Emma Gonzalez's Speeches. *Elle Magazine*, Retrieved from: https://www.elle.com/uk/life-and-culture/a21051343/emma-gonzalez-elle-list-2018/.
25. NPR.org (December 17, 2017). The Arab Spring: A Year of Revolution. NPR.org. Retrieved from: https://www.npr.org/2011/12/17/143897126/the-arab-spring-a-year-of-revolution.
26. Alperstein, N. & Jones, T. (2020). The Online Social Movement of #NeverAgain: How social networks build a sense of membership, influence, support and emotional connection on Twitter. *The Journal of Social Media in Society*. 9:2, pp. 127–149.
27. Takhteyev, Y., Gruzd, A. & B. Wellman. (2012). "Geography of Twitter Networks." *Social Networks*, 34 (1): pp. 73–81. Retrieved from: https://doi.org/10.1016/j.socnet.2011.05.006.
28. Burch, A. & Mazze, P. (2018, February 14). Death Toll Is at 17 and Could Rise in Florida School Shooting. *The New York Times*. Retrieved from: https://www.nytimes.com/2018/02/14/us/parkland-school-shooting.html.

29. Robinson, M. (2018, March 25). A generation under siege. *The Atlantic*. Retrieved from: https://www.theatlantic.com/politics/archive/2018/03/march-for-our-lives/556475/.
30. Isa, D., & Himelboim, I. (2018). A Social Networks Approach to Online Social Movement: Social Mediators and Mediated Content in #FreeAJStaff Twitter Network. *Social Media + Society*. Retrieved from: https://doi.org/10.1177/2056305118760807. P. 4.
31. Filipovic, J. (2018, April 10). The right's insane sliming of David Hogg. *CNN.com*. Retrieved from: https://www.cnn.com/2018/04/10/opinions/insane-right-wing-sliming-of-david-hogg-filipovic/index.html.
32. Newkirk, V. (2018, February 22). The power of the Parkland Town Hall. *The Atlantic*. Retrieved from: https://www.theatlantic.com/politics/archive/2018/02/the-power-of-the-parkland-town-hall/553949/.
33. Isa, D., & Himelboim, I. (2018). Ibid.

CHAPTER 3

Social Influencers, Content Creators, and Network Mediators in Social Movements

In what turned out to be a feeble attempt at socially responsibility, the Pepsi® brand of soft drinks in April 2017 launched an advertising campaign featuring Kendall Jenner, a model and celebrity most noteworthy for her relationship to the infamous Kardashian family. The advertisement, part of a larger campaign "Live for Now—Moments," depicted bringing people together with the product as the symbolic connection between a social issue and the brand with a celebrity, who in combination with the issue and the product, were meant to converge into a single message. The meta-approach included the 21-year-old supermodel taking part in a photo shoot within the commercial as she "jumps in"—the title of this particular commercial—with a group apparently protesting police brutality. Jenner hands one of the police officers a Pepsi in an attempt to mollify his concerns over the contrived protest, an approach that advertisers often use to simplify and typify social issues. Social media was having none of this, as people condemned the commercial for co-opting actual social movements against police brutality, and as a result of the social media onslaught, the commercial was withdrawn shortly after its release on both television and the internet.[1] The moral of this tale is that in the age of media activism, it's important for brands to match their celebrity spokespeople and social issues in perfect alignment otherwise fans and followers will see the act as merely performative.

It has been said that "with great power comes great responsibility." Whoever's version of the quote you prefer—Voltaire, Uncle Ben from the

N. Alperstein, *Performing Media Activism in the Digital Age*,
https://doi.org/10.1007/978-3-030-73804-4_3

movie *Spiderman*, or Winston Churchill, this chapter considers the meaning of great power with regard to those who are social movement influencers, opinion leaders, mediators, and moderators in the digital age. This chapter will bring focus to bonafide celebrities and microcelebrities, as well as other media figures who play a key role in drawing attention to an issue or cause and have the power to amplify the message in both mainstream and digital media. Also considered are those ordinary people who for various reasons are thrust into the spotlight and take on a role of key mediators in the social network. Interest extends to social capital as well as the multi-step flow of opinion leadership exemplified in the digital age by influencers, not necessarily because of their expertise or talent they bring to a social movement, but perhaps are influential because of the amount of content they disseminate or the ways in which content they create is curated by others, retweets, for example, across social networks. Whether it is actresses Jane Fonda or Alyssa Milano, Swedish teen Greta Thunberg, actor Terry Crews, or sports figures like Colin Kaepernick, among many others, their relationship to and influence upon specific social movements in the digital age cannot be denied. The case study for this chapter looks at the network of news media organizations that form around the #ClimateStrike movement and a network analysis of climate activist Greta Thunberg is presented.

Context Collapse

When reflecting on the inconsistency demonstrated in the Pepsi advertisement featuring celebrity Kendall Jenner mixing celebrity status, commercial spectacle, and social movement, the fallout can be deemed context collapse (see Fig. 3.1). Context collapse refers to a situation in which

Fig. 3.1 Context Collapse at the intersection of personal, spectacle, and social issue

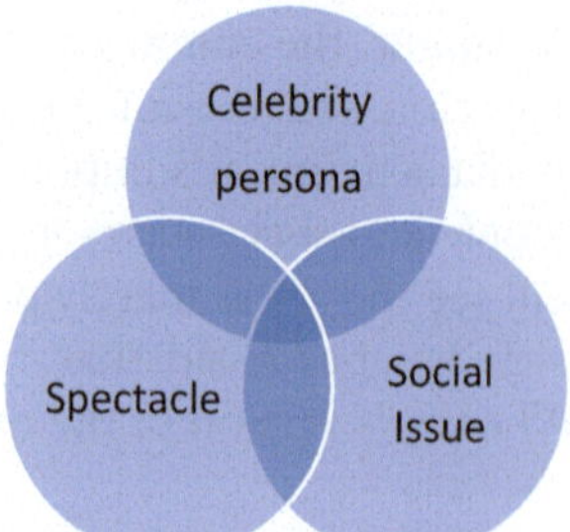

multiple contexts collapse into a single moment, sometimes as in the case of this celebrity resulting in a collision that audiences—fans, followers as well as detractors—take advantage of in order to express their dismay at the clash between what they know and believe about a social issue and the intrusion of the celebrity into that belief system. The elaboration of commentary on social media in particular can be swift, where virality and connectivity can do their work, as in the instance described above. Context collapse, the flattening of contexts, can be intentional or unintentional. Sometimes when a celebrity or media figure speaks out on an issue and the audience or audiences perceive inconsistencies between the performative nature of their appearance and their own perception of the issue, it can backfire. This is so even if there is intentionality behind the performative nature of their appearance. The mixing of social issue and the celebrity persona represents a kind of blurring between what we know the celebrity or media figure to be, an actor or athlete, for example, and their assumed presence in the context of a social issue. It is the difference between the "reel" and "real" life of a celebrity.

What is going on here is what Goffman referred to as "face-work," that we may define as the strategic management of performance. The continuum of the idealized persona that extends from intentional or unintentional presentations of self is a function of infinite flux or the authenticating self—the self always in motion and in need of management. It should not be taken for granted that the celebrity has, because of their standing or notoriety, an automatic pass to join or lead the movement, as even the most highly managed persona needs to find consistency between their image—the face they put on it—and context, that is the issue they wish to support.

From Two-Step to Multiple Step Flow

The two-step flow theory developed in the 1940s by Paul Lazarsfeld and later modified by Elihu Katz and Lazarsfeld assumes that news and information flows from mass media to opinion leaders and then on to wider audiences, rather than flowing directly from mass media to the audience. Katz's three dimensions of opinion leadership include who one is, what one knows, and who one knows (Fig. 3.2). Those opinion leaders have two qualities that distinguish them from the rest of the population: first, they pay closer attention to news and information, in particular they may focus more on what has been referred to as elite media, like opinion or

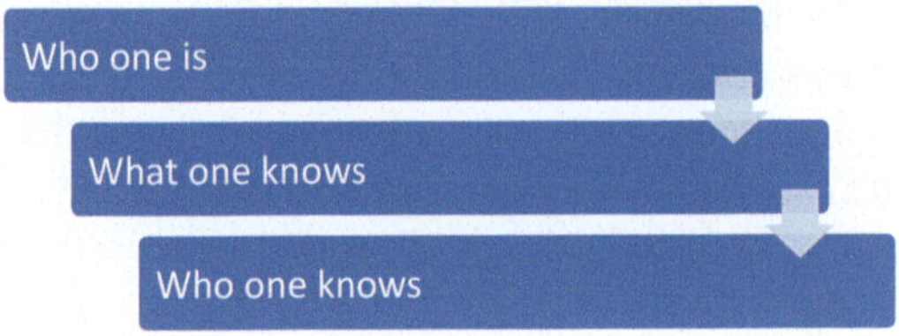

Fig. 3.2 Elihu Katz's dimensions of opinion leadership

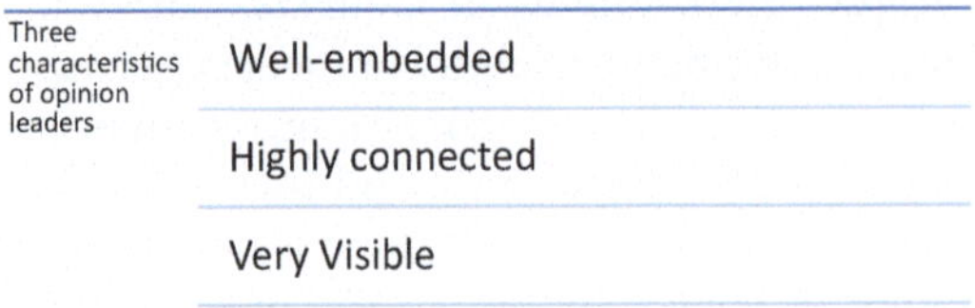

Fig. 3.3 Qualities of opinion leaders

op-ed essays, as opposed to general news items; and second, they operate in social circles where they will likely have more opportunities than others to spread those ideas. Hence, the two-step flow theory.

However, direct effects of media upon audiences may be hampered based on "social interactions, audience selectivity in exposure, perception and retention."[2] Figure 3.3 lists the three characteristics of opinion leaders: well-embedded, highly connected, and very visible. Because of their attention to news and information as well as their sociality, opinion leaders are in a better position to influence others than if individuals with whom they have contact would get their opinions from general media sources, like newspapers or television. We tend to think of opinion leaders as literally leaders—people of a certain social standing, like an elected official, authority figure, celebrity, or other prominent individual, but that is not necessarily the case, especially not in the digital age.

Taking the term "leadership," for example, to mean someone in authority, one might think that former US Vice President Al Gore's 2006 award-winning documentary film *An Inconvenient Truth* would place him in a good position to affect people's attitudes about climate change, and for some people, he well may have influenced their attitudes. But in a world of social media, a good internet connection can allow anyone regardless of status to spread news, information, and opinions with lightning speed. In such a somewhat democratized world, the term "opinion leader" need not operate from a "top-down" hierarchical structure based on social standing with regard to one's ability to influence others, as the flow of information and opinions may be bottom up or multidirectional. In that sense, in a networked environment, influencers on social media might operate somewhat differently than opinion leaders were thought to have operated within the two-step flow model.

Alternatively, with regard to the multiple step flow of information, Ognyanova suggests looking at the structure of the social network to see how ideas are spread. The researcher also describes the changing mediator roles that media as well as individuals play in a digital world in which there is no opinion leadership, at least not as Lazarsfeld and Katz described it, where both individual influencers and media operate on co-equal terms. The concept of social capital in the digital age refers to an individual's position in a group within a social network whose role is to strengthen the community. Although social capital means different things to different people, for example, brands calculate social capital as the value of their online social networks, the term can be applied to other contexts like social movements as well. The value of social capital in online networks can, for example, be measured by the trust placed in influencers. The value of social capital can also be measured through the alignment of beliefs held by those engaged in the movement, what is called homophily or euphemistically known as "birds of a feather flock together." Also, degree of cooperation among those engaged in the social movement can be measured through interpersonal connections that grow as the social network expands, as a digital movement may start with a seed, perhaps even a solo protester, and over time grow into a broader and more complex network. Social influence and opinion leadership have much in common, as both refer an individual's ability to affect attitudes and actions of others. The impact on attitudes Ognyanova claims, however, is more likely to come from friends or close associates, whereas the latter (actions) are "domain specific."[3] She cites as the distinguishing characteristic Katz's three dimensions—who one is, what one knows, and who one knows—that differentiate opinion leaders from others in a social group.[4] It may be argued, however, based on Granovetter's strength of weak ties theory, in digitally based social networks where influencers serve the role of mediator that closeness may not be a key consideration, and in fact, it may hinder attitude formation or change.

The Power of Worker Protest

Over many years, sports figures have played a significant role in social protest, most notably in recent years is Colin Kaepernick, a former quarterback for the San Francisco 49ers American football team who in August 2016 refused to stand in reverence for the American national anthem, in other words he "took a knee" to protest racial injustice and police brutality. "I am not going to stand up to show pride in a flag for a country that oppresses black people and people of color," was his response. He added, "To me this is bigger than football, and it would be selfish on my part to look the other way." Kaepernick serves as another example of context collapse that takes place at the intersection of his media figure persona, sports spectacle, and social justice issue. As Kaepernick's stance drew notoriety and the scorn of the then president of the United States, controversy grew as other players and other teams also took a knee prior to the start of National Football League games during the playing of the American national anthem. The action cost Kaepernick his football career.[5]

There is a very long history, dating back as far as 532 AD of sports figures engaged in activism that is present in contemporary societies in many parts of the world. For example, during the COVID-19 pandemic, players in the US National Basketball League walked off the court prior to the start of a game to protest the shooting of a Black man, Jacob Blake, in Kenosha, Wisconsin. LaBron James, an icon of the National Basketball Association (NBA) who is quite active on social issues lent his support to the boycott (see Fig. 3.4). Other leagues, in support of the NBA teams, like the Women's National Basketball League (WNBA) as well as three major league baseball games were not held in support of the action by the NBA teams.[6]

Because of their connection to spectacle, sports figures are considered media figures, celebrities who hold the power to draw attention to social issues and injustices. In the book *Media Spectacle*, author Douglas Kellner writes about Michael Jordan who he describes as an "icon of media spectacle, combining extraordinary athletic achievement, an unrivaled record of success and winning, high entertainment value, and an ability to exploit his image into highly impressive business success."[7] The same description could be applied to many other contemporary sports figures. Kellner claims that the nature of spectacle in the digital age has its origins in identity politics and the social movements of the 1970s, "especially as more separatist strains of feminism surface, various nationalisms appeared in

Fig. 3.4 LaBron James Tweeting in the aftermath of James Black Shooting

ethnic and race-based movements, and gay and lesbian movements highlighted connections between sexuality and identity, while a general fragmentation and splitting of different groups emerged in a politics of difference."[8] Spectacular infotainment as Kellner refers to media spectacles, vis-à-vis the role that sports figures and celebrities play in social movements, are transformed into megaspectacles that "divert attention from the actual causes of inequality and injustice and the social and political movements that attempt to address them."[9] Consistent with the idea of performing media activism, Debord in the late 1960s wrote: "The present stage is bringing about a general shift from *having* to *appearing*—all 'having' must now derive its immediate prestige and its ultimate purpose from appearances." While Debord wrote *The Society of the Spectacle* in the pre-social media era, it can be argued presently that the use of social media to spread and sustain a social movement and the ability of celebrities and other media figures to mediate messaging have changed the nature of media spectacle that extends from bonafide celebrities to include ordinary people who for various reasons become microcelebrities.

Unlike sports figures, whose notoriety may preclude them from suffering the vagaries of corporate policies regarding speaking out on public issues, employee activism on the part of workers at all levels might feel it is their right and perhaps duty to speak out on public issues. As well, surveys show there is a growing expectation for corporations to speak out as well.[10] Where the power balance in the past may have tipped toward corporate interests, in today's digital media environment, celebrities and other media figures are more empowered as their social networks which may comprise 100 million or more followers on a platform like Instagram, for example, as they are able to demonstrate the ability to gain attention, spark interest, further the conversation on social issues like systemic racism, and extend the conversation as well, all without the help of mainstream media, although they may take part in or mediate the control that corporate interests might have wielded in the past. Indeed, corporations and organizations like the national sports leagues have been forced to show solidarity with players as well as employees and citizens of their respective hometowns in the movement toward racial justice. It is not clear whether the prominent role taken by celebrities boosts awareness of social issues or further polarizes people but their willingness to stick their necks out, so to speak, with regard to social issues marks a departure from a more restrained role they may have played in a pre-digital media era, one where media and corporate interests may have suppressed engagement on social issues.

Microcelebrities and Social Movements

Consistent with the idea of performing media activism, Marwick and boyd conceptualize celebrity as a practice that they describe as both the appearance in social media and in reference to Erving Goffman's dramaturgical view as a performance of backstage access. The performance requires what Goffman referred to as strategic "impression management," described as the control (or lack of control) and communication of information through performance.[11] By looking at networked celebrity activity, the power and influence of performance can be revealed. Celebrities in their social media performances reveal things about themselves—personal information—that creates a feeling of intimacy between the celebrity and their followers. As it is not their primary role as actor, sports figure, and so on, engaging in a social movement exposes the celebrity's values in ways that meet or are opposed to those value positions of their fans or followers. It is the candid presentation of self that provides a glimpse of the celebrity behind the scenes. Marwick and boyd go on to suggest that this creates an "indeterminate authenticity," or to put it another way, a demonstration of the authenticating self in which the persona is always in flux. "While celebrity practice is theoretically open to all, it is not an equalizer or democratizing discourse. Indeed, in order to successfully practice celebrity, fans must recognize the power differentials intrinsic to the relationship."[12]

The power differential they describe however is different for microcelebrities, whose authenticating requirements are more significant with regard to self-disclosure as well as posting practices. As a symbolic interactionist, Goffman was interested in Durkheim's concept of spontaneity, which can be linked not only to performance but the kind of spectacle that is necessary, particularly in social media, to attract and maintain attention to a social issue. To that end the climate activist Greta Thunberg might be categorized as a microcelebrity, and it should be pointed out, there are even more nuanced categories including micro-influencers and nano-influencers, the latter refers to those who are active on Instagram or YouTube, for example, who have an audience that is perhaps as small as 1000 followers but make up for size based on their ability to gain intimacy with their small audience. It was 2001 when researcher Theresa Senft coined the term "microcelebrity" that she described as a new style of online performance in which people employ webcams, video, audio, blogs, and social network sites to "amp up" their popularity among readers and viewers.[13] The difference between a bonafide celebrity or media figure whose appeal may be to broader audiences and a micro-influencer is that the latter may experience more intense involvement with those engaged in the social movement. The reference to micro influence extends to subcultural, niche, or even local level microcelebrities. There is a process associated with growing one's role as influencer in the digital age, as one might begin by creating a social presence, effectively utilizing social media mimicking the style and tactics of bonafide celebrities, creating spectacle perhaps in the form of a solo protest, for example, with the goal of reaching beyond friends and family toward building a larger audience. An example would be when in 2019 Greta Thunberg seeking to limit her carbon footprint chose to sail on a yacht from the United States to Spain to attend a European conference.[14] The advent of influencers in social networks is founded in the so-called democratization of social media, as such media have become part of the fabric of everyday life, what may be called mediated social connections, because media mediates our cultural experiences, and it mediates our relationships with others engaged with various digital media platforms.[15] This is no less so for those engaged in performing media activism in the digital age.

Mediators and Moderators

The terms "mediators" and "moderators" were introduced in Chap. 2 as those actants who mediate relationships or moderate news and information serving as intermediary between a social movement and its publics or audiences. Mediators can be categorized as elites (celebrities and media), non-elites (ordinary people), or core (those directly impacted by the issue) mediators. Of relevance to this chapter, one way to think about a moderator role within a social movement is to consider the strength an individual may have to influence the connectivity among people in the movement. This certainly sounds like the role that opinion leaders or bonafide celebrities may play in a social movement. Mediators, on the other hand, take on more of an explainer role in which such individuals are able to change people's minds; they mediate outcomes. It is the very intermediary role of news and information on digital platforms related to issues of concern to a movement that serves as a moderating vehicle. Within this perspective social media, along with mainstream electronic and print media, play a moderating role of their own, and so to do influencers that elaborate upon and curate others' content on social media platforms. It is through their moderation that mediation takes place. It is in this way that social media activism becomes one form of collective action. As Himelboim and colleagues point out, social mediators are "highly effective in making bridging relationships and are highly connected in their own clusters." They go on to say that "social mediators are influential key actors who attract more attention in their own clusters," and they serve as a bridge between two clusters in a social network.[16]

Performative Activism

When it comes to digital activism, Goffman's dramaturgical application to everyday life may be applied to online "performance" as individuals craft identities curating other people's content or posting their own original content; a performance that can be as simple as clicking on a thumbs up to give approval or giving a post a thumbs down expressing disapproval. These efforts to create an impression or play a role in an online social movement, given the amount of time that many people spend on social media, become part of a continuous effort to perform media activism. To that point, there is much written about demonstrating one's "authentic" self on social media. But the continual self-expression and attempts to create an impression are all part of a performance that is not so much about authentic expression but rather denotes the authenticating self, a continual process of authentication. The idea that social media is a stage upon which people perform activism has significance for clicktivists or slacktivists, but it may have special import for social influencers, as there is an expectation that they will present themselves in alignment with the particular social movement to which they connect their own political or social position, values, and beliefs, all of which is based on the persona the influencer wants to project onto the movement. Indeed, there is an expectation among fans and followers that celebrities will take on greater responsibility when speaking on behalf of a social issue. Having said that, performative activism (not to be confused with performing activism) takes on a rather pejorative meaning because the term is associated with increasing one's social capital rather than activism based on altruism. The irony in all this is that the influencer through their performative act can neither reveal their authentic self nor conceal their true self, which is the basis for the process associated with the authenticating self, a self that is always in flux. An example of performative activism would be when the actress Emma Watson posted as part of the #BlackOutTuesday hashtag campaign on her Instagram account a black image in support of the Black Lives Matter movement. She was roundly criticized for using an image instead of posting informative and perhaps more meaningful content; she was accused of performative activism.[17]

Up Chain and Down Chain Amplification

On the other hand, there is actress Jane Fonda who is no stranger to civil disobedience in the name of various social and political movements in which she has over many years been involved. As a bonafide celebrity, she exemplifies the kind of media figure that has the prowess to command media attention—her presence at a protest or rally creates a media spectacle—perhaps drawing the attention of a polarized audience. Therefore, while some social movements begin in social media, perhaps with a hashtag campaign, and ultimately move from one social media platform to another and up the chain to mainstream media, other movements work in the opposite direction and yet others operate in both directions—up chain/down chain—simultaneously. Strategic amplification plays significant role in growing "shares" or other metrics used to measure amplification. Aligned with the #Climatestrike movement, Fonda made news in 2019 by

Fig. 3.5 Actress Jane Fonda supporting the climate change movement

moving her home at least temporarily to Washington, DC, so she could participate in weekly "Fire Drill Fridays" climate protests held in front of the US Capitol. The spectacle of her and other celebrities being arrested, in her case she was arrested five times (see Fig. 3.5), traveled across mainstream and social media platforms. Moreover, her activism that netted her a weekly arrest, metaphorically demonstrated that she puts her money where her mouth is, so to speak.[18] In other words, she demonstrated the kind of courage and integrity associated with the concept of the authenticating self; moreover, she made the needle move, amplifying attention to the cause of climate change and the Fire Drill Fridays movement.

Case Study: Greta Thunberg/Climate Change

It was December 2018 when then 15-year-old Swedish climate change activist Greta Thunberg addressed the United Nations Climate Change Conference, launching her as a powerful influencer on this environmental, social, and economic issue. By mid-2019, over 1.5 million students from 125 countries had participated in the #ClimateStrike and #Fridays4Future movement. The sustaining campaign Thunberg created serves to illustrate how a solo protester became a worldwide microcelebrity in the cause of the climate crisis. Thunberg began the #Fridays4Future campaign as a personal yet public demonstration in which she refused to attend school on Fridays in order to bring attention to the world's climate crisis. By September 2019 participation in protests grew to include over four million people worldwide. As a profile in the *New York Times* states: "In that short time, Thunberg, a 17-year-old Swede, has become a figure of international standing, able to meet with sympathetic world leaders and rattle the unsympathetic. Her compelling clarity about the scale of the crisis and moral indignation at the inadequate political response have been hugely influential in shifting public opinion."[19] Along with her fans and followers, in the process of growing a social network and championing this movement, she has been unmoved by detractors and those who attack her. The vigilance she demonstrates is apparent in the 2020 documentary, "I am Greta."[20] Drawing worldwide attention to the climate crisis, being nominated for the Nobel Peace Prize, speaking to the United Nations on climate issues, among many other accomplishments of note, culminated into being referred to by numerous people as "the Greta effect."

As the climate change movement is quite dynamic, the conversation around the issue as well as the conversation around Greta Thunberg has changed. In a study of mis/disinformation associated with Thunberg, five narratives were identified that cut across several social media platforms: Facebook, Twitter, Reddit, YouTube, and articles posted on US-based news organizations on the Web. The five narratives included: mental stability, antifa, George Soros, being a puppet, and the industrial climate complex. The first, mental ability, refers to Thunberg's Asperger's syndrome diagnosis. The second relates to a t-shirt she was photographed wearing with the slogan Antifascist Allstars. The third refers to her supposed connection to George Soros, who is often the subject of conspiracy theorists stemming from the far right. Thunberg has also been accused of being a puppet, controlled by her parents and other organizations or businesses. And the fifth narrative involves the climate industrial complex, which refers to a loose set of corporate interests and nonprofits to which she has supposedly been linked.[21] Based on a query in Media Cloud, Fig. 3.6 provides a chart of the number of stories between August 2018 and 2019 that mention Greta Thunberg. In total, during the 2018–2019

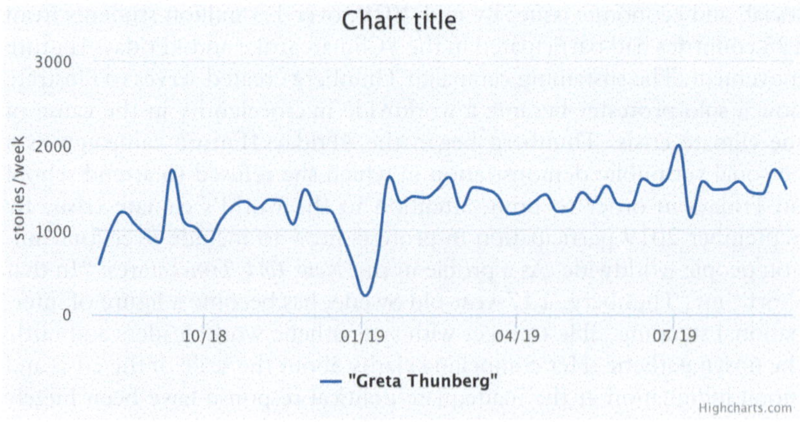

Fig. 3.6 Number of Greta Thunberg Media Stories 2018–2019

period, 75,000 stories were published with at least one sentence that included Greta Thunberg. There were three periods of particular interest: the first school strike, her appearance at the United Nations, and the worldwide school strikes. At the time of the first school strike in August 2018, there were 1221 stories published in the top US digital native sources. By December 14, when she appeared before the United Nations, there were 1223 stories that mentioned her. And in March 14, the beginning of the school strikes, there were 1487 stories that mentioned Greta Thunberg.

Link Analysis

Table 3.1 lists the ten stories with the most inlinks. Time magazine was the most inlinked source, perhaps because the link is to the issue in which Greta Thunberg was named Time's Person of the Year. In addition to mainstream media sites, the FridaysForFuture.org website, along with left-leaning NPR and right-leaning fox40.com, is listed. According to the Media Cloud analysis, Table 3.2 lists the top media sources ranked by quantity of inlinks. The table also indicates the political leanings of the media. All of the ones on the list lean either center or center left, except one course, archive.org; however, the latter is merely a repository of historical internet documents.

Table 3.1 Top 10 media stories online ranked by quantity of inlinks from 2018 to 2020

Rank	*Title*	*Publish_ date*	*Media*	*InLink count*	*Facebook share count*
1	Greta Thunberg is TIMES' Person of the Year	2019-12-15	Time	37	1,55,364
2	Teen climate change activist endorses Joe Biden	2020-10-12	WFLA	25	93
3	Global Climate Strike: Greta Thunberg and Huge Crowds Protest	2019-09-20	Forbes	22	58
4	After two years of school strikes, the world is still in a state of climate crisis denial	2020-08-19	Guardian	25	7944
5	FridaysForFuture	2019-07-05	Fridaysforfuture.org	25	9768
6	Greta Thunberg Twitter	2019-09-24	Twitter	19	731
7	Greta Thunberg's Speech at the U.N. Climate Action Summit	2019-09-23	NPR	20	0
8	Greta Thunberg on Twitter	2020-10-12	Twitter	14	4751
9	Teen climate change activist Greta Thunberg endorses Joe Biden	2020-10-12	Fox40.com	12	26
10	Greta Thunberg returns to school in Sweden after year off	2020-08-25	AP	12	5

By far the most mentioned influencer in the climate crisis news network is Greta Thunberg, who is mentioned in 3500 stories, accounting for 94 percent of the mentions. She is followed by Donald Trump (25 percent), Joe Biden (13 percent), and Angela Merkel 7 percent.

The network visualization in Fig. 3.7 depicts the interconnectedness of the media covering the climate crisis. The analysis reveals the clusters of content that use the same narrative. This visualization depicts how media sources are linked to one another. The multiplex of mainstream and alternative media presented should be viewed with the second part of the case study in which the Facebook Climate Strike social network is described and analyzed.

Table 3.2 Top ten media sources online ranked by quantity of inlinks from 2018 to 2020

Name	*InLink count*	*OutLink count*	*Story count*	*Facebook shares*	*Media InLink count*	*Twitter partisanship*
Guardian	145	6	99	5,19,772	72	Center left
Twitter	74	13	39	8353	50	Center
Archive.org	72	0	86	2	2	Center right
Time	69	3	22	3,45,215	52	Center left
YouTube	54	0	40	3,13,973	43	Center
AP	44	0	10	488	17	Center
BBC	34	0	33	68,977	22	Center
Instagram.com	33	0	17	286	20	Center
Reuters	30	0	19	10,737	25	Center
Tomdispatch.com	28	16	14	73	10	Left

Climate Crisis on Facebook

In order to better understand the Climate Strike movement and the role of influencers, in particular Greta Thunberg as mediator in the network, this case study researched the following hashtags—#climateaction, #climatecrisis, #Fridaysforfuture, #climatejustice, #climatechange, #ClimateStrike, @gretathunbergsweden—that produced a list of 208 Facebook pages. The data was obtained from CrowdTangle, a public insights tool owned and operated by Facebook that included public posts for pages between October 2019 and October 2020.[22] During that period, there were recorded 1.2 million interactions, 56,000 comments, and 200,000 shares. The types of posts included photos (77 percent), links (11 percent), statuses (2 percent), Facebook videos (9 percent), and YouTube and other videos (0.7 percent).

While Greta Thunberg is an important or core mediator within the broader climate crisis social network, there are other key actors that represent varying areas of interest. In fact, those areas of interest are wide, ranging from corporate interests on both sides of the climate argument to nonprofit or informal organizations to individuals who based on their status, celebrity, or microcelebrity play a role in the formation and dynamic nature of this online social network.

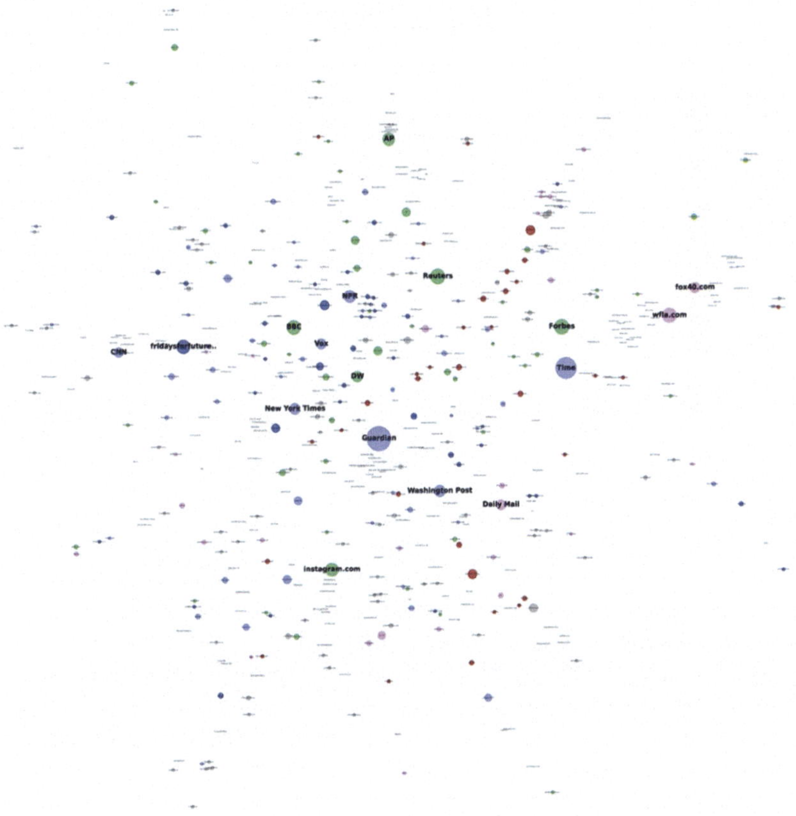

Fig. 3.7 Network Map of Media Covering Greta Thunberg (MediaCloud.org)

Beside Greta Thunberg, there are other influencers who are mediating or moderating the discussion on Facebook. As indicated in Fig. 3.8, over 62 percent of the Facebook pages are from nongovernment or volunteer organizations, like Moms Clean Air Force, while 10 percent are of individuals, including Greta Thunberg. Moms Clean Air Force is a lobbying organization that seeks to develop policy on a national and local level regarding protecting children from air pollution and climate change. They describe themselves as a "mompartisan" group of over one million.[23]

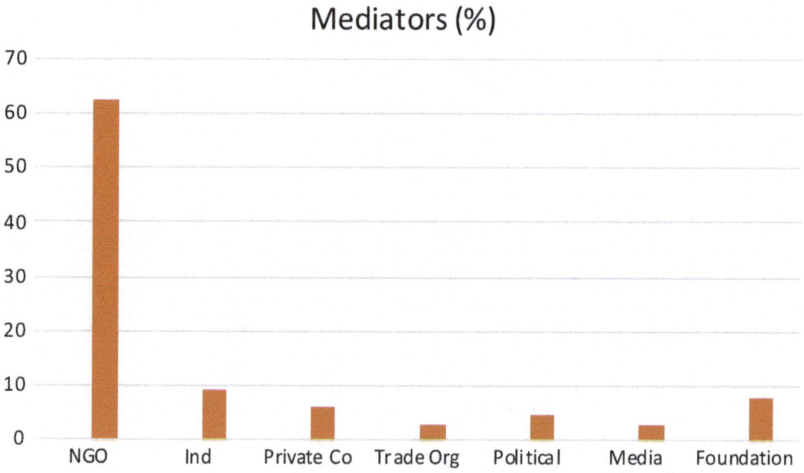

Fig. 3.8 Types of social mediators

Table 3.3 provides a sampling of mediators by type in the broader climate crisis social network, that include individuals, NGOs, foundations, trade organizations, political figures, and media.

For example, the Sanjay Mishra Facebook page includes a photo of the Indian actor as part of the promotion of a film *Kadvi Hawa* (translation: Bitter Wind), a Hindi-language drama based on the theme of climate change. The film stars Sanjay Mishra. The comments on the photo of the actor on Facebook includes comments from fans like:

> Thank you so much Sir for giving us a film like Kadvi Hawa. I hope one day we will have better audiences in masses to make these kind of films turn into blockbusters. I hope.
>
> Awesome movie, I watched it 3 times. Sir, love your perfection towards character. Every teenager must watch this movie. Climate change is real issue nowadays but we are focussing on some foolish issues. Salute you sir.

Greta Thunberg posted the following on her Facebook page, along with a photo of the sculpture by Isaac Cordal titled Follow the Leaders or Politicians Discussing Global Warming.

Table 3.3 Type of Mediators and Examples

Individuals	Greta Thunberg
	William J. Barber, II (religious activist)
	Sandra Steingraber (author)
	Laura Turner Seydel (Ted Turner's daughter)
	Sanjay Mishra (actor)
NGO	UN Environment Programme North America
	Scientists for Future Regionalgruppe Aachen
	Moms Clean Air Force
	John Muir Project of Earth Island Institute
	Heiltsuk Oppose Oil Pipelines and Super Oil Tankers
Foundations	The White Feather Foundation
	The Kresge Foundation
	Outrider Foundation
	Environmental Justice Foundation Deutschland
Trade Organizations	Outdoor Industry Association
	Our Maryland
Political	Representative Mike Levin
	IATSE Members For Bernie Sanders 2020
	Herefordshire Green Party
	Councillor Chas Booth
Media	The Hill

The thought of us giving up on the 1.5 or well below 2°C-targets of the Paris Agreement—without people even knowing what the full consequences of that would mean to future generations and to the most affected people and areas—is simply unacceptable.

The way the global aspect of equity and climate justice is being systematically and completely ignored in the European debate is shameful.

Yes, WE might be able to "adapt", for a while. We have the infrastructure and the resources.

But the global majority has not.

When the EU's climate policies and targets are being discussed, the aspect of equity doesn't even seem to exist. Apparently it's not even worth a mention. And yet, climate justice is the very heart of the Paris Agreement. And we have clearly signed up to lead the way.

#mapa #climatejustice
#FaceTheClimateEmergency

Get Your Geek on, which describes itself as a broadcasting and media production company specializing in memes, posted the following which garnered a significant amount of attention.

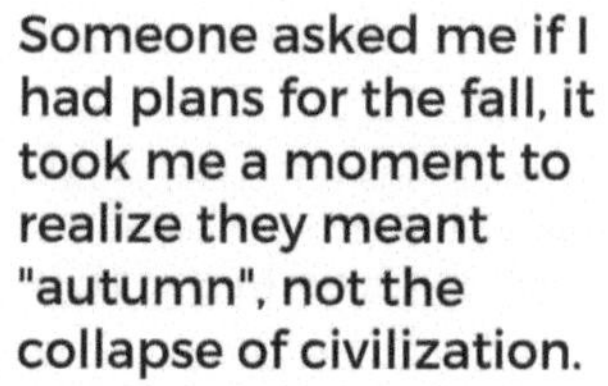

This particular meme above attracted almost 182,000 interactions and almost 40 percent of the interactions from the data set utilized in this case study. Table 3.4 lists the top Facebook pages associated with the climate crisis movement. Sentiment associated with these Facebook pages indicates the type of reactions caused by the posts. For example, the Get Your Geek On page garnered a significant number of laughs while Greta Thunberg's post of the sculpture photo indicated a large number of sad reactions. Context is important, as the post in the form of a meme is offered with a sense of irony; it garnered 181,000 interactions, accounting for 39 percent of the reactions among those active in the data set, while the photo of the sculpture posted by Thunberg meant to strike a more serious tone had 109,000 reactions or 24 percent of total interactions within the data set.

A social network forms when nodes, which are the social actors described above as mediators and moderators, form links with others. In its most simple form a "like," although clicktivist in nature, exemplifies how nodes connect to one another. The social network emerges as a set of clusters or communities that are formed into subgroups with their own interconnections. But those clusters may be dynamic in that they may grow in size or actors may move from one cluster to another, as those likes along with mentions, in the case of Twitter retweets, posts, and comments emerge over time. As this case study is about a core influencer in the climate change movement, Greta Thunberg, the theory of structural holes can be applied to further understand how social capital expended by the influencers within the social network communicates across those clusters extending social boundaries.[24] Generally speaking, someone with a lot of "shares" on Facebook demonstrates the power, which can be defined as social capital, to influence a social network. In the climate crisis social network, Greta Thunberg's post had approximately 6700 shares and almost 65,000 likes. Likes and shares are standard metrics utilized to measure the amplification of someone in the social network.

Table 3.4 Top Facebook Pages/Groups: Interactions and Sentiment

	Likes	*Comments*	*Shares*	*Love*	*Wow*	*HaHa*	*Sad*	*Angry*	*Care*	*Tot. interactions/%*
Get Your Geek On	58,312	1789	47,208	1153	252	72,421	294	6	222	181,657/39
Sanjay Mishra	57,837	472	62	3544	73	42	6	3	215	62,254/13
Greta Thunberg	64,697	3071	6760	6778	217	288	6725	397	1489	109,393/24
Yuumei	15,784	172	2464	11,493	192	16	74	0	621	43,245/9
China Xinhua News	24,920	34	70	319	61	7	3	3	23	30,816/7
Moms Clean Air Force	18,271	1229	1766	1113	71	79	10	19	62	25,440/6
Sunrise El Paso	744	143	19,058	158	5	1	4	5	16	22,620/5
Occupy Democrats	7132	1388	5480	1490	23	175	69	68	180	20,134/4
Dilmah conservation	9516	23	518	105	13	31	2319	14	38	16,005/3

At first glance these social actors appear unconnected as they represent particular interests; however, because of their one common interest in climate issues, they form an interconnection with one another, a public with a common interest in climate change. Within the larger social network, clusters are formed based on particular aspects of climate but they also share common traits, in this case an interest in climate issues or associated political ideology. This means that followers in one cluster may be exposed to information or messages from another cluster, although the interconnectedness of messages will likely be limited based on exposure. While followers are mostly limited by interactions in their immediate cluster, but because they are not entirely disconnected, some of those engaged on these pages will serve as bridges between clusters and in the process pass information from one cluster to another. The theory of structural holes accounts for those "brokers" who contribute to the flow of information across social boundaries. Social mediators of these Facebook pages because of the structure of their social networks serve as what are referred to as hubs that have the ability to bridge relationships. As Himelboim and colleagues state: "key actors who attract more attention in their own clusters (defined by in-degree centrality) act as a bridge between two clusters (defined by betweenness centrality). This unique position in the network allows them to spread information within their own clusters and to other clusters that would otherwise be devoid of that information."[25]

Social Network Analysis

As the concern here is for structural influences, algorithms calculate betweenness centrality by identifying the shortest paths connecting people in the network and counting the number of paths through the influencer. "Brokering" is the term utilized to describe what these influencers do in the network to connect disconnected groups. With regard to the influencer, such brokers are likely to hold information that other people in the movement do not have or know about in which case the influencer plays an important role in making connections within the social movement. The ability to broker the flow of information in the network suggests the influencer has the social capital of an opinion leader. As the opinion leader helps to establish a hierarchy within the network, it becomes clear that all connections are not of equal importance, which can be measured by the fourth characteristic, eigenvector centrality. This measure, Ognyanova points out, indicates that "people have more influence when their social ties are also highly influential ... For instance, if two social media users have the same number of ties, the one whose contacts are more popular and well-connected would have a higher eigenvector centrality."[26] All of these measures help to better understand the role of influencers within a social movement. The chapter started out by raising the issue of power within the movement. Now we can point to the measures that indicate the structural relationships within the social network to better understand who, including the media, is driving the conversation. Whether the individual or individuals are bone fide celebrities, microcelebrities, other media figures, or other types of mediators, the ability to influence the movement may be analyzed and visualized within the social structure of the network.

Density measures how close nodes are in a network, while reciprocity measures two-way communication or how much nodes are talking to each other. Centralization measures the extent to which a few nodes dominate the conversation. Each node has a centrality measure: indegree (based on times it has been mentioned or replied to), outdegree (based on times it has mentioned or replied to others), and total degree (the sum of both). Finally, modularity measures the fragmentation of a network into distinct communities. For all of these measures, values range from zero (lowest) to one (highest). For example, modularity values closer to one indicate clear divisions between communities, whereas values less than 0.5 suggest that the communities "overlap more; the network is more likely to consist of a core group of nodes. A high modularity value reflects greater separation between communities of conversation. A network that is low in centrality means that there are many mediators and influencers making it less centralized. Networks that are close-knit and homophilous tend to disseminate information. Heterogeneous networks that are more spread out (larger in diameter), loosely connected (low in density and reciprocity), and fragmented (high in modularity) could lead to slower diffusion of information and threaten widespread adoption of beliefs about climate change.

In order to visualize influence within the social network, the Facebook data derived through Crowdtangle was formatted for use in Gephi an open-source network mapping tool. In the climate crisis Facebook social network, there are 13,933 nodes in the network, and there are 9913 edges. Nodes in the social network are visualized as colored dots in a network map indicating clustering. In this case, nodes are both Facebook accounts and links. Edges are illustrated by the lines that connect the nodes. In this case, the edges are the connection between the entity and the URL that it shared in the directed network. In order to focus on the major component in the network connections, the giant component was filtered in this case, which comprised 471 nodes and 487 edges or 3.38 percent of the nodes in the network and 487 edges or 4.91 percent of the network.

The calculation for closeness centrality indicates that 65 percent of those engaged in the network were connected to what might be referred to as the "Greta cluster" while the remaining 35 percent of those engaged belonged to a cluster whose key influencer is 1,000,000 Strong Against Offshore Drilling. This suggests that while Greta Thunberg exhibits greater influence within the climate crisis network, there are other key mediators who command attention and disseminate information of particular interest to those within their clusters. As pointed out earlier there is spillover from one cluster to another, as they are both part of a larger social network.

As the interest here is to look at Greta Thundberg as influencer within the climate crisis network, a network map was created based on what may be referred to as an ego network (see Fig. 3.9). As the term "ego" implies, there is a node that is central to the network and there are other nodes that are connected to that node. The ego network is illustrative of the influence that, in this case, Greta Thunberg has on the social movement. In addition to the 1,000,000 Strong Against Offshore Drilling, there is another large cluster within the social network, an organization, Extinction Rebellion, that describes itself as a decentralized, international, nonpartisan movement using civil disobedience to effect climate change and related environmental issues.[27] XR, as it is commonly known, is a movement to highlight climate and ecological issues, deeming them urgent enough to hold protests in London over the past two years, bring the city to a "standstill for days, printing presses of rightwing newspapers blockaded and fossil fuel companies targeted."[28]

In this case study of influence within the climate crisis digital network, the focus was on Greta Thunberg as a core influencer. The case revealed that there are a diverse set of independent actors both publishing and passively consuming content based on particular interests those actors represent. In addition to the mainstream publishers' network described and illustrated based on the Media Cloud data, we can see representation from the political right and left. Other types of organizations are also represented in the network including loosely as well as highly connected organizations, prominent individuals, nongovernmental organizations, as well

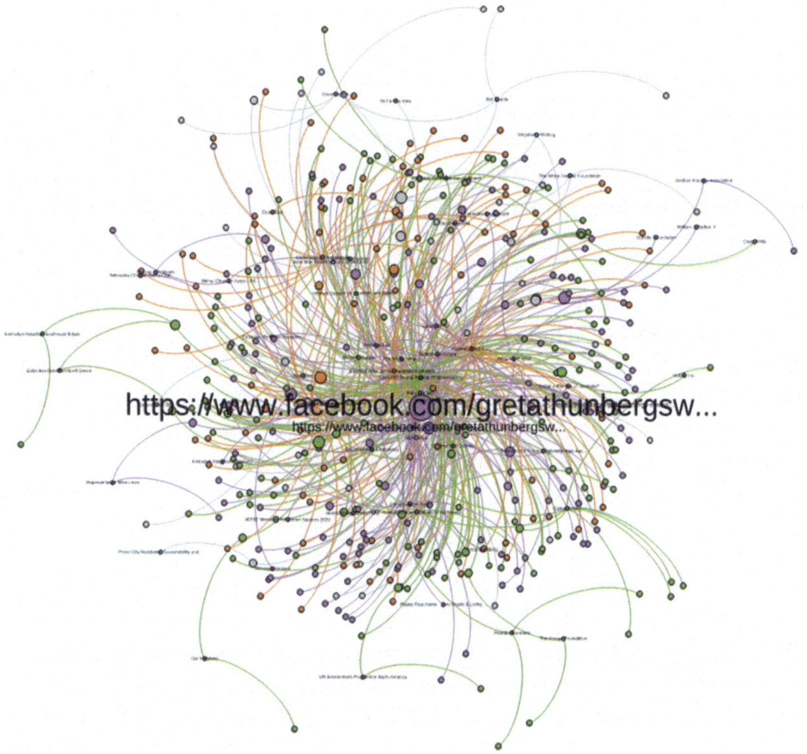

Fig. 3.9 Greta Thunberg ego network visualization

as Greta Thunberg. In other words, the climate crisis social network is complex, and as a result clusters form within the network that present varying viewpoints on the crisis, and the posted content is situationally relevant both to the poster of that content, whether it be a meme, video, or post, and to those who consume that content expressed in the form of interactions and sentiment toward the content and the content provider. The conversation around the climate crisis is shaped not by one individual but by the confluence of social engagements within the network and the sharing of content of interest and by clicking on content shared by others. What makes the complexity of the network interesting is that it is not the single influencer who dominates the network but rather the networked public that determines what it relevant credible and worthy of online engagement, independent of the strength of one individual to proffer an argument regarding the climate crisis. The implications for those developing strategies for social movements need to consider that while social media are not democratic in the sense that not everyone has equal access, they are nevertheless networked spaces where a diversity of opinion is represented by actors who are elite as well as non-elite. The ability of a single influencer to strategically amplify a particular position needs to be tempered with the understanding that social networks are diverse, complex organisms where some people operate within an echo chamber-like cluster and at the same time information may spill over from cluster within the network to another. The term "influence," and in that influencer, is reminiscent of the concept of control. The concept of control needs to be understood as a place or point of negotiation or to put it another way, the space where culture does its work and the space where we do our own work with what is presented in whatever form it is offered.

Conclusion

This chapter explored the role that influencers play in digital social movements. Digital influencers come in several forms from bonafide celebrities, like Jane Fonda, whose climate strike protests garnered much attention to those referred to as microcelebrities, like Greta Thunberg who began her climate strike protest as a solo affair, but the movement grew into an international phenomenon. Sports figures throughout the millennium have engaged in social movements and the basketball icon LaBron James or the quarterback Colin Kaepernick are no exceptions. These influencers, and many other media figures along with new media themselves, serve as both mediators and moderators in digitally based social movements. With regard to the role that media play in the development and furtherance of a social movement, the use of Media Cloud provided evidence that news media play a role in amplifying the social issue and likely influence the discourse, sentiment, and response to the climate crisis. The social network that forms around the climate crisis social movement provides a platform that reflects the concerns of the networked public regardless of the position they take on the issue as people form clusters, sometimes around individuals like Greta Thunberg. But there are multiple clusters within the social network, and sometimes there is spillover as fears and concerns of one cluster may traverse to another. There is both an echo-chamber effect as well as the possibility if not the opportunity to amplify messaging in a particular direction. That is the role that influencers may play in the development of a social movement.

Chapter 4 investigates pockets of resistance, what we might refer to as anti-movements with a specific focus on contentious politics. The case study for the chapter, "Conflict and Contentiousness," looks at toxicity on the platform Reddit in light of discussions of vaccine hesitancy and vaccine resistance and the emerging movement surrounding that social issue.

Notes

1. Astute.com (n.d.) Case study: PepsiCo & Kendall Jenner's controversial commercial. https://astute.co/pepsi-kendall-jenner-commercial/.
2. Ognyanova, K. (2017). Multistep flow of communication: Network effects. In P. Roessler, C. Hoffner, & L. van Zoonen (Eds.), *The International Encyclopedia of Media Effects* (pp. 1-10). New York, NY: Wiley-Blackwell.
3. Ibid., p. 3.
4. Katz, E. (1957). The two-step flow of communication: An up-to-date report on a hypothesis. *Public Opinion Quarterly*, pp. 61–78. doi: https://doi.org/10.1086/266687.
5. Wulf, S. (January 30, 2019). Athletes and activism: The long, defiant history of sports protests. *TheUndefeated.com*. Retrieved from: https://theundefeated.com/features/athletes-and-activism-the-long-defiant-history-of-sports-protests/.
6. McCarriston, S. (August 28, 2020). NBA boycott: LeBron James, other stars react to players' decision not to take court for playoff games. *CBSsports.com*. Retrieved from: https://www.cbssports.com/nba/news/nba-boycott-lebron-james-other-stars-react-to-players-decision-not-to-take-court-for-playoff-games/.
7. Kellner, D. (2003). *Media Spectacle*. New York: Routledge, p. 64.
8. Kellner, p. 94.
9. Kellner, p. 96.
10. JustCapital.com (n.d.). SURVEY: What Americans Want from Corporate America During the Response, Reopening, and Reset Phases of the Coronavirus Crisis. Retrieved from: https://justcapital.com/reports/survey-what-americans-want-from-corporate-america-during-the-response-reopening-and-reset-phases-of-the-coronavirus-crisis/.
11. Goffman, E. *The Presentation of Self in Everyday Life*. Doubleday: Garden City, New York, 1959.

12. Marwick, A. & boyd, d. (2011). To See and Be Seen: Celebrity Practice on Twitter. *Convergence: The International Journal of Research into New Media Technologies.*17:2, pp. 139–158.
13. Senft, T. (2008). *Camgirls: Celebrity and Community in the Age of Social Networks Digital Formations.* New York: Peter Lang.
14. Alperstein, N. (February 21, 2020). Micro-celebrities can't "shake it off". *MediatedSocialConnections.com.* Retrieved from: http://mediatedsocialconnections.com/index.php/2020/02/21/micro-celebrities-cant-shake-it-off/.
15. Alperstein, N. (2019). Celebrity and Mediated Social Connections: Fans, Friends and Followers in the Digital Age. Switzerland: Palgrave Macmillan.
16. Himelboim, I., Golan, G. J., Suto, R. J., & Moon, B. B. (2014). A social networks approach to public relations on Twitter: Social mediators and mediated public relations. *Journal of Public Relations Research.* 26, pp. 359–379.
17. Singh, O. (June 3, 2020). Emma Watson is being criticized for 'performative activism' after altering black squares for Blackout Tuesday to seemingly fit her Instagram aesthetic. *MSN.com.* Retrieve from: https://www.msn.com/en-us/lifestyle/lifestyle-buzz/emma-watson-is-being-criticized-for-performative-activism-after-altering-black-squares-for blackout-tuesday-to-seemingly-fit-her-instagram-aesthetic/ar-BB14WkjL.
18. Revanche, J. (November 2, 2019). Jane Fonda is white, wealthy and privileged—and she's using that power for good. *The Guardian.com.* Retrieved from: https://www.theguardian.com/commentisfree/2019/nov/02/jane-fonda-is-white-wealthy-and-privileged-and-shes-using-that-power-for-good.
19. Marchese, D. (October 30, 2020). Greta Thunberg Hears Your Excuses. She Is Not Impressed. *The New York Times.* Retrieved from: https://www.nytimes.com/interactive/2020/11/02/magazine/greta-thunberg-interview.html.
20. IBMD.com. (2020). *I am Greta.* Retrieved from: https://www.imdb.com/title/tt10394738/.
21. Dave, A., Boardman Ndulue, E., & Schwartz-Henderson, L, (2020). Targeting Greta Thunberg: A Case Study in Online Mis/Disinformation. The German Marshall Fund of the United States. July, No.11. Retrieved from: https://www.gmfus.org/file/29635/download.
22. CrowdTangle Team (2020). CrowdTangle. Facebook, Menlo Park, California, United States.
23. Moms Clean Air Force. (n.d.). https://www.momscleanairforce.org/our-mission/.

24. Burt, R. S. (2001). Structural holes versus network closure at social capital. In R. Burt, K. Cook, & N. Lin (Eds.), *Social capital: Theory and research* (pp. 31–55). New York: Aldine de Gruyter.
25. Isa, D. & Himelboim, I. (2018). A Social Networks Approach to Online Social Movement: Social Mediators and Mediated Content in #FreeAJStaff Twitter Network. *Social Media and Society.* January-March, p. 4.
26. Ognyanova (2017). Multistep Flow of Communication. p. 6.
27. Rebellion Extinction (n.d.). https://rebellion.global/about-us/.
28. Taylor, M. (January 8, 2021). More than 1,000 Extinction Rebellion activists taken to court. TheGuardian.com. Retrieved from: https://www.theguardian.com/environment/2021/jan/08/more-than-1000-extinction-rebellion-activists-taken-to-court.

CHAPTER 4

Conflict and Contentiousness: Network Connections and Pockets of Resistance in Social Movements

"Populism" is a term heard about a lot, as it reflects the political positions of Marine La Pen in France, Jair Bolsonaro in Brazil, and Donald Trump in the United States, among many others. But the populism of today is pretty much the opposite of the "common man" populism of the late 1800s. A Google nGram (Fig. 4.1) indicates that the term "populism" didn't begin to show up in books until around the 1880s and had a slight peak around the time that William Jennings Bryant ran as a US presidential candidate on a populist platform.

It wasn't until the 1930s that a Depression-era populist wave emerged. Historically populism may have its roots as a "common man" movement; however, there have been waves of anti-populist movements as well, leading to today's style of plutocratic populism that in the United States is not being led by poor farmers from the mid-West or rural South, as was the case in earlier movements, but by what might be characterized as the business elite. It is an odd paring, for sure, but it might be said that for every populist there is an anti-populist. Populism is to a degree like a pendulum that swings in tune with the times. In a time of economic upheaval, populist outrage looks to make sweeping societal changes, perhaps seeking outsiders like Donald Trump, who in 2016 promised to "drain the swamp" referring to entrenched bureaucrats in the federal government. But as populist governments fail to meet their promised changes, populist movements tend to move toward the center, in essence moving against that which they rebelled against in the first place. As a *New York Times* column

N. Alperstein, *Performing Media Activism in the Digital Age*,
https://doi.org/10.1007/978-3-030-73804-4_4

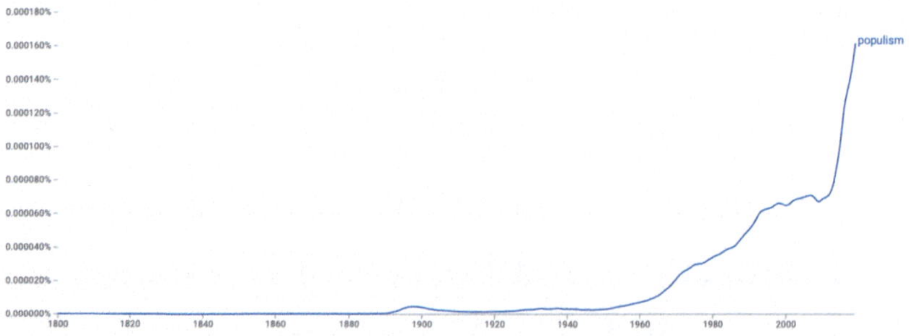

Fig. 4.1 The rise of the term "populism" (Google nGram)

points out: "But these unwelcome changes or dangers all have one thing in common: They are experienced as dispossessing a particular subset of society. When that happens, people cling more tightly to the group identity that feels under threat, which primes them to see the world as divided between 'us' and 'them.' Who better to protect 'us' than the angry populists who promise to punish and control "them"—and also promise to take on establishment centrists whose old-school liberal ideals demand equal protections?"

In light of this polarizing effect, consider the impact of cable TV news—MSNBC, Fox, and CNN. Using the Stanford Cable TV News Analyzer, readers can see in Fig. 4.2 the screen time given to "populism," "nationalism," and "immigration," three polarizing issues. The peak for immigration in the world of cable TV news was January 2018, as immigration was an issue that factored in the US mid-term elections. At that time there were 53 videos regarding populism, 59 regarding nationalism, and 1593 videos on immigration.

Writing in his book *The People, Yes*, Thomas Frank describes anti-populism championed by a range of supporters from the Robber Barons of the late nineteenth century to the liberal elites of today both share a disdain for populism. Frank refers to that disdain as "the Democracy Scare," in which elites do not believe the masses—the uneducated or unwashed, so to speak—have the capacity to decide democratic elections. In other words, Donald Trump and populism make strange bedfellows. Not just in the US, we can see contentious politics under the guise of populist movements in France, Brazil, the UK, and Germany, as the far-right wing German Afd political party conflates mask wearing, a topic this

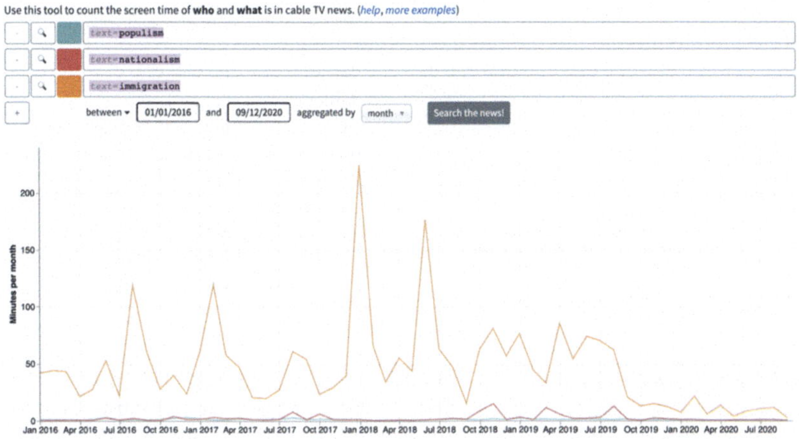

Fig. 4.2 Stanford cable TV news analyzer

book will take up below, with its anti-government rhetoric. It has been reported that "While some AfD members have made a splash in attending the recent demonstrations, anecdotal evidence suggests that they are simply one faction of a motley crew made up of pandemic denialists, anti-vaxxers, far-right agitators, libertarians, nationalists, and affiliates of the *Reichsbürger* movement, which claims that the German government created after World War II is illegitimate."[1] The Gilets Jaunes or Yellow Vest movement in France is somewhat different in that it is not a nationalist movement aligned with any political persuasion, right or left wing, nor does it focus on a societal issue like immigration, and there is no single leader of the movement. Rather, it is an economic class movement.[2] Populism in the form of "anti" movements (see Table 4.1), whether it is the AfD, Yellow Vests, Five Star, Freedom Party, Independence Party, Nationalist Front, Podemos, Syriza are flourishing.

These movements alone or in combination represent anti-austerity, anti-government, anti-Eurozone, anti-establishment, anti-European Union, anti-immigration, or anti-Islam.[3] Inequality makes for fertile ground for populist movements, from both the left and the right and in Europe as well as Latin America, to thrive. In addition to populism, immigration or rather anti-immigration populists in Poland and Italy could rise based on the direction the economies and the COVID19 pandemic take. This chapter explores pockets of resistance in social movements of which

Table 4.1 European populist movements

Country	*Populist movement*
Spain	Podemos
Greece	Syriza
Italy	Five Star Movement
Britain	UK Independence Party
France	National Front
Netherlands	Freedom Party
Germany	AfD
Austria	Freedom Party

populist movements might be one. The focus is on countermovements as exemplars of contentious politics, whether the movement is the #NeverTrump digital Lincoln Project, the anti-gun March for Our Lives youth movement to end gun violence, or anti-apartheid, anti-capitalism, or anti-fascism movements, among many others. These are movements where social norms collide. In this chapter's case study, the social network analysis (SNA) approach is applied to the anti-vaccine movement, characterized by the World Health Organization as vaccine hesitancy. To illustrate the phenomenon of performing activism in the digital age, the network connections among members of the #Vaxxhappens subreddit on the Reddit platform are analyzed to investigate levels of toxicity in the social discourse around vaccines.

Contentious Politics

The concept of contentious politics, coined in the 1970s by the late Charles Tilly during a time of social upheaval, serves as a blanket to many contemporary social movements. "The concept of contentious politics encompasses social movements but extends to a wider range of conflictual phenomena, including strike waves, civil wars, revolutions, and insurgencies. It shifts the focus from the subjects and objects of contention to the mechanisms that connect them to each other and to broader institutions and actors." Tarrow cites the work of Tilly, who developed his Dynamics of Contentious project in which he described five areas of research including relational dynamics within movements, relations between movements and political parties, the process of radicalization, the mechanisms that drive civil wars, and the transition from mobilization to civil wars.[4] There is a fitting connection between the dynamics of contentiousness and cyberconflict theory that was introduced in Chap. 1 of this book, as both relate to the connective tissue that binds non-state actors who operate within digital networks, and those outside of the dominant forces in society, namely government and corporations. Athina Karatzogianni theorizes cyberconflict as conflict that takes place within computer-mediated environments; namely, by digital activists. The theory of cyberconflict suggests that performing media activism in the context of contentious politics is not a function or result of technological developments but rather a political effect. I would argue that it is also a cultural effect as bias plays a significant role in shaping one's adherence to group membership within a social network, and it plays a role in shape-shifting one's personal identity, as one seeks to align or bend one's personal beliefs or resist the norms of a group.

Normative Social Behavior

Rimal and Real studied how behaviors are shaped by perceived norms. Their theory of normative social behavior has application in the context of contentious nature of social issues and associated social movements.[5] First consider two types of norms: descriptive and injunctive. Descriptive norms are typical patterns of behavior with the expectation that people will behave accordingly. Sometimes, however, descriptive norms can be contested. They also relate to the individual's belief about the prevalence of a behavior. In order words, if I see others performing in a certain way, it may impact my own beliefs about performing in the prescribed manner or taking a particular ideological position. On social media, for example, following a litany of retweets on a social issue, one may choose to like a tweet or retweet on an issue. The mere act of retweeting, and in that joining others who are doing the same, is confirmation of the validity of the message contained in the tweet. You can imagine this process taking place as a tweet goes viral or a TikTok video obtains tens of thousands of views, serving as confirmation of the position taken in the content. Another way of looking at this phenomenon is based on the idea that the more people harbor exaggerated perceptions within their social network about an issue, the more likely they will perceive their own behavior as normative.

Injunctive norms are prescriptive (or proscriptive) rules regarding behavior that ought (or ought not) to be performed. With regard to performing digital activism, injunctive norms are dependent upon the group, community, or cluster to which one belongs. Injunctive norms refer to the extent which individuals perceive that external influence is the expectation to behave in a particular manner, otherwise they must consider the consequences, like not being part of the group, a form of punishment. Injunctive norms encourage the individual toward conformity. For example, what we call influencers on social media, those with social capital, or perhaps opinion leaders, set expectations for other to behave in a particular manner and by implication sanctions will be incurred if they do not comply. During the COVID-19 pandemic, many colleges and universities were hiring "influencers" to post images and messages on social media platforms that promote safe behaviors like wearing a mask, routine hand washing, and social or physical distancing.[6] We can also see this phenomenon played out with a movement like QAnon whose activities are described below.

Sanctions in this sense might have to do with group membership, like being excluded from the group, or sanctions may impact one's identity, like the loss of status compared to others. Here social comparison theory provides some guidance. This theory developed in 1954 by Leon Festinger states that individuals measure their own *social* and personal standing based on how they stack up against others. The question might be raised: what is the cost, figuratively speaking, of membership in an offline or online social network? Who would approve or disapprove of one's engagement in an online social movement? In an odd way, there is the potential of descriptive and injunctive norms to operate simultaneously when an individual believes both that many others engage in a behavior and that others would disapprove of them enacting the behavior, although there is usually congruence between the two types of norms. Specifically, people may believe that wearing a mask during the COVID-19 pandemic, for example, is widespread (high descriptive norm) and at the same time they may believe that they should not wear a mask (strong injunctive norm). In order to bridge the inconsistency, influencers play a role in addressing misinformation or ambiguities. We can see that culture plays a large role in this process as culture tells us a lot about how or why normative influences occur in either individualistic or collectivistic cultures. Ramal and Real's theory of normative social behavior is based on the premise that descriptive norms (people's perceptions about the prevalence of a behavior) affect individuals' own behaviors through interactions with three normative mechanisms: injunctive norms, outcome expectations, and group identity. Additionally, the researchers point out that these three mechanisms serve as mediators. Mediators in social media are either media themselves, opinion leaders or authority figures, and celebrities, among others serving as influencers who may invoke those mechanisms. The role of moderator in a social network would be consistent with the strength of weak ties theory in which people we do not know well may have greater influence than those we are close to in our social network.

Associated with the theory of normative social behavior is Floyd Allport's concept of pluralistic ignorance, whereby individuals operating within a group privately reject an idea but believe that other members of the group believe the idea, so they decide to accept it; this can lead to rapid change. "When everybody believes that he is the only one who thinks something, and does not talk about his opinion for fear of violating a moral taboo or an authoritarian ruler, or of just being unpopular, it sometimes happens that a wave of publicity will sweep through the community, informing people that everybody else (or many others) think as they do."[7] As the groups to which we belong tend to be homophilic, that is made up of like-minded people, we tend to go along with the "bunch" when we see them angry or upset or oppositional to something; this phenomenon is referred to as the spiral of silence. As there is so much vitriol online that is outrage, anger, and oppositionality that social media becomes a form of political theater. And because of the amplification of such vitriolic metaphors, memes, and tweets, over time people shift their opinions, what Ramal and Real call descriptive norms, so they align more closely with the group to which we belong.

Anti-mask Movement and Normative Social Behavior

At the beginning of the COVID-19 outbreak in early 2020, with little experience with pandemics, some governments recommended that people wear masks and use social or physical distancing as measures to prevent or slow down the spread of the virus. In many countries, citizens complied especially in some Asian countries, like China, Hong Kong, Japan, South Korea, Thailand, and Taiwan, where wearing a mask was already an accepted norm, particularly based on both culture and history (see Fig. 4.3).[8]

The United States was another matter. Divisions arose among mask wearers and those who resisted or refused to wear a mask, even after several months of virus spread and some state and local governments mandating the use of masks and evidence that wearing masks makes a difference in combating the spread of the virus. What arose in the United States and UK in particular was an anti-mask movement, apparently in response to violating people's freedom; also, there is an accompanying disbelief

Fig. 4.3 Pro-mask wearing tweet

regarding the severity of the virus as if people are in denial, an expression of the divisiveness seen in some social movements. The anti-mask movement (not an official name) as this is an amorphous conglomeration of individuals is steeped in conspiracy theories, some of which are intertwined with the anti-vaccine movement that is the subject of the case study presented in this chapter. Those conspiracy theories emerge around fears of Big Pharma, YouTube, Bill Gates, and George Soros to name a few. Some of the confusion regarding the efficacy of wearing a mask may have derived from conflicting messages from government leaders, especially in the early days of the outbreak when the president of the United States refused to wear a mask. But there is also evidence that the knowledge base of the anti-mask movement comes from information gleaned from social media or reinforced in social media. To some degree the question isn't even about masks; rather the issue relates to the fact that people, especially many in the United States, don't want to be told what to do. But there are deeper cultural issues at work too, like the contention among some people that it isn't "manly" to wear a mask. To that end, Zagury-Orly suggests four major reasons for mask resistance (Fig. 4.4).[9] In addition to gender issues related to mask wearing, culture plays a significant role. In many Asian cultures that might be characterized as collectivistic, mask wearing was common even before the outbreak of COVID-19. The United States, in contrast, would be considered an individualistic culture, as described above, people don't want to be told what to do seeing the right not to wear a mask as a constitutionally protected one. However, to place culture in a binary such as this is too simplistic, as it doesn't go against individualism to want to expose other people to risk. Bias, the third reason, has to do with perceived norms. It may have to do with group membership, and it may have to do with identity. Finally, influential others play a significant role. Not only do opinion leaders serve as mediators of networked

Reasons for Mask Resistance	Gender - it's not manly
	Culture - individualistic vs. collectivistic
	Bias - to wear or not wear based on a perceived norm
	Influence - Formal organizations may offer conflicting information

Fig. 4.4 Four reasons for mask resistance

communities, but mediators go beyond authority figures or experts or bonafide celebrities to include the type of influencers, like those individuals popular on YouTube or Instagram. In the end, it may be all four of these reasons that impacts mask wearing; however, it may be the weight of bias and influence that nudges people in a particular direction.

The anti-mask movement is not new; however, as out of the 1918 Spanish flu epidemic, the Anti-mask League of San Francisco emerged, and some of the rationale for not wearing a mask then is eerily similar to the positions taken by those engaged in the anti-mask movement associated with COVID-19.[10] During the Spanish flu epidemic, resistors to wearing a mask expressed concern regarding their appearance, comfort, and similar to today's mandate resistance is connected to a sense of freedom. It was reported that even celebrities were against wearing masks, for fear they would go about their business unrecognized.[11] The Anti-mask League of San Francisco was short-lived, attracting few people and having the proverbial rug pulled out from under it shortly after the league was organized when the Mayor of San Francisco removed the mandate to wear a mask. What is also striking is the connection to the women's suffrage movement. The 2018 flu epidemic was taking place at the same time as the women's suffrage movement in the United States was in full swing, and the wearing of masks represented in a symbolic manner the stifling of women's voices, resulting in their resistance to wearing a mask. The COVID-19 pandemic, a trigger event, and the related issue of mask wearing should give us pause to consider whether this history of the anti-mask movement during the Spanish Flu of 1918 is repeating itself, as there are similar concerns that cut across both the earlier flu epidemic and the current COVID-19 pandemic.

Performing QAnon

QAnon is not the first conspiracy theory and leaderless social movement to take hold, but it is perhaps the first to use digital media as a primary tool to spread its message. What may have begun in 2017 as a fringe movement has evolved into a major one where we can see the theory of normative social behavior (TNSB) play out in the guise of performing activism. In addition to what are called "drops" which are messages of conspiracy posted on social media, the movement utilizes all manner of commercial spectacle, including selling Q-related merchandise, although Amazon announced in early 2021 that it would stop selling Q merchandise. The convergence of commercialism and conspiracy movement can be seen in what is referred to as "pastel QAnon." The example of a fashion influencer on Instagram with 50,000 followers illustrates how mixing messages of fashion and beauty, with discussions of mental health, and the WWG1WGA—"Where we go one, we go all"—motto used by adherents of QAnon Pastel, the movement operates even if subtly within the concept of spectacle.[12] The conspiracy movement began on a message board called 4Chan and later moved to another called 8Chan, later changed to 8Kun. But the movement also was active on Facebook and Twitter spreading conspiracy messages related to "Pizzagate," a conspiracy theory that alleged there was a child sex trafficking operation in the basement of a popular pizza restaurant in Washington, DC. However, Pizzagate is not enough to sustain a movement and so Q, as it is often referred to, latched onto the wave of anti-mask wearers and focused on conspiracies related to Bill and Melinda Gates. The movement is partially fueled by Facebook groups, many of this writing have been booted off the platform, that include "bakers" who decode Q's posts and other topics of interest to the group. But in need of something with substance, the movement co-opted a legitimate Save the Children online fundraising movement to address trafficking of children to meet their own ends.[13]

Metaphorically speaking, social media is a stage where diffused audiences are not located in a physical space like a theater; they can be anywhere their internet connection allows. On the social media stage, individuals play roles that Goffman described as "patterns of action." In a stage play that is offered up to its audience over and over again, players seek to perform their part with consistency, but on the stage of social media consistency is not a requirement. This translates into Goffman's terms that the "performance takes place," and that the performance “works” as a function of social interaction. That the performance takes place may be a function of posting to Twitter and the notion of “works” would be a function of the complicity of followers, comments, DMs, and retweets. As such, unlike a stage play, those engaged in social media play shifting roles to changing audiences. The instability of this system is problematic on the level of group interaction and the impact it has on identity. As was pointed out in Chap. 1, Kate Hawkins in her article, “Browsing the Performative: A Search for Sincerity,” distinguishes between performance and performative.[14] She likens a performance to a stage play in that it can be repeated; however, the experience of the performance will not be the same. Performative, on the other hand, Hawkins claims is the act of doing that does not require an audience in the theatrical sense but does hold importance when considering the nature of social media and the ways in which those engaged in an online social movement navigate that terrain. So, how does performative behavior play out on the QAnon stage? Using Google Trends, various conspiracy theories advanced by QAnon can be tracked over time. In addition to Save the Children, there is the Fall Cabal, Pizzagate, Out of the Shadows, and FrazzleDrip conspiracies. Figure 4.5 represents the trends of the four conspiracies on YouTube. During a 90-day period, the Fall Cabal (indicated in red) was trending on YouTube.

Figure 4.6, however, indicates during the same period in general web searches Pizzagate (indicated in yellow) was trending higher. Save the

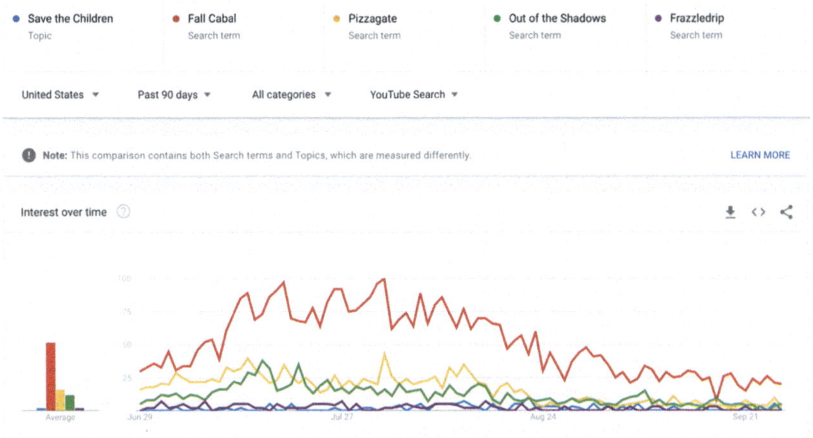

Fig. 4.5 QAnon trending conspiracies on YouTube

Children (indicated in blue) was trending on the web during the month of July.

One of the tactics utilized by QAnon is both content and hashtag hijacking as is the case with Save the Children. Marc Andre-Argentino, who tracks QAnon activity on Facebook identified 61 anti-child tracking groups but claims they are predominantly QAnon pages where they share Fall Cabal, Out of Shadows, and Pedowood videos, as well as Qdrops. All of this activity constitutes reinforcement of descriptive and injunctive norms and the behavioral outcomes are suggestive of the performative nature of online activism in which anti-movements or those that operate on the periphery drive followers deeper into their corner. As of October 2020, Facebook decided to ban any groups related to the QAnon as it considers this a "militarized social movement."[15] While this might be a righteous move on the part of the platform, eliminating extremist groups from the social media platform will not end such movements. It's important to keep in mind that QAnon began on one message board and then moved to another. In other words, the movement, because it is made up of diffuse audiences has the ability or rather flexibility to move from platform to platform. Indeed, QAnon followers have drifted to lesser-known platforms like Gab, MeWe, and VK, all three of which are Facebook clones. And since the Facebook ban, European followers of QAnon have moved on to Telegram, another Facebook-like platform. But the migration to

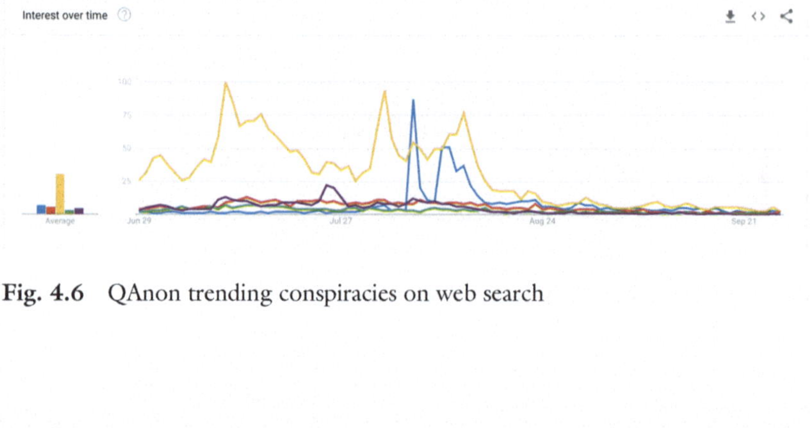

Fig. 4.6 QAnon trending conspiracies on web search

these other platforms is driven by the particular Facebook community to which these Q-followers belong. Argentino describes how Q-followers who were banned from Reddit, moved to a Reddit-like platform Voat. Parler is another platform for a time that Q-followers utilized, as have other conservative and right-wing movements that do not find the more mainstream Twitter platform as hospitable, although as of this writing both Apple and Google and Amazon Web Services have deplatformed the service. Interestingly, Q-followers on Instagram are stuck in a manner of speaking, as there is no alternative, that is open platform, to which they may migrate.

Social Amplification: Organic and Strategic

The kind of cross-contamination in which a diffuse movement like QAnon posts "drops" and shares content not only on Facebook and the alternative platforms mentioned above, are an effort to strategically amplify their message. Performing media activism is both an effect, because of social media's performative nature and a cause, as the nature of social media is to serve as an amplifier. What you see on social media, in other words, what you are looking at reading or observing, is what you get, the content of which is what is driving the messaging on social media. "Amplification on digital media" is a term that is usually employed by marketers attempting to get a commercial message across to particular groups of consumers, usually based on a demographic, psychographic, or behavioristic profile. This type of amplification would be characterized as strategic because it is intentional in that it seeks to measure outcomes that may range from awareness to behavior (sales of products or services). But strategic amplification can also be applied to extremists or those who attempt to antagonize or manipulate messaging on social media.[16] The concept of amplification can also be applied to social movements as Snow and colleagues identify amplification as one of four concepts associated with growing a social movement. The model of frame alignment (Fig. 4.7), updated to consider the more dynamic aspects of framing, refers to the "an ongoing and intentional means of recruiting participants to the movement"; amplification, as the term implies, is an attempt to expand appeal.[17,18] The other concepts include bridging, extension and transformation. Bridging is an attempt to bring together disconnected groups or those not yet involved in a social movement but includes organizations that have similar interests. Extension refers to bringing two groups

Fig. 4.7 Models of frame alignment

together even though their organizations goals do not align. Transformation relates to the stages of social movement development described in Chap. 1 of this book in that as social movements lose their proverbial steam; they need to be invigorated with new life and energy perhaps by seeking new themes or positions. The latter is exemplified by the co-opting by QAnon of the hashtag #SaveTheChildren. Amplification is the process of growing awareness of a social movement and attempting to engage and perhaps mobilize people to become active for a cause. It is this fourth model that is of interest here, as amplification requires the use of spectacle in order to gain attention, create awareness and to use a term direct out of marketing, "break through the clutter."

Jonah Berger, author of the book *Contagion*, maintains that content elicits an emotional reaction—makes your heart race—tends to get shared, especially when compared to content that evokes negative feelings. Creating a sense of awe or wonder as compared to content that makes people feel sad or angry is likely to get talked about, even more so than the use of influencers. At the same time, angry content is more likely to be shared than sad content due to "greater emotional arousal or activation."[19] This position is consistent with the theory of negative dominance that suggests humans give greater weight to negative entities as opposed to positivity bias. While arousing content may be the key, the model for achieving activation is amplification. Strategic amplification, utilized by commercial interests is sometimes organic, perhaps as the result of a spontaneous expression or outburst that catches people's attention and is perhaps worthy of a retweet, like, or comments, what Berger would refer to as a "trigger." Furthermore, in the realm of social media sometimes under some circumstances some things go viral. While organic amplification cannot be controlled, strategic communication can, especially if it is in the form of a promoted tweet, paid search, or part of an organized campaign. Organic amplification is uncontrolled in the sense that no one can predict what will catch on. Take, for example, TikToktivists who, in what appeared to be a spontaneous approach, utilized the platform in an attempt to degrade the Trump 2020 campaign app with negative reviews. Performing activism of this nature comes in the form of TikTok videos and spills over into other social media platforms in an attempt to amplify the message.[20] One TikTok user, with 750,000 followers, posted a step-by-step primer regarding how to post negative reviews of the Trump election app on the Apple App store that garnered 5.6 million views. TikTok has also been utilized by the Black Lives Matter movement with almost 5 million views immediately after the death of George Floyd, and others have used the app to raise awareness about the death of Ahmaud Arbery and the broader issue of racial and in that social injustice. Entertainment-based TikTok videos provide instructions to protesters to bring water and food with them when attending rallies. Pop culture spills over into the medium when, for example, performer Lizzo posted a video to let people know where to donate to the George Floyd Memorial Fund, and the song "This Is America" a song about racism by the actor and musician Donald Glover who raps under the name Childish Gambino was also posted on TikTok.[21]

Emotive content has the possibility of evoking a sense of wonder in the individual engaged in digital activism. Wonder is a quality that relates to the use of celebrities, as in the examples of pop singers above, among other creative approaches or tactics that in words, images and sounds comprise performative behavior that encourages activists and would-be activists to consent to participate. This is the model (see Fig. 4.8) utilized by advertisers, a magic show of sorts that encourages people into the discussion and as they engage with the content, people employ their own discourse strategies in the direction of normative or perhaps anti-normative behavior. In other words, much content in social media encourages people to ask: "which side are you on?" The simple act of pressing the like button

Fig. 4.8 A simplified model of mediated engagement

or up or down voting a comment are expressions of an individual's discourse strategy. Ambiguity is an important characteristic in the dialogic nature of posting and replying as competing positions lead to discomfort and as a result people seek closure, continuity, and conformity. In essence, am I for police tactics to keep law and order or do I support the movement to defund (however that term is defined) the police? Existing somewhere in the middle ground encourages people to wonder about their own position on this or any matter of social or political import that is before them. Wonder leads to engagement, which may initially take the form of elaboration in one's own mind, in the sense that people engaged or seeking to engage in a social movement agree to consider the messaging that serves as an inducement in the process of engagement that is likely to move the individual in one direction or another. Individuals employ their own tactics of complicity and resistance as they engage with celebrities or other influencers, among other techniques that are part of the grab-bag of tools available to the online communicator. As an example of how the concept of wonder works with amplification, an anti-mask rally in the state of Utah in the United States was so outrageous that it moved from the local news station that reported the rally as a result of the tweet in which the video of the rally, likened to a skit on the TV program Saturday Night Live, went viral.[22]

Context Collapse in Social Networks

With regard to social movements for which there are pro and anti-movement participants, we can view this confluence—two rivers running together—within the concept of context collapse, a topic introduced in Chap. 3, which has particular import for those engaged in digital activism. Context collapse is a sociological phenomenon that describes what happens when many social groups exist in one space. In online social movements and hybrid movements where diffuse audiences gather, the nature of communication changes from the more intimate one-to-one give and take of conversation—friend to friend, for example—to the explosion of voices all speaking at once. Online experiences call upon users to take on a persona or personas that reflect the context in which they are engaged. The shifting of identity or identities is work; moreover, it is performative in nature. Shaking part of one's identity loose in order to accommodate the beliefs of others in a community has the effect of opening one up to uncertainty or being exposed to ambiguous messages through which one can adapt to normative behaviors presented by the group or cluster to which one becomes aligned. "Some techniques of audience management resemble the practices of 'micro-celebrity' and personal branding, both strategic self-commodification. Writing about context collapse boyd and Marwick maintain "out model of the networked audience assumes a many-to-many communication through which individuals conceptualize an imagined audience evoked through their tweets."[23]

Context collapse is more likely to occur as networks increase in size and heterogeneity. As this growth in the network takes place, connections between segmented groups may occur. As such those engaged in the online social network begin to share content with the entire network, but performative behavior may be fraught with issues ranging from awkwardness to inappropriate behavior that drives people to different subgroups. Clusters form through the process of homophily in which like-minded people join in a cluster to reinforce existing beliefs and associated behavior. This phenomenon is a function of social bias—doing something or not because it is a perceived norm. The uncertainty that exists within the tension created by such norms becomes a form of social proof in which the individual establishes a belief that "others know best" therefore in order to maintain membership in the cluster one has to perform to the expected norm. Reluctance to wear a mask during the COVID-19 pandemic may take the form of reactance bias in which people form a cluster within the broader social network that perceives mask wearing as an attack on personal freedom, and at the same time another cluster (audience segment) may be supportive of wearing masks during a health crisis. In the UK during the month of July 2020 when the British government mandated mask wearing in shops, the use of the hashtag #NoMasks spiked, which might indicate that sentiment was leaning in the direction of negative dominance. But other information suggested that the vast majority of people were supportive of mask wearing. This is an example of strategic amplification when engagement in a hashtag movement is measured by the number of tweets using the hashtag that may not be reflective of anything other than the massive number of tweets.[24]

On Facebook such clusters come in the form of Facebook Groups which may be public or private. For example, one anti-mask Facebook group—ReOpen NC started an online "Burn Your Facemask Challenge."[25] This example of resistance bias comes on the heels of the governor of North Carolina issuing a mandate for citizens to wear masks; the group grew to 10,000 within a few weeks.[26] And based on a rule about posting misinformation, Facebook banned a group Unmasking America! that had approximately 10,000 members. But there is additional evidence that anti-mask wearing operates in the same social sphere as pro-mask wearers, creating online tensions in which one cluster may actually fuel growth in the other, as extreme views push those engaged in a movement further to one side or another. Even within one's own social network, much content is shared that could create not only awkwardness but posting or tweeting might be construed as inappropriate behavior for the broader network but find support within a cluster. Context collapse, therefore, can affect what one engaged on a social media platform posts or comments upon, but those posts or comments can come back to haunt the individual. Individuals engaged in an online social movement develop strategies to manage their self-presentation in order to offset context collapse.[27] Whether one practices self-censorship or changes their messaging or even adjusts their privacy settings (which is quite rare), all of this and more are part of performative behavior.

Individuals who are engaged in an online movement, in order to make themselves heard above the fray, have to amplify their voices. Creating spectacle, a topic covered in Chap. 1, refers to the "dazzle" that one can create, usually reserved for commercial interests, but within the context of today's social media, may be utilized by ordinary citizens or to use social media parlance, influencers. Spectacle and the desire to "break through the clutter," as they say in advertising, requires extreme measures, performances that might be visual, audio, or language that is extreme. Part of creating spectacle is standing out in a crowd and part of it is screaming over the heads of others, but it is also about getting the message out to others in the hope that it will receive comments or retweets. In her essay "Media Manipulation, Strategic Amplification, and Responsible Journalism," media scholar danah boyd describes three things media manipulators use to strategize: (1) create spectacle, using social media to get news media coverage; (2) frame the spectacle through phrases that drive new audiences to find your frames; and (3) become a "digital martyr" to help radicalize others.[28]

With regard to engagement in a social movement, people tend toward being either pro or anti—we seek extremes because the tension that exists in the middle is uncomfortable. Exacerbating extreme positions are bots. We know that social media have become a place for collective social action to occur worldwide. But we also know that not everybody engaged in a social movement has the same intent, which opens up the possibility of false actors pushing agendas that may support a government or other organization's interests, in an effort to manipulate public opinion, at least public opinion as it exists online. This phenomenon has been referred to as "astroturfing" or "false amplification," and sometimes disinformation or misinformation campaigns that drive people to the extremes are managed by "troll farms," which are accounts operating under false identities and manned by employees to fabricate or manipulate conversations on Twitter. Camille Francois and colleagues refer to this as fabricated collective action, "a form of social media behavior that seeks to create the impression of genuine collective sentiment (waves of panic, support or dissent from a particular agenda, etc.)."[29] The problem is, however, that people engaged in an online social movement cannot tell a bot from an actual person and they cannot distinguish between accurate information and false information disseminated by troll farms. All of this leads to what might be called connected contentiousness. Although not referring to bots or troll farms, the term "conflictual phenomena" introduced by Tilley seems apropos of the situation. Generally speaking, people seek stability and that comes to a degree from membership, adherence to group norms and through personal identity, that is, identifying with one or the other aspect of a cause or issue. Within such a siloed world of social media, there is little room for the back and forth and give and take of discussion that we might expect may take place in an offline discussion. However, the online behavior I am describing has a spillover effect onto everyday conversations in which, for example, within the same family Trump supporters and #NeverTrumpers express contentiousness in the same physical space. The role played by bots and troll farms is significant in nudging people into such silos or online clusters that may be gendered, racial in make-up, and location bound, as well as temporal clustering.

Categorizing Social Movements

Building on the definitions of social movements described in Chap. 1, anthropologist David Aberle in his 1966 book *The Peyote Religion Among the Navajo* described four broad movement categories: alternative, redemptive, reformative, and revolutionary (see Fig. 4.9). In short, some social movements are created to promote social change while others are created to prevent change or maintain the status quo. And the nature or degree of changes sought by those engaged in a social movement may be minor (partial change) or radical (total change) in nature. Furthermore, change as it is being referred to here may be at the individual or societal level. Aberle offers a simple definition:

> A social movement is an organized effort by a group of human beings to effect change in the face of resistance by other human beings. By this definition, a social movement is differentiated from purely individual efforts, from unorganized group efforts such as crowd action (if indeed these efforts are truly unorganized), and from efforts at technological change which proceed only against the resistance of the material world. Under the heading of resistance by other human beings is included passive resistance or apathy. It should be noted that the definition does not require that the resistance be organized.[30]

For example, in what is categorized as an alternative movement, like Mothers Against Drunk Drivers, only a partial change in behavior is sought. Sometimes a coalition may be formed as was the case with a corporation like AT&T and its employees, along with several other groups including the National Organizations for Youth Safety (NOYS), Students Against Destructive Decisions (SADD), and Mothers Against Drunk Driving (MADD). Government agencies, such as the Governors Highway Safety Association (GHSA), can also get involved in the digital campaign, "It Can Wait" for which there is a dedicated webpage as well as a hashtag useful in spreading the message on Twitter and Facebook.[31] There is a behavioral component to this campaign in which visitors to the webpage are asked to take a pledge not to text while driving; when they do so, in effect, they have signed on to the movement.

Efforts to encourage recycling serve as another example of an alternative movement. A religious movement would qualify as redemptive, as it seeks to persuade individuals to change their inner state of being. Christian

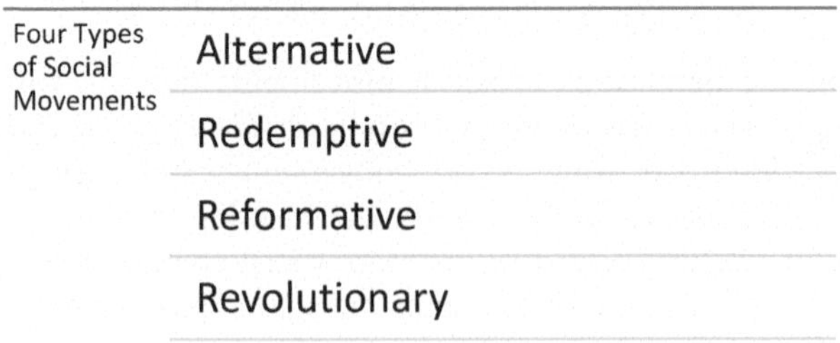

Fig. 4.9 Aberle's four categories of social movements

missionaries, for example, have been at this type of movement since the 1500s. A reformative movement seeks a partial change in the social system; the women's suffrage movement would serve as an example and so would the more recent movement to change laws to accommodate same-sex marriage. A transformative movement would seek a total change in the social system. The Medicare for All movement, because of its association with Socialism, serves as a contemporary example, because it seeks to change the private medical system currently operating in the United States.[32]

The 3.5 Percent Rule

Harvard political scientist Erica Chenoweth investigated hundreds of social movement campaigns over the last century and found that nonviolent campaigns are twice as likely to achieve their goals as violent campaigns. She describes nonviolent movements as a "method of struggle in which unarmed people confront an adversary by using collective action—including protests, demonstrations, strikes, and noncooperation—to build power and achieve political goals." This approach to civil resistance has become a "mainstay of political action across the globe."[33] Furthermore, she developed the 3.5 percent rule based on her research that suggests that it takes 3.5 percent of the population to actively participate in a social movement to effect political change.[34] Reflecting on social movements in 2020, Chenoweth claims that while nonviolent resistance campaigns may have peaked in popularity, they have become less effective due to structural changes to the movements themselves. The January 6, 2021, insurrection at the US Capitol in which five people were killed and the building rampaged stands in contrast to nonviolent resistance. Civil resistance, she says, is fueled by new technologies that allow more people to have access to news and information, including online newspapers, dedicated websites, and social media. And that access extends beyond Western countries with perhaps a more developed communication infrastructure to countries in Africa and Eastern Asia who can communicate and learn from one another and, as Chenoweth says, inspire one another. Furthermore, as we have seen in a number of social movements like the Egyptian uprising of 2011, political elites and traditional media outlets can be bypassed allowing for what at least on the surface looks like more democratic participation.[35]

Consider the experience of Zeynep Tufekci, author of the book, *Twitter and Tear Gas: The Power and Fragility of Networked Protest*, who utilized Twitter to help move medical supplies to protesters who were wounded in the melee that took place in Tahrir Square. With regard to the use of digital media, she maintained large numbers of people can be brought together with little organization or coordination. The question she raises regards how digital technologies help movements develop quickly through early stages "without compromising the organizational and collective capacities of the movements and their ability to deal with inevitable future challenges. Understanding this complex relationship is essential for the success of networked protests as governments continue to adjust their repressive strategies."[36] Contentious politics around social movements in China, Russia and Iran have utilized blocking tactics on digital media platforms to avoid the spread of anti-government messaging and perhaps confuse as well as overwhelm audiences. In his critique of Tufekci's book, Maxwell Adjei maintains that "several conditions (such as collective offline agitation, presence of a triggering event/strong rallying point, etc.) may be necessary for online activism to effectively draw large crowds for a movement. There is certainly a reason why not every popular 'pro-protest hashtag' on the internet results in a successful movement. Without the presence of the right conditions—economic, cultural, religious, commercial, political, etc.—it is difficult for digital tools to successfully initiate mass movements."[37] Chenowith echoes this sentiment when she says, "Taking advantage of this sudden lapse in conventional forms of popular resistance, a host of governments across the world have pushed forward divisive policies that range from the suspension of free speech to controversial judicial appointments to bans on immigrant or refugee admissions."[38] Fueling resistance may not be the collective action Chenowith describes but rather the connective action associated with performing media activism.

Among several reasons Chenowith gives for changes in the nature of social movements is new technologies that make it easier to become aware of events that might otherwise have gone unnoticed. This can be attributed to the widespread availability of online information through among other outlets, social media. And the awareness of a movement may not just be internal, as access in many instances can be global in nature. People over much of the world could see the pro-democracy protests in Hong Kong that began in March 2019 on any number of platforms from Twitter to TikTok. And the overtaking of the US Capitol was livestreamed on multiple platforms as events unfolded. Of great importance is the ability of ordinary people to communicate through social media platforms bypassing government gatekeepers, as well as mainstream new media.

Case Study: Anti-vaccine Communities on Reddit

Digital media has changed the healthcare system in that patients in many instances have usurped the authority of medical caregivers as they take to social media to discuss their personal beliefs and decisions regarding their healthcare. Personal responsibility can take many forms including joining movements related to mask wearing during a global pandemic described above. In the book *Celebrity and Mediated Social Connections*, I write about the medicalization and pharmaceuticalization of culture and the ways in which individuals utilize social media to inform their healthcare decisions. In addition to direct-to-consumer prescription drug advertising (DTCA) and dedicated websites like WebMD, there are ePatients who utilize digital resources to empower themselves and engage with others regarding health-oriented decisions.[39] Sometimes issues related to healthcare take on significance when groups become mobilized around healthcare reform, disabilities and health, gender and health, or healthcare activism like the Medicare for All movement in the United States. The following case study applies social network analysis to the Reddit platform to better understand vaccine hesitancy.

The ability of individuals to take their own healthcare upon themselves is nothing new as anti-vaccine movement, for example, has been around for more than 200 years. Writing about the history of vaccines, the College of Physicians of Philadelphia states: "Critics of vaccination have taken a variety of positions, including opposition to the smallpox vaccine in England and the United States in the mid to late 1800s, and the resulting anti-vaccination leagues; as well as more recent vaccination controversies such as those surrounding the safety and efficacy of the diphtheria, tetanus, and pertussis (DTP) immunization, the measles, mumps, and rubella (MMR) vaccine, and the use of a mercury-containing preservative called thimerosal."[40] As we enter the second decade of the twenty-first century, vaccine hesitancy is still one of the top threats to global health, according to the World Health Organization. The *New York Times* reports: "Though the situation may seem improbable to some, anti-vaccine sentiment has been building for decades, a byproduct of an internet humming with rumor and misinformation; the backlash against Big Pharma; an infatuation with celebrities that gives special credence to the anti-immunization statements from actors like Jenny McCarthy, Jim Carrey and Alicia Silverstone, the rapper Kevin Gates and Robert F. Kennedy Jr. And now, the Trump administration's anti-science rhetoric."[41] Some attribute the growth of the anti-vaccine movement to actress Jenny McCarthy who in 2007 publicized the belief that her son's autism was caused by vaccines.

Jennifer Reich, author of *Calling the Shots: Why Parents Reject Vaccines*, maintains that the women's health movement was among those forces that repositioned expertise within the individual, and conversely, experts seek to empower individuals to be "self-efficacious" sometimes encouraging parents to turn to social media.[42] For example, the organization Voices for Vaccines seeks to counter the anti-vaccine movement by creating an online forum to discuss science-based vaccine-related information.[43] The Center for Countering Digital Hate, based in the UK conducted an assessment of the influence of anti-vaccination content on social media platforms since the outset of the COVID-19 pandemic, between May and June 2020. Among their findings, misinformation regarding a COVID-19 vaccine has been prevalent on Facebook, as well as other social media platforms.[44] There is contentious politics at work on the issue as almost all states in the US have anti-vaccination groups, including some states in which there are political action committees (PAC) set up to further the political interests of the anti-vaccine community. As well there are anti-vaccine groups operating on Facebook; in other words, social media has become a prime arena where the forces of pro and anti-vaccine rhetoric compete.

Reddit is not often seen as a subject of much social media analysis as popular platforms like Twitter are much more accessible to researchers because of the many tools available to them collect and analyze content. Reddit, however, is an online community comprised of what are referred to as subreddits of which there are over two million that cover myriad topics.[45] The community is driven by users who may up or downvote a comment increasing or diminishing its influence. In other words, the most popular comments rise to the top of the subreddit, conversely the least popular fall to the bottom. To make all this work smoothly, moderators are user-appointed for each subreddit and rules determining what type of content is appropriate are developed for each subreddit. For example, the anti-vax subreddit has eight rules, of which the following is one: "If you disagree with any article or opinion posted in this subreddit, you are more than welcome to comment whilst keeping things civil. We remind you of reddiquette."[46] Relevant to this case study, O'Kane and colleagues studied discourse on reddit regarding HPV vaccination.[47] These researchers found that much can be understood about attitudes toward vaccination by studying comments on public forums such as reddit; comments that may influence decision making. These researchers concluded based on their analysis of 22,000 comments that attitudes toward HPV vaccination are not gender specific, and they concluded that analyzing data from online discussions can help to both understand attitudes toward vaccination and help to shape policy when it comes to health communication. Despite the fact that there are rules regarding what members of a subreddit community can and cannot post, a number of researchers have pointed out the toxic culture that may exist within online communities. To better understand toxicity on Reddit, Communalytic, a tool developed by Anatoly Gruzd and colleagues is useful to investigate such toxicity on Reddit.[48] A full description of Communalytic and its application can be found in the last chapter of this book.

For this case study, 1985 posts drawn during the August 8–10, 2020, period from the Vaxxhappens subreddit were analyzed. Figures 4.10 and 4.11 represent the posts per day as well as a word cloud derived from the subreddit data.

Toxicity Analysis

An analysis of toxicity was conducted based on the Vaxxhappens data set. Based on the Perspective API, Communalytic generates nine types of antisocial scores (between 0 and 1) for each post in the data set, with scores closer to one indicating higher levels of toxicity. Communalytic uses the following scores as provided by Perspective: toxicity, severe toxicity, insult, identity attack, profanity, threat, and attack on commenter. Table 4.2 defines each characteristic of toxicity and provides a sample post for each category from the data set.

In total, there were 1985 posts, including 113 submissions (posts that start a new thread) to the Vaxxhappens subreddit, and 1143 replies. The top ten posters and the percentage of their activity on the subreddit are depicted in Fig. 4.12. For example, k_money55, who was responsible for 15 percent of the posts in the subreddit posted the following submission: "Stop comparing getting vaccines for your own good to the Holocaust." Which generated 77 comments. And, while Genb7 was responsible for 14

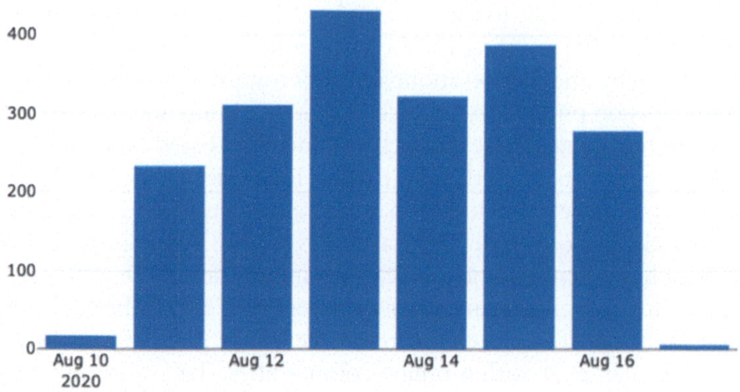

Fig. 4.10 Vaxxhappens subreddit posts per day

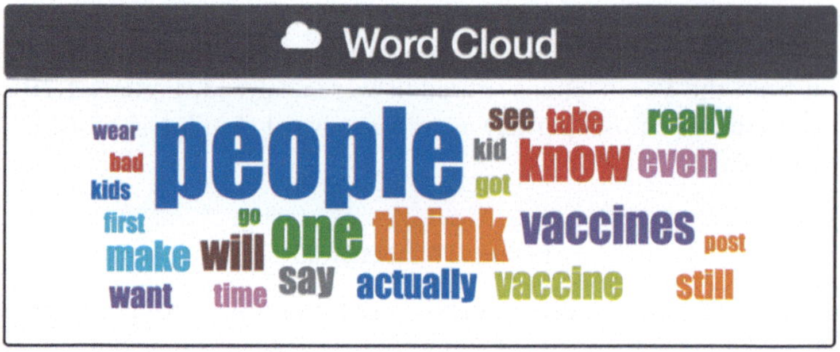

Fig. 4.11 Vaxxhappens subreddit word cloud

percent of the activity in the subreddit, the posts were either in the form of comments or replies to others, not original submissions.

Table 4.3 indicates the number of posts that were automatically classified as one or more of the Perspective's anti-social scores that are available on Communalytic. For example, 4–11 percent of the posts were characterized as *toxic*, while 16 percent were characterized as an *attack on the commenter*, the categories with the largest number of posts, this was followed by *insults*, which were between 3 percent and 9 percent of the posts. While it might have been expected that given the nature of the social issue that anti-social behavior would comprise a larger fraction of the posts. It is important to remember that subreddits are moderated, and therefore the

Table 4.2 Nine categories of anti-social acts from perspective API[a] available for analysis in Communalytic, their definitions and examples

	Definition	*Sample*
Toxicity	Rude, disrespectful, or unreasonable post	*I fucking hate their "I've done my research!!!!!!" bullshit*
Severe toxicity	Very hateful, aggressive, disrespectful post. This score is less sensitive to posts that include positive uses of curse words	*No. Science is rooted in experimentation and the proof/disproof of hypotheses. Your claim is that vaccines are harmful. Prove it. Can't? Then shut up, fuck off and stop trying to get people killed. No debate involved.*
Insult	Insulting, inflammatory, or negative post toward an individual or a group	*Anti Vaxxers always say we assume they're stupid No Karen we don't assume you're stupid, we know you're stupid*
Identity attack	Negative post attacking someone because of their identity (including race, gender, sexual orientation, ideology, religion, nationality, etc.)	*I'm Jewish, Ashkenazi to be specific, and it makes my blood BOIL when I see posts like that.*
Profanity	Post with swear words or other obscene language	*I fucking hate their "I've done my research!!!!!!" bullshit*
Threat	Post with an intention to inflict pain, injury, or violence against an individual or group	*Ah yes, let your children die because the weak don't deserve proper lives.*
Attack on commenter	Post directly attacking another user	*We get you're not a smart person, no need to proudly display your ignorance.*
Sexually explicit	Sexually Explicit model scores on the basis of presence of references to sexual acts, body parts, or other lewd content.	*I think the poster has sex with sheep. I don't have proof of it, but that's just because I haven't looked.*
Flirtation	Flirtation model scores on the basis of presence of pickup lines, complimenting appearance, subtle sexual innuendos, etc.	*I had literally forgotten all about this chick. I was a big fan until she got pregnant, and then she became absolutely insufferable and I unfollowed her everywhere. Glad to hear her baby is apparently doing OK though.*

[a]As defined by Perspective API https://github.com/conversationai/perspectiveapi/blob/master/2-api/models.md

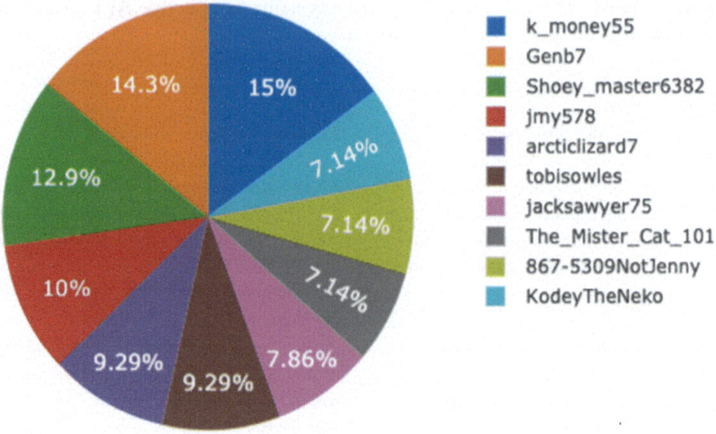

Fig. 4.12 Top ten vaxxhappens subreddit posters

Table 4.3 Number and percentage of toxic posts

Number and percentage of posts with their scores						
Threshold >0.07 >0.08 >0.9						
Toxicity	204	11	142	2	71	4
Severe toxicity	72	4	26	1	0	0
Insult	180	9	104	5	55	3
Identity attack	39	2	15	0	2	0
Threat	63	3	33	1	8	0
Attack on commenter	308	16	178	9	112	6
Flirtatious	18	1	7	0	3	0
Sexually explicit	22	6	16	0	7	0

level of toxicity may be different than other subreddits that would be under the "rules" established by their moderators.

The Communalytic tool provides an overview of the anti-social behavior in this data set. Average scores and the distribution of scores for all posts are indicated in Fig. 4.13. Figure 4.14 represents a distribution table of toxicity scores showing that the toxicity score for most posts is under 3 percent.

The toxicity summary (Fig. 4.3) shows the counts based on the three different thresholds: 0.7, 0.8, and 0.9. The table indicates that toxicity levels are not terribly high, although one-third of the posts in this data set are attacks on the commenter, which is defined as a post attacking another user.

While Perspective calculates several different scores, some of them are interrelated. For example, based on correlation analyses (see Table 4.4), the following four scores are highly correlated with each other (Pearson correlation > 0.9): *toxicity*, *severe toxicity*, *insult*, and *profanity*.

Social Network Analysis

The toxicity analysis above provides insights into the anti-social behavior of the s/vaxxhappens group as a whole. But the question remains as to how posts, replies, and comments are coordinated among the group or clusters within the social network. On Reddit this is known as brigading that occurs when a group of users, invade a subreddit to flood it with downvotes to affect its karma dynamics.[49] The communication network is mapped (Fig. 4.15) to show who replies to whom by looking at the nodes and edges in the network data to visualize the dynamics of the r/vaxxhappens network.

While the data in the discussion of toxicity was extracted from Reddit and analyzed using Communalytic, Gephi is employed as a tool to create the network visualization.[50] Through the use of Gephi, the level and

	Average for dataset	Highest value	Lowest value
Toxicity	0.26	0.99	0.01
Severe toxicity	0.16	0.87	0.00
Identity attack	0.17	0.94	0.00
Insult	0.23	0.98	0.00
Profanity	0.20	0.99	0.00
Threat	0.22	0.95	0.01
Sexually Explicit	0.13	0.98	0.01
Flirtation	0.26	0.95	0.02
Attack On Commenter	0.33	0.97	0.00

Fig. 4.13 Toxicity analysis summary table for r/vaxxhappens subreddit

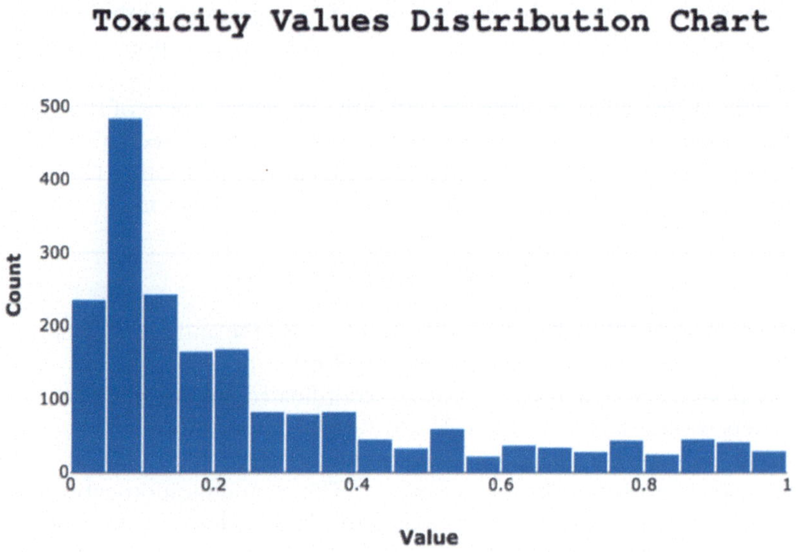

Fig. 4.14 The distribution of toxicity scores for r/vaxxhappens subreddit, showing that the toxicity score for most posts is under 0.3. (*Y* axis: post count; *X* axis: toxicity score)

quality of group engagement can be demonstrated. In this network, there are 1112 nodes and 1818 edges visualized in Fig. 4.15. The size of the node is a representation of each redditor on the network and the edges represent posts or replies. The size of the nodes corresponds to the number of other users that replied to or received replies from other users on the network. Betweenness centrality is a way to measure the path of one node in the network to another. The larger the node, the higher the betweenness centrality measure, as these nodes serve the purpose of linking to others in the network. As the visualization indicates there are several active clusters in the network that are posting and replying to one another, and there are fewer active members along the periphery of the network.

To better understand the communities operating in the network, modularity along with other network metrics is utilized to describe the network structure (see Table 4.5). In this subreddit, there are 42 communities or clusters. The value of modularity is 0.793 which is indicative of conversations among different groups of users. The measure of modularity ranges

Table 4.4 Pearson correlation analysis among perspective API scores analysis among perspective API scores

	Toxicity	*Severe toxicity*	*Profane*	*Identity attack*	*Insult*	*Threat*	*Sexually explicit*	*Flirtation*	*Attack on consumer*
Toxicity	1.0								
Severe toxicity	0.94	1.0							
Profane	0.96	0.92	1.0						
Identity attack	0.65	0.67	0.54	1.0					
Insult	0.96	0.88	0.92	0.68	1.0				
Threat	0.47	0.54	0.36	0.49	0.40	1.0			
Sexually explicit	0.54	0.62	0.56	0.33	0.47	0.38	1.0		
Flirtation	0.28	0.34	0.25	0.29	0.25	0.49	0.63	1.0	
Attack on consumer	0.13	0.06	0.04	0.03	0.16	0.07	-0.01	0.01	1.0

Note: All correlation values are significant at the 0.01 level (2-tailed)

from 0 to 1 where a value closer to 0 suggests a highly connected network.[51] In this case the network is not highly connected, as such groups pair off so to speak, forming clusters, in order to engage on issues that are situationally relevant to that cluster.

Based on the visualization of the r/vaxxhappens subreddit, patterns of interactions have been explored within the vaxxhappens community on reddit. This case study has demonstrated that anti-social behavior is prevalent within this social network; it reflects the darker side of citizen engagement in social and political issues. The tool utilized in this case study provides insight into this particular social network as it works through issues related to the vaccine hesitancy movement. The toxicity scores in the VaxxHappens subreddit represent anti-social acts. If an act is defined as a "manifestation of anti-social behavior on social media," the term "act" may be replaced with the concept of performing digital activism advanced in this book. Performing anti-social acts is a representation of a need. What kind of need? The need to be noticed; seen by others. The need to stand out from the crowd. The need to feel important. The need to feel like one is a member of a group. All of these needs are psycho-social in nature and are a reflection of the engagement in social media in

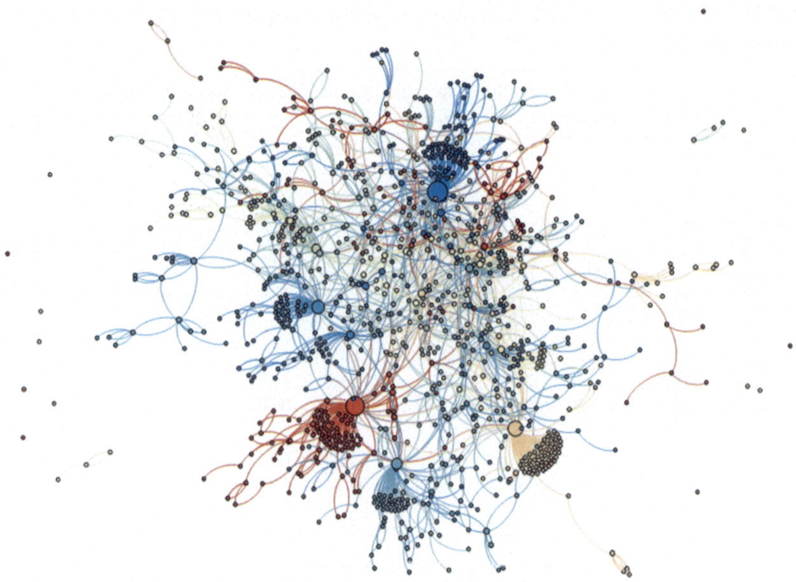

Fig. 4.15 Network visualization of r/vaxxhappens subreddit social network

Table 4.5 Network-level properties and metrics for r/vaxxhappens subreddit

Nodes	*1112*
Edges	1818
Density	0.001
Clusters	43
Degree	1.635
Modularity	0.793

contemporary society. Although the term "spectacle" has become somewhat of a cliché, it is useful in the present context as individuals representing themselves in social media are commodities. In the same way that products and services are sold, so to do individuals "sell" themselves using tactics and techniques that are not dissimilar to those utilized in commercial culture, which is especially so when the individual is the product, in this case expressing themself in the form of a toxic representation. As each toxicity score represents a specific anti-social act, it's important to keep in mind that as all subreddits are moderated, the level of toxicity may also be actively moderated; that is to say if the performance goes beyond certain boundaries set by the moderators the commenter can be banned from the subreddit. As Gruzd and colleagues state: "A darker side of social media has emerged and remains evident today, with various countries, governing bodies, and citizens grappling with the impending normalization of aggressive behaviour, hostility, and negative discourse in online spaces. This realization has led to an influx of research examining the patterns of 'anti-social' in online communities, as well as the development of the necessary tools required for systematic investigations."[52]

Conclusion

This chapter set out to present a discussion of conflict and contentiousness in social movements with an eye toward pockets of resistance or what might be referred to as countermovements, movements that may go against an established norm. The chapter began with a reflection of populist movements and tracked the rise of such movements historically until today, and in addition to a discussion of populist movements a review of terms like "nationalism" and "immigration"—hot button topics—were tracked through their use of cable TV news. Anti-movements, like the #NeverTrump Lincoln Project, were presented to illustrate the role that contentious politics and conflictual phenomena play in contemporary movements. The theory of normative social behavior was utilized to describe how two types of norms, descriptive and injunctive, may move those engaged in a social movement from the periphery to the center, as seeing tweets or posts and corresponding likes and DMs move actants in one ideological direction or another. Social comparison theory was also introduced to describe how not adhering to group norms may lead to sanctions that impact not only one's social standing in a group but also their personal identity as they measure how they stack up against others in the social network. Influencers, in this case, play an important role in people's perceptions about the prevalence of a behavior or intention to behave. To illustrate how the theory of normative social behavior works when applied to a social movement, the chapter explored the anti-mask movement that reared its ugly head during the COVID-19 pandemic and focused on the reasons people give for mask resistance. The chapter also looked at QAnon that has grown into a major movement with an eye toward the ways those engaged in the movement perform digital activism through "drops" and other elements of spectacle to draw attention and adherents to their belief system. The concept of amplification, both organic and strategic, was considered as characteristics of performing digital activism. And, context collapse, a sociological phenomenon referring to the collision of many groups operating in the same digital space is discussed as it may lead to both information overload and misinformation as well as ambiguity regarding messaging that social movements are attempting to convey. Rounding out the chapter is a case study of a vaccine hesitancy community on Reddit. That case study was based on a toxicity analysis performed with the Communalytic social network analysis tool.

In the next chapter, issues related to social justice and data activism will be explored through among other topics, a case study of the brutal murder of George Floyd and the global social justice movement that emerged as a result of his death.

Notes

1. Debinski, G (September 20, 2020). What's going on with the far right in Germany? *GZeromedia.com*. Retrieved from: https://www.gzeromedia.com/whats-going-on-with-the-far-right-in-germany.
2. Nossiter, A. (December 5, 2018). How France's 'Yellow Vests' Differ from Populist Movements Elsewhere. *The New York Times*. Retrieved from: https://www.nytimes.com/2018/12/05/world/europe/yellow-vests-france.html.
3. Ashkenas, J. & Aisch, G. (December 5, 2016). European Populism in the Age of Donald Trump. *The New York Times*. Retrieved from: https://www.nytimes.com/interactive/2016/12/05/world/europe/populism-in-age-of-trump.html.
4. Tarrow, S., (2015). *Contentious Politics. The Oxford Handbook of Social Movements*. Eds. Donatella Della Porta & Mario Diani.
5. Rimal, R. & Real, K. (2005). How Behaviors are Influenced by Perceived Norms. A Test of the Theory of Normative Social Behavior. *Communication Research*. 32:3, pp. 389–414.
6. Marcus, E. (September 26, 2020. Colleges Are Hiring Their Own Students as Covid-19 Safety Influencers. *The New York Times*. Retrieved from: https://www.nytimes.com/2020/09/26/style/coronavirus-campus-influencers.html.
7. Katz E. (1981) Publicity and Pluralistic Ignorance: Notes on 'The Spiral of Silence'. In: Baier H., Kepplinger H.M., Reumann K. (eds) *Öffentliche Meinung und sozialer Wandel/Public Opinion*

and Social Change. VS Verlag für Sozialwissenschaften. https://doi.org/10.1007/978-3-322-87749-9_2.

8. Wong, T. (May 12, 2020). Coronavirus: Why some countries wear face masks and others don't. *BBC.com*. Retrieved from: https://www.bbc.com/news/world-52015486#:~:text=Yet%20in%20some%20parts%20of,the%20virus%2C%20even%20healthy%20people.
9. Zagury-Orly, I. (2020). Unmasking reasons for face mask resistance. *Global Biosecurity*, 1:4, Retrieved from: https://jglobalbiosecurity.com/articles/10.31646/gbio.80/.
10. Smith, K. (April 20, 2020). Protesting During A Pandemic Isn't New: Meet The Anti-Mask League Of 1918. *Forbes.com*. Retrieved from: https://www.forbes.com/sites/kionasmith/2020/04/29/protesting-during-a-pandemic-isnt-new-meet-the-anti-mask-league/#22ec0aa212f9.
11. Hauser, C. (August 3, 2020). The Mask Slackers of 1918. *The New York Times*. Retrieved from: https://www.nytimes.com/2020/08/03/us/mask-protests-1918.html.
12. Tiffany, K. (August 2020). The Women Making Conspiracy Theories Beautiful: How the domestic aesthetics of Instagram repackage QAnon for the masses. *The Atlantic*. Retrieved from https://www.theatlantic.com/technology/archive/2020/08/how-instagram-aesthetics-repackage-qanon/615364.
13. Roose, K. (September 28, 2020). How 'Save the Children' Is Keeping QAnon Alive. *The New York Times*. Retrieved from: https://www.nytimes.com/2020/09/28/technology/save-the-children-qanon.html.
14. Hawkins, K. (n.d.). *Browsing the Performative: A Search for Sincerity*. Retrieved from: http://www.katehawkins.co.uk/images/TEXTS/BROWSING%20THE%20PERFORMATIVE%20-%20A%20SEARCH%20FOR%20SINCERITY.pdf.
15. Newton, C. (October 8, 2020). Why did Facebook ban QAnon now? Platformer.com. Retrieved from: https://www.platformer.news/p/why-did-facebook-ban-qanon-now.
16. Phillips, W. (May 22, 2018). The Oxygen of Amplification. DataandSociety.com, Retrieved from: https://datasociety.net/library/oxygen-of-amplification/.
17. Snow, D. Rochford, Jr., E. Worden, S. & Benford. R. (1986.) Frame Alignment Processes, Micromobilization, and Movement Participation. *American Sociological Review*. 51:4 pp. 464–81.
18. Snow, D., Benford, R. McCammon, H., Hewitt, L. & Fitzgerald, S. (2014). The Emergence, Development, and Future of the Framing Perspectives: 25+ Years since "Frame Alignment." *Mobilization: An International Quarterly*. 19:1 pp. 23–45.

19. Berger, J. (April 14, 2015). The Secret to Online Success: What Makes Content Go Viral. ScientificAmerican.com. Retrieved from: https://www.scientificamerican.com/article/the-secret-to-online-success-what-makes-content-go-viral/.
20. Banjo, S. Egkolfopoulou, M. (July 10, 2020), TikTok Teens Are 'Going to War' Against the Trump Campaign After Republicans Call to Ban the App. Time.com. Retrieved from: https://time.com/5865261/tiktok-trump-campaign-app/.
21. Janfaza, R. (June 4, 2020). TikTok serves as hub for #blacklivesmatter activism. Cnn.com. Retrieved from: https://www.cnn.com/2020/06/04/politics/tik-tok-black-lives-matter/index.html.
22. Stopera, M. (September 14, 2020). A News Report From A Utah Anti-Mask Rally Is Going Viral Because It Almost Feels Like An "SNL" Sketch. Buzzfeed.com. Retrieved from: https://www.buzzfeed.com/mjs538/anti-mask-rally-utah.
23. Marwick, A.E., boyd, d. (2011). I tweet honestly, I tweet passionately: Twitter users, context collapse, and the imagined audience. *New Media & Society*. 13:1, pp. 114–133. doi:10.1177/1461444810365313.
24. Dotto, C., & Morish, L. (August 20, 2020). Coronavirus: How pro-mask posts boost the anti-mask movement. Retrieved from: https://firstdraftnews.org/latest/coronavirus-how-pro-mask-posts-boost-the-anti-mask-movement/.
25. Castrodale, J. (June 18, 2020). The 'Burn Your Mask' Challenge Is Even Dumber Than Eating Tide Pods. *Vice.com*. Retrieved from: https://www.vice.com/en_us/article/bv8jm5/the-burn-your-mask-challenge-is-even-dumber-than-eating-tide-pods.
26. Tiffany, K. (July 14, 2020). Facebook's Pandemic Feuds Are Getting Ugly. *The Atlantic*. Retrieved from: https://www.theatlantic.com/technology/archive/2020/07/facebook-reopen-north-carolina-masks/613978/.
27. Marwick, A.E., boyd, d. (2011). Ibid.
28. boyd, d. (September 14, 2018). Media Manipulation, Strategic Amplification, and Responsible Journalism. *Points.DataandSociety.net*. Retrieved from: https://points.datasociety.net/media-manipulation-strategic-amplification-and-responsible-journalism-95f4d611f462.
29. Francois, C., Barash, C., & Kelly, J. (August 2017). Measuring coordinated vs. spontaneous activity in online social movements. Retrieved from: https://osf.io/preprints/socarxiv/ba8t6/.
30. Aberle, D. (1991). *The Peyote Religion Among the Navajo*. Norman, OK: University of Oklahoma Press.
31. It Can Wait. (n.d.). Digitally based alternative movement. Retrieved from: https://www.itcanwait.com/home.

32. Lee, N. (August 2, 2019). Four Types of Social Movements. *Medium.com*. Retrieved from: https://medium.com/@nicklee3/the-four-types-of-social-movements-8db910192573.
33. Chenoweth, E. (2020). The Future of Nonviolent Resistance. *Journal of Democracy*, 31: 3, p. 70.
34. Robson, D. (May 13, 2019). The '3.5% rule': How a small minority can change the world. *BBC.com*. Retrieved from: https://www.bbc.com/future/article/20190513-it-only-takes-35-of-people-to-change-the-world.
35. Chenoweth, E. (2020). pp. 69–84.
36. Zeynep Tufekci. (2017). *Twitter and Tear Gas: The Power and Fragility of Networked Protest*. New Haven, CT: Yale University Press, p. 234.
37. Adjei, M. (2019). Book Review: Twitter and Tear Gas: The Power and Fragility of Networked Protest, *Peace & Change*, 01490508, 44:2, p. 284.
38. Chenowith, E. (2020). P. 270.
39. Alperstein, N. (2019). *Celebrity and Mediated Social Connections: Fans, Friends and Followers in the Digital Age*. Palgrave Macmillan.
40. The History of Vaccines (n.d.). History of Vaccines.org. Retrieved from: https://www.historyofvaccines.org/content/articles/history-anti-vaccination-movements.
41. Hoffman, J. (September 23, 2019). How Anti-Vaccine Sentiment Took Hold in the United States. *The New York Times*. Retrieved from: https://www.nytimes.com/2019/09/23/health/anti-vaccination-movement-us.html.
42. Reich, J. (2016). Calling the Shots: Why Parents Reject Vaccines. New York: New York University Press.
43. Voices for Vaccines. (n.d.). https://www.voicesforvaccines.org/.
44. Center for Countering Digital Hate (n.d.). *The Anti-Vaxx Industry: How Big Tech powers and profits from vaccine misinformation*. Retrieved from: https://252f2edd-1c8b-49f5-9bb2-cb57bb47e4ba.filesusr.com/ugd/f4d9b9_7aa1bf9819904295a0493a013b285a6b.pdf.
45. Redditmetrics.com (n.d.). Retrieved from: https://redditmetrics.com/.
46. Anti-vax subreddit (n.d.). Retrieved from: https://www.reddit.com/r/antivax/.
47. Lama Y, Hu D, Jamison A, Quinn SC, Broniatowski DA. (2019). Characterizing Trends in Human Papillomavirus Vaccine Discourse on Reddit (2007–2015): An Observational Study. *JMIR Public Health Surveill*ance 5(1):e12480. doi:10.2196/12480.
48. Communalytic is developed by the Social Media Lab at Ryerson University, and is available for use at https://communalytic.com.
49. Reddit.com. (n.d.). What is "Brigading" and how do you do it? Reddit.com. Retrieved from: https://www.reddit.com/r/OutOfTheLoop/comments/36xhxc/what_is_brigading_and_how_do_you_do_it/.

50. Gephi (n.d.). Gephi the open graph viz Platform. Retrieved from: https://gephi.org/.
51. Gruzd, A., Paulin, D., & Haythornthwaite, C. (2016). Analyzing Social Media and Learning Through Content and Social Network Analysis: A Faceted Methodological Approach. *Journal of Learning Analytics*, 3(3), pp. 46–71. https://doi.org/.10.18608/jla.2016.33.4.
52. Gruzd, A., Mai, P., & Vahed, Z. (June 2020). Studying Anti-Social Behaviour on Reddit with Communalytic. Retrieved from: https://advance.sagepub.com/articles/Studying_Anti-Social_Behaviour_on_Reddit_with_Communalytic/12453749.

CHAPTER 5

Exploring Issues of Social Justice and Data Activism: The Personal Cost of Network Connections in the Digital Age

In the age of the Internet of Things (IOT), it seems as though much of daily life is connected to and through digital appliances from mobile phones to automobiles to refrigerators; however, what's important here is that they all collect data. When thinking about the leakiness of all that data, two dimensions of global data justice come to the fore in the form of function creep and market making. When information is utilized for purposes other than those originally specified, it may be referred to as function creep. Of course, what happens to all that data is a matter of concern, as it is not clear who owns our data, where it is stored, and how it is utilized down the line impacting, among other things, our privacy. While not originally intended to catch protesters in the act, during the 2019 and 2020 protests in Hong Kong, for example, facial recognition technology was utilized to match faces from video footage of protesters to images held in police databases, with the intent of disincentivizing protesters.

Social justice in the digital age refers to those human rights and individuals whose freedoms that have been curtailed, who have received inequitable treatment with regard to opportunities and resources, and are discriminated against because of their class, gender, race, or sexual orientation. For migrant communities and refugees, border policing, asylum processes, and access to government support are key issues related to social justice. As there is much data being collected about marginalized communities, concerns over data colonialism have grown. In reaction, data activism has emerged as a critique of the actors and practices, including governments

N. Alperstein, *Performing Media Activism in the Digital Age*,
https://doi.org/10.1007/978-3-030-73804-4_5

and corporations, associated with treating human life as a resource. Algorithms trained over time to impact marginalized people are created in a way that makes it difficult to even determine authorship, as machine learning increases the algorithm's power in the form of algorithmic bias. This bias creates data inequities affecting housing, for example. While much work has been done in the area of ethics, autonomy, trust, accountability, governance, and citizenship, this chapter extends the discussion to consider datafication in the US, Europe, Asia, Africa, and Latin America.

Artificial intelligence (AI) can be utilized for myriad purposes from something seemingly benign like monitoring traffic and in that catching speeders to locating lost children. However, there are more insidious uses, as cameras surveil protests and monitor people through facial recognition, like they did to those protesters engaged in the Hong Kong pro-democracy political movement. As an indication of just how pervasive this is, one company that makes facial recognition technology says they operate in 50 countries.[1] While governments might say they use body scanning technology at airports to thwart terrorist threats or it is utilized by police departments to apprehend criminals, such technology can be utilized for other purposes, especially as the data collected is without individual consent. As a form of data resistance, during those Hong Kong protests government attempts at surveillance resulted in activists taking down lampposts housing the AI face recognition technology. This example is reflective of the tensions that exist between privacy and security, issues of acute interest to data activism, and social justice issues. The issue of technology injustice extends beyond AI. While not a matter of invading one's privacy through the acquisition of personal data, in a quite different example of the use of AI, in 2018, police in Dixmont, Maine, in the United States used a "bomb squad robot" to kill a Black man engaged in a shootout with police. There was a similar use of a robot to kill a man in Dallas, Texas, involved in a police confrontation; the police chief called the use of the robot justified. Where does the use of all this technology lead those engaged in offline or online social movements?

Market Making

The second related issue is market making in which corporations—software developers—create apps or other technologies to benefit commercially from surveillance enterprises or what has been referred to as surveillance capitalism. All the data collected through these technologies can be packaged or repackaged and sold for purposes other than those for which it may have been originally intended. As we are still in the nascent stages of IOT and related technology development, from a data justice perspective the moral or ethical aspects of surveillance capitalism are not clear. But smart phones, digital thermostats, and digital assistants like Alexa or Siri are fraught with issues in a first world environment, and surveillance technologies impact not only the digital "haves" but the "have-nots" as well. As Shoshana Zuboff writes in her book *The Age of Surveillance Capitalism*, "Surveillance capitalism unilaterally claims human experience as free raw material for translation into behavioral data. Although some of these data are applied to product or service improvement, the rest are declared as a proprietary behavioral surplus, fed into advanced manufacturing processes known as 'machine intelligence,' and fabricated into prediction products that anticipate what you will do now, soon, and later."[2] In one example based on social monitoring, intelligence analysts working for Amazon use social media tracking to gather information about environmental activism that the company sees as a threat to the continuity of its operations, including Greta Thunberg's global climate strike and the Fridays for Future movement. Amazon also monitored the 2019 *gilet jaunes* or Yellow Vests movement for economic justice fearing it could be a threat to their operations. Such corporate monitoring extended beyond France to solidarity movements in Austria and Iran where there were protests against state repression.[3] Zuboff argues the attention economy, which is propagated by Google and Facebook, promotes user participation so that data can be collected with the goal of optimizing advertising and nudging consumer activity.

Speaking at a Techonomy conference in 2010, Eric Schmidt, formerly of Google stated: "There were five exabytes of information created by the entire world between the dawn of civilization and 2003. Now that same amount of information is created every two days."[4] Undoubtedly, today we are inundated with data, so much data that it requires companies to develop software that can manage that data, integrating disparate kinds of data in order to yield insights for governments and corporations. One company, Palantir, has done just that, and while much of its work based on proprietary software is on behalf of governments and commercial companies, it has been utilized in what is referred to as predictive policing. "To critics, data-driven policing encourages overly aggressive tactics and reinforces racial biases that have long plagued the criminal-justice system. Palantir's effort to market its software to police departments can also be regarded as an example of how weapons originally meant for the war on terrorism are now being deployed on American streets."[5] But the software can be utilized beyond that to identify undocumented workers that were targeted in ICE raids. Palantir is often described as the company that knows everything about you.[6] The company that went public in the fall of 2020 is not without controversy. One major investor, George Soros, decided to divest his shares in the company because he "does not approve of Palantir's business practices."[7] Government agencies from many parts of the world contract with the company to use its technology for spying purposes. The company was co-founded in 2003 by entrepreneur and venture capitalist Peter Thiel. A headline in a Bloomberg news article puts it this way: "Peter Thiel's data-mining company is using War on Terror tools to track American citizens. The scary thing? Palantir is desperate for new customers."[8]

Algorithms: Just Math

Machine intelligence is based on algorithms, which are in their simplest form a set of instructions designed to perform a specific task. At base, an algorithm is just math. On the one hand there is math fairness that is simply the algorithm performing its function, and on the other hand, there is social fairness that may not be accounted for in or considered by the algorithm. The distinction is important. To take this a step further, while fairness equals justice, mathematical fairness does not equal social justice. An example of machine learning gone awry is the International Baccalaureate program whose in-person testing was substituted, because of the COVID-19, by an algorithm that measured a number of extraneous factors, like a student's grades on assignments or comparative grades from other graduates of the school, to predict the score they might have achieved had they taken the in-person test. The secret algorithm impacted the ability of many students to attend university.[9]

When you plug in a term to Google search, for example, it is an algorithm that delivers the list of links to you. Some algorithms are quite simple, while others are complex. You might recall a 2014 movie about the life of cryptanalyst Alan Turing. "The Imitation Game" alludes to the Turing Test, in which a user having a conversation through a computer—something akin to a computer chat—tries to determine whether the correspondent on the other end is a person or a program. In an early formulation, the participant wasn't trying to distinguish between human and machine, but between a man and a woman. This test was called "the imitation game." In fact, "One of his early mathematics papers explores the reliability of certain algorithms that would later be central to computations for things like the PageRank algorithm, on which Google's search engine is based."[10] The goal of most algorithms is to achieve efficiency, but efficiency is based on a number of factors ranging from the power of the computer doing the processing to the number of steps required of the algorithm to conduct the assigned task.

There is built-in bias, a technochauvinism to algorithms based on the idea that technology is superior to people. But people create algorithms, and they embed, even if inadvertently, their bias into technology. It should not be lost that gender plays a role in the creation of algorithms. Additionally, algorithms because of their very nature, like in the International Baccalaureate example above, often don't get it right on the first attempt. Facial recognition, for example, has been weaponized against vulnerable communities. Humans are needed to intervene in order to make adjustments, but that doesn't always happen and not in a timely manner before damage is done. Most important, we have to acknowledge the limits of technology, AI, and machine learning in a radical rebuild of these systems in order to root out bias. It is worth noting that Google fired AI ethicist, Timnit Gebru, co-founder of Black in AI, whose mission is to increase the number of people of color in the artificial intelligence community, which highlighted the tensions between the company and worker activists.[11]

Consider that Google search mentioned above and think about how plugging in your search terms efficiently reveals an answer to your query. Algorithms are utilized for many purposes beyond that Google search, including Uber, for example, and the uses extend to many fields, from agriculture to transportation to various fields of science. And while working of an algorithm sometimes is equated with magic, there is a need to keep in mind that when human judgment is taken out of the equation, as is the case with predictive modeling, societies skirt the edge of digital ethics.[12] Sometimes algorithmic magic becomes too complicated, which is where machine learning comes into play. Based on past decisions the algorithm has made, it can learn to make recommendations and predictions. The implications for social movements are significant, as Safiya Noble puts it in her book *Algorithms of Oppression*, search engine algorithms can reinforce racism.

One response to ethical concerns for AI comes in the form of the Markup, a nonprofit journalistic enterprise engaged in data-driven investigations regarding how big organizations are using technology in ways that impact society. In an investigation of fair housing practices, it was found that landlords, realtors, developers, insurers, or lenders utilize predictive algorithms to discriminate against applicants for housing. While there have been court judgments against such practices, there is no algorithmic responsibility in this instance as the US Supreme Court and the US Department of Housing and Urban Development seem to be at loggerheads on the issue.[13] The ethical and moral imperative that digital technologies and in that the networked society be inclusive and democratic gives way to a more sinister outlook that views such technologies are parasitic and asymmetric with regard to the imbalance of power associated with big data and their propensity toward behavior modification. Referring to behavior modification, Zuboff suggests that technology firms, like Google, have unprecedented access to personal data, and this in turn allows them to produce knowledge about citizens that is so accurate that it can predict behavior. While predictive analytics can be used for the good, like tracking down fraud, predictive modeling and machine learning can process both current and historical data to make predictions about the future. This view of predictive analytics is not presented as a dystopian view of society; rather it is a function of data science and machine learning. It is in that manner that surveillance capital is in itself merely instrumental. In the Chinese social credit system, an example of predictive analytics, citizens are scored on their behavior from jaywalking to playing music too loud, as well as their trustworthiness. The consequence of not adhering to the "program" could be the loss of certain rights. The system can even impact one's friendships, as in the case where a friend is a jaywalker, for example, and loses social credits, their lowered social status can impact your social credit score. The role in behavior modification is quite evident, as who would want to be or be associated with a jaywalker? It is easy to imagine the implications for such a system in the context of activism around social and political issues. But it's important to recognize that data-based reward systems are fairly ubiquitous especially in the developed world, as one's credit score may impact the amount of money one might want to borrow to purchase a home, or impact something as simple as reward points accumulated on a credit card for purchase of products and services.

Data Inequities

During the COVID-19 pandemic, there has been a lot of societal upheaval, individually and collectively. Clearly, under such circumstance healthcare is a primary concern but so too is unemployment as layoffs reached into the millions. In 2020 as the pandemic spread and conditions worsened, many people took their grievances online regarding socioeconomic conditions in order to express solidarity with others and to consider actions to protect health and livelihoods. Although capitalist societies are inherently inequitable, the pandemic exposed the extreme differences especially with regard to marginalized groups. Housing is just one area of primary economic concern, as many people who lost their paychecks may have been subject to eviction or foreclosure. In one instance, hashtag activism around the issue of housing grew with the use of hashtags #RentStrike, #CancelRent, #CancelMortgages, and #NoIncomeNoRent, as well as dedicated websites and Facebook groups that were established like Rentstrike2020 and WeStrikeTogether, to produce an emergent social movement that was worldwide in scope.

Inequities extend beyond economic ones, like housing, to consider broader inequities like access to digital media in order to participate in online activism. In other words, digital media is a place where inequity is practiced. In her study of the rent strike movement, Margherita Massarenti, raises the question: “So how does the mobilizing capacity of worse-off groups change in an historical phase that allows little if no physical collective action to happen?”[14] There is a false belief that digital media are more democratic, meaning they are more easily accessible or widely available enabling anyone who wants to participate in online public discourse the ability to do so, but that is in reality not the case. As Massarenti points out, the same inequity that affects a broad array of inequities, including housing, also afflicts the “digital experience of marginalized or disadvantaged communities” offline.[15] Massarenti’s analysis of the Twitter network that utilized the #RentStrike hashtag supports the conclusion that those who are disadvantaged in their actual communities are also disadvantaged in the digital sphere. The social network she describes is one that is dominated by politicians, media or other institutions, what have been referred to as elite mediators; the network is not a space for inclusive discussion among individuals affected by the issues at hand. In other words, there is a digital class struggle at work. Media activists, she concludes, need to be aware of the need to build coalition and community offline as well as online in order to achieve needed inclusiveness in digital movements. What this research tells us is that digital activism is not something that is unique or stands separate but rather digital activism needs to be understood within the larger context in which it exists reflecting both issues of social justice and highlighting injustice. In her book *Weapons of Math Destruction*, Cathy O'Neil echoes the concerns of others working in this field describing algorithms that affect much of our daily lives as "opaque, unregulated and uncontestable even when they are wrong," culminating in what she calls a "toxic cocktail for democracy." A more ominous sound is echoed from as Virginia Eubanks writes in *Automating Inequality* that data pretty much rules our daily lives, impacting those less fortunate.[16]

Social Glue Versus Social Fragmentation

It can be said that social issues come to the fore when news media, both mainstream and digital, bring attention to an audience that coalesces around the issue and thus potentially begins the formation of a social movement. Reference to those with the ability to bring issues to the top of the public agenda is to institutions, individuals, or news organizations, because of their mediator roles that sets the news agenda for social issues, which can lead to some movements becoming more successful than others in terms of claiming their share of voice in both mainstream (radio, TV, and print) and digital media platforms. In other words: Why are some social movement organizations more successful than others at gaining media coverage? Furthermore, what does media coverage even mean when the media and the audience are fragmented? Abercrombie and Longhurst describe audiences of digital media platforms as diffused.[17] They distinguish diffused audiences from simple or mass audiences in the following: Diffused audiences may access digital media anytime and anywhere, which means individuals have access to greater amounts of content leading to greater opportunities for people to "perform" by retweeting a news item, for example. The diffused audience is one that is based on the devolution of the private into the public sphere as the possibilities of engagement are continual, open-ended. As messaging, videos and tweets no matter who is the source have the potential to go viral, without much thoughtfulness or consideration, as a result several platforms in order to address inequities have sought to slow down the spread of messages in particular when they spread misinformation or disinformation. The messaging platform WhatsApp, for example, limits users' ability to forward messages, and TikTok reviews videos before they reach the main feed. Facebook has what they call a "virality circuit breaker" that allows the platform to moderate some of the messaging to ensure it meets community standards. And Twitter encourages users to add some commentary before merely hitting the retweet button; again, with the idea of creating more thoughtful and perhaps reasoned conversation.[18] The implications for all of these changes is to interrupt the flow of misinformation and perhaps limit some of the anger that is seen as an endemic part of social media and replace the vitriol with more reasoned commentary.

With regard to mainstream media, including radio, television, and print, we look to the agenda-setting function in which gatekeepers—editors and reporters—set the news agenda. In their research on local news organizations, Andrews and Caren found that "local news media favor professional and formalized groups that employ routine advocacy tactics, mobilize large numbers of people, and work on issues that overlap with newspapers' focus on local economic growth and well-being. Groups that are confrontational, volunteer-led, or advocate on behalf of novel issues do not garner as much attention in local media outlets."[19] However, Ferreira's extended view of McCombs classic theory of agenda setting with a view toward the digital age questions whether an audience that is distributed through infinite subjects and fragmented media—an audience that is diffused—can be considered an audience at all.[20] While major media outlets collectively disseminate a rather redundant set of issues or topics, digital media and their empowered audiences create and currate content in a way that fractures that model. Along the way, topics and issues that may include take on a life of their own, including mis- or disinformation. In the context of agenda setting, it is important to stress the role that YouTube, Facebook, and Twitter play as gatekeepers of social activism. Tweets about a social protest, for example, may be disseminated on social media before a story reaches mainstream media, signifying the role of citizen journalists, so-called influencers, or anyone on the scene with a mobile phone and internet connection who can livestream an event. As the audience for social media is diffused, so too are the gatekeepers whose agendas as well as their motivations are varied. But as hashtag warriors or digital activists, individuals tend to communicate within their own social bubbles, which brings up the issue of social glue, the binding substance that traditionally may have held society together, as people would likely have been exposed to varying opinions on a subject rather than only being exposed to information (and in that misinformation) from those within one's digitally based social network. While social movements on the right or left can move digital activists in the direction of either reformist or social justice, algorithms also can reinforce racism.[21]

Cloud Protesting

Associated with the idea of a diffused audience in the digital age is the concept of cloud protesting, a kind of one size fits all approach to digital dissent. The cloud refers to a computing environment that includes a number of services ranging from computer servers to databases, analytics, and others, that are all delivered over the internet. Simple enough. In contemporary society, social movements have changed from in-person protests to hybrid movements that combine both in-person and online engagement in an issue most directly through social media, but cloud protesting is the employment of the services identified above in order to manage a social movement. Stephania Milan who has studied cloud protesting states:

> What has the cloud to do with protesting? Contemporary protest is best described as a cloud where a set of ingredients enabling mobilization coexist—identities, narratives, frames and meanings, know-how, and other 'soft' resources. They are fundamentally different from the 'old' pre-packaged ideals and beliefs soaked in ideology, because they can be customized by and for individuals. Resources are in the cloud to be shared in a 'pick and choose' fashion, allowing each individual to tailor his or her participation. Anyone can join anytime; one can bring along his or her identity, cultural and political background, grievances and claims, and even groups of friends. Anyone fits in the broad narrative of the cloud, anyone can contribute. Identities, resources, narratives are negotiated on and offline, but they mostly 'live' online. They are mediated by the web interface offered by commercial social media.[22]

In the digital age, most social movements are characterized as diffused as the internet and social media in particular enable people to organize informally, create multiple and flexible identities, and operate without formal hierarchical leadership. Social movements based on these characteristics could be quite mobile and move across borders fairly easily. What has been referred to as the Arab Spring of 2011, for example, started out as an antigovernment protest in Tunisia, but then spread to Libya, Egypt, Syria, and Bahrain. Although governments attempted to shut down the internet, digital activists moved from Facebook to Twitter, YouTube, and beyond in an attempt to thwart oppression and achieve the social justice aims of the movement based on the slogan, "Bread, freedom and social justice." Cloud protesting, in other words, is a place for algorithmic resistance, a kind of counter-cloud politics.

What is also of interest here is the connection between cloud protesting and normative social behavior, a topic taken up in Chap. 4 of this book. Descriptive norms are typical patterns of behavior with the expectation that people will behave accordingly. Injunctive norms are prescriptive (or proscriptive) rules regarding behavior that ought (or ought not) to be performed. With regard to performing digital activism, injunctive norms are dependent upon on the group, community, or cluster to which one belongs. In line with this thinking, Milan states: "The cultural and normative production of the movement(s), a crucial step towards norm change, which all movements seek, was no longer monopolized by resource-rich large-scale organizations, but the different nodes would voice their claims and build their narratives in a number of scattered websites and online self-organized platforms, bypassing mainstream media."[23]

In an environment of cloud protests it is possible that the media become so fragmented and the audience so diffused that the end result can become a social movement of one, a solo movement. Consider the #ClimateStrike movement started by Swedish teenager Greta Thunberg. What began as a solo campaign eventually became a transnational climate strike movement. Solo protests, some of which like #ClimateStrike move beyond the solo stage to coalesce into social justice movements.[24] Solo protests, while may be few in number, according to two researchers at Vanderbilt University, are often undertaken by young people or older adults who may not have the wherewithal to launch a broader movement; however, "the force of their symbolism and the drama of the confrontations they sometimes invite, lone acts of political defiance can end up having an outsized impact," as was the case with Thunberg, whose solo performance was picked up and amplified by social media and has been retold in mainstream media. Milan contends that the cloud provides easy access to individual activists, which provides one explanation for the rise in solo protesting. Working on an individual basis, a citizen seeking social justice can form a loose hybrid collective, albeit a transient one, with the ability to customize the narrative and shape the normative behavior. In other words, in a cloud environment, it does not take an organized movement to create social change, rather a loose confederacy that provides a "sense of belonging but less responsibility—in short, the cloud has no strings attached."[25]

Hashtag Activism

Digital platforms have been harnessed by social causes to launch and bring to the forefront movements particularly in the form of hashtag activism. Mainstream news media as well as digital media tend to pay attention to charges of high emotion rather than rational discussion. But whether the social movement begins with the uninformed or the ill-informed, an energized hashtag campaign can lead to enthusiasm. The point here is that activists cannot stir up distress regarding a social issue if there is no issue to stir up. And although many if not most hashtags are ephemeral, lasting perhaps no longer than a few days, some hashtags have real staying power, like the #BlackLivesMatter hashtag movement. The movement, like its hashtag emerged after a young Florida man was gunned down by a private citizen who was subsequently acquitted of murder. That incident—the acquittal—sparked a Facebook post that included the phrase "our lives matter."[26] It was on June 13, 2013, that Alicia Garza published the post as an expression of her condemnation of the verdict. In response, her friend commented back with the hashtag #BlackLivesMatter, which inadvertently led to the emergent stage of the movement. As a nascent movement, the hashtag as one might have expected did go viral, as it has been referred to as the hashtag heard all around the world. Figure 5.1, based on Google Trends data from 2013 to 2020, compares the use of hashtags #BlackLivesMatter, #AllLivesMatter, and #BlueLivesMatter, the latter referring to support for law enforcement officers.

Charlton Mcllwain writes in *Black Software: The Internet & Racial Justice, from the AfroNet to Black Lives Matter* about the dual-edged sword of the role that African Americans played in the creation and evolution of the internet, but points out the limitations of digital technology experienced by many who seek to push for racial justice. Technology, he says, has been utilized against Black people who oppose the status quo, but on the flip side demonstrate how Black people have utilized technology toward their own ends.[27]

The hashtag #BlackLivesMatter didn't become prominent as a calling card for the nascent movement until the next incident in which a young Black man Michael Brown was killed by a policeman in Ferguson, Missouri. According to the Pew Research Center, the use of the hashtag went from

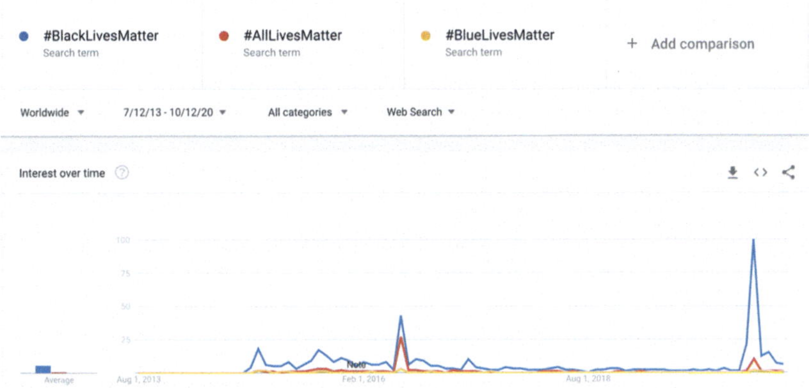

Fig. 5.1 BlackLivesMatter hashtags used over time

5000 to almost 60,000 tweets per day. And at the time when the police officer in that killing was acquitted, the hashtag garnered almost two million posts in a three-week period.[28] Such hashtag campaigns, digital media scholar Alice Marwick says, are what she characterized as "low overhead actions." She described hashtag activism in the following manner: "They can retweet a message about Black Lives Matter. They can change their profile picture on Facebook… And these might not be people who would go to a protest or who would necessarily donate money to a bail fund, but it creates the sort of sense of consensus and this idea of a very broad movement with a wide, wide social base."[29] The use of the hashtag continues as there have been additional unfortunate incidents of racial injustice, including the death of George Floyd that has resulted in not only a hybrid movement that extends not only to US streets but the movement has taken off in many places around the world.

In Nigeria, where half of the population is under 30 years of age, with a median age around 18, and unemployment and underemployment in 2020 stands at 63 percent, young Nigerians have taken to the streets to demand economic change and social justice. According to Statcounter, Nigeria is a connected society as 56 percent of Nigerians use Facebook, 21 percent use Twitter, and another 22 percent use Pinterest, YouTube, and LinkedIn, which is to say that social media is easily accessible in this highly developed African country (see Fig. 5.2).

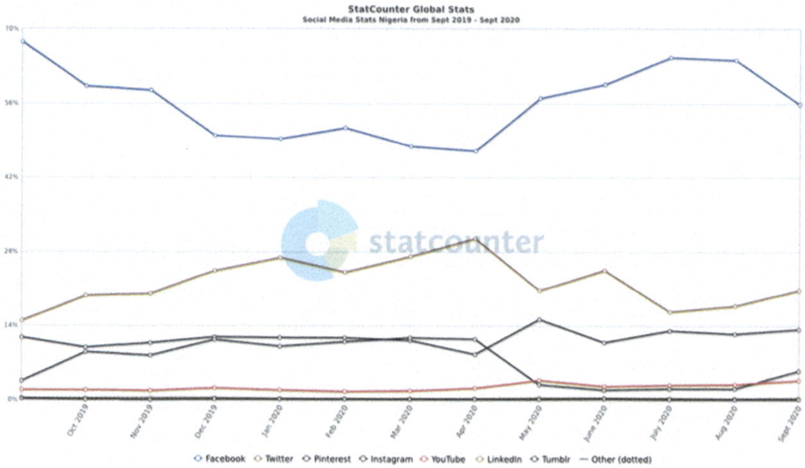

Fig. 5.2 Social media use in Nigeria. (Statcounter.com. (October 21, 2020). Social Media Use in Nigeria. Retrieved from: https://gs.statcounter.com/social-media-stats/all/nigeria.)

In the context of a growing transnational Black Lives Matter movement, hashtag activists posted a video the Special Anti-Robbery Squad, better known as SARS. #ENDSARS was spread by Influencers both from Nigeria as well as international celebrities, including Kanye West and Cardi B.[30] Writing for the online site *The Conversation*, Sakiru Adebayo states: "I argue that the protest placards demonstrate the idea that #ENDSARS on social media and on the streets is as much an expression of a will to modernity by Nigerian youths as it is a yearning to be treated with dignity." The kinds of issues raised by this hybrid movement are similar to the issues regarding police brutality that parallel the Black Lives Movement in the United States and elsewhere, but some aspects are unique to Nigeria because of its youth culture moving from a traditional to modern society.[31] Another theme of this movement is the phrase "to be modern is not a crime," in reaction to Nigerian police profiling people who wear Nike apparel or have iPhones. The movement is part of a long-term struggle, and SARS has over the years been disbanded and resurrected several times. In a variation of Black Lives Matter, in response to populist and racist anti-immigrant sentiments in Dutch politics and public debate, a Black Lives Matter movement emerged to address problems in the Netherlands.

Historically, the Dutch have viewed themselves as a tolerant people, but economic pressures, educational issues, language issues, among others gave rise to a more prominent racist position. What may have sparked protests is an age-old celebration, Black Pete, that has racist overtones.[32] The Black Lives Matter movement found footing in France, too, in solidarity with the death of George Floyd and what his death symbolized regarding racism and police brutality. The French are also confronting questions regarding Black rights and racism in general.[33]

Hashtag campaigns are widely utilized in African countries to support various social and political issues. For example, a Namibia campaign against violence against women used the hashtag #ShutItAllDownNamibia to draw international attention and led to street protests in the country. In the Democratic Republic of Congo (DRC), the hashtag campaign #CongoIsBleeding was launched to draw attention to long-standing issues related in the country related to armed group violence as well as violence against women and exploitation of child labor. In Zimbabwe, the hashtag #ZimbabweanLivesMatter gained strength as the country's security forces clamped down on protests against a number of social issues ranging from censorship, economic conditions, and human rights violations. And, in Cameroon, a French-speaking country, the #EndAnglophoneCrisis hashtag campaign was launched to raise awareness of discrimination against non-French speakers.[34]

Platformitization

Beyond cloud protesting and hashtag activism is the infrastructure that makes all this possible—platforms. To begin, platforms are simply computational infrastructures that rely heavily on users to contribute content while the platform manages interactions through interfaces, algorithms, and policies. We can see that at work in social movements where activists provide live or nearly live feeds to mainstream news organizations in the context of an event or protest. As most mainstream news media treat social movement events as episodic, it means that the movement's organization has to employ a strategic understanding of how social media platforms operate within the broader media context; that is the only way in which movements can be sustained and in that be maintained in the public's eye. If tweets and posts are fast, quick, and too short lived, like most hashtag campaigns, the only way that movements can sustain themselves is by extending their reach not only through third-party media platforms, working with mainstream media and in conjunction using social media platforms, they also must create "owned" media, like blogsites where they can post material at will, extending beyond the cable news cycle with the goal of sustaining the movement. There is a tug and pull at work, as media platforms are structured for the short term, whereas social movements are in it for the long term, if they can sustain the messaging by going beyond traditional outlets.

Platformitization refers to the transformative ability to extend the platforms further into the economic landscape of the web. For Blanke and Pybus the issue concerns a platform's ability to control, stabilize, and extend their ability to alter existing infrastructures. For example, Amazon began as a bookseller but was able to extend their capacity to web services, and AirBnB extended their software model to include additional distributed services. The process is one of decomposition and recomposition to form a number of interconnected parts. This perspective, Blanke and Pybus contend is the way platforms have come to be defined, hence the notion of platformitization.[35] Anne Helmond who has studied this phenomenon suggests that implications regard who has access to the platforms, which would include de-platformitization in which the platform is removed from the system, as the lines between amateur and professional practices become blurred.[36] Amateurs, she suggests, may want to skirt the rules by working around platform governance, like a band that seeks strategic engagement on TikTok. With regard to Black Lives Matter on TikTok, there is an abundance of content, but it isn't the amount of content that determines how much users see; rather it is the users' habits that make that determination. TikTok's algorithm is unique among social media platforms in that the "For You" tab predicts what users will like based on who they followed, liked, or watched. Based on the algorithm, by design, TikTok cuts out large amounts of content that users will not likely see. Furthermore, the platform has the power to declare that if a user doesn't comply with the rules they won't be allowed on the platform or similarly that an app won't be allowed in the app store. We would under most circumstances view this phenomenon as a function of platform capitalism, as it is associated with monetization of platforms. But the tension exists between open and closed infrastructures that have impact on the political economy as well, as there is a tendency toward creating monopolies. These extended platforms are part of larger ecosystems that operate without accountability or transparency.

As an example of how surveillance society operates, the NGO Tactical Tech, which describes itself as "an international NGO that engages with citizens and civil-society organisations to explore and mitigate the impacts of technology on society," wrote about protests in both the UK and US regarding educational surveillance. In the first instance, UK students launched a protest regarding the use of an algorithm to predict their end-of-year grades. In many instances grades were lowered resulting in some students not getting into the university of their choosing. In the second instance, students at 12 universities in the United States protested the use of facial recognition software that falsely recognized people on campus. Both represent instances of algorithmic bias. Furthermore, the data can be packaged and sold as third-party data sets that can be utilized by large platforms like Google or Facebook. In addition to Tactical Tech, there are the Fight for the Future campaign, Big Brother Watch, and the Electronic Frontier Foundation that are engaged in this movement related to predictive technologies.[37] What these organizations are calling for is a systemic literacy so that young people, in particular, know who is collecting their data and what those platforms are doing with it. Apps, on the other hand, do not ask permission to access data, as permission is a condition of utilizing the app; if a user does not give permission, the app become inoperable. Rieder and Hofmann maintain that the idea that algorithms are an openable "black box" suggests that transparency is a panacea; rather, they proposed three regulatory guidelines that can provide greater accountability. The guidelines include observability, not to be confused with transparency, establishment of normative evidence regarding what is acceptable within the concept of public interest, and continuous observation.[38]

Datafication extends beyond computer-based platforms, like Facebook and Twitter, to enter the mobile ecosystem through apps. The distinction is important in two ways: first, privacy on websites is to a degree regulated at least in the EU by GDPR, while apps do not have to adhere to GDPR protocols; and second, websites track users based on cookies, while apps track user data through software development kits (SDK) which are embedded into apps. Most computer users have grown used to cookies, even the permissions requested seem innocuous. But if one gives an app access to a photo, for example, the user may actually be giving permission to access all the photos on their mobile device. Furthermore, such data is not contained by either the app or the platform; rather, data is aggregated, packaged, and sold to various enterprises or government entities. In that sense one's data is not just one person's data, moreover, there is an accompanying loss of anonymity. The implications for those who engage in social movements are significant. Kings College in London developed a web app that identifies the various types of permissions associated with an app. They are categorized as follows: normal, dangerous, signature, or unknown.[39]

Ruha Benjamin, in her book *Race After Technology*, takes up this charge as she conceptualizes the benign surface of technologies that belie their racist underpinnings under the guise of "New Jim Code," a reference to Jim Crow laws and practices in the nineteenth and twentieth centuries in the United States aimed at segregation. She describes how discriminatory designs encode inequity that in turn amplifies racial differences. From her personal experience, she says choosing to give her newborn son an Arabic name "guarantees he will be flagged anytime he tries to fly."[40] This process only replicates existing social divisions. While the algorithmic intent may be pure, the outcome rather than eliminating racial bias only serves to amplify it, all of which leads to a technological architecture that stratifies and sanctifies social injustice. She lays the blame at the foot of those who "encode judgments into technical systems but claim that the racist results of their designs are entirely exterior to the encoding process. Racism thus becomes doubled—magnified and buried under layers of digital denial."[41] Benjamin defines the New Jim Code as "the employment of new technologies that reflect and reproduce existing inequities but that are promoted and perceived as more objective or progressive than the discriminatory systems of a previous era." In coming up with this label, Benjamin was referencing others who have worked in this area, what she refers to as "cousin concepts" like "racialized surveillance," "technochauvinism," "algorithms of oppression," and "algorithmic inequity."[42] The application of the New Jim Code has implications for banking, home ownership, law enforcement, political disenfranchisement, among other insidious applications of algorithmic bias.

Case Study: Police Brutality and Social Justice

George Floyd Part I

While societies all around the world grapple with issues related to racial discrimination, nothing has amplified the issue more than the death of Black people at the hands of police officers. Any discussion of racial bias, however, must include a discussion of the use of artificial intelligence. In policework the use of AI has come under increased scrutiny in that AI tools often times are accused of mistaking people's identity, and this is more so when it comes to people of color. This process is referred to as "predictive policing" and it is directly associated with targeting communities of color and the resulting arrests. Moreover, data of those arrests are utilized to build databases that over time result in not only targeting bias but sentencing bias within the court systems. Biased AI becomes part of a feedback loop in which more data collected leads to more predictive policing with communities of color getting the proverbial short end of the stick.[43] As a result of data discrimination, and in the wake of the death of George Floyd, companies like IBM have opted out of the facial recognition business and a broader discussion regarding the use of AI and data discrimination continues.[44]

In the matter of George Floyd, a Black man whose brutal murder by Minneapolis police on May 26, 2020, was captured on a now infamous eight-minute video of a police officer who utilized a knee chokehold on Floyd's neck, as the victim repeatedly called out, "I can't breathe."[45] The bystander video of the incident was posted on social media and spurred not only local protests but protests in various parts of the world. The phrase "I can't breathe" became a rallying cry for the Black Lives Matter movement. While George Floyd's murder may not be directly attributable to AI, the systemic racism associated with racial data certainly contributed to the attitudes of the police officers involved in this incident. Ayanna Howard, a roboticist at Georgia Tech declared "bias is the original sin of A.I."[46]

On May 26, 2020, both mainstream and alternative media had their eye on the public spectacle surrounding George Floyd's death. This case study begins by analyzing the role of news media in public discourse around the #GeorgeFloyd hashtag. Media Cloud, an open-source platform for studying media ecosystems, was utilized in order to identify stories that were published on US digital media platforms for the time period, May 25–November 18, 2020.[47] The goal of this first part of the case study is to look closely at the network structure of media reporting on the death of George Floyd and, in the aftermath, the ensuing protests. In the same way that individuals engaged in performing activism form network structures, so to do media create network structures. During a six-month period, beginning with the death of George Floyd, Media Cloud identified 29,760 stories, from 2406 media sources. There were 27,030 story links and 11,891 media links. From a social network perspective, a story link is a hyperlink of one story to another, and a media link is when one media source links any number of times to another media source. For example, a story in the *New York Times*, "8 Minutes and 46 Seconds: How George Floyd Was Killed in Police Custody," had 87 media links and over 88,000 Facebook shares. Figure 5.3 shows the total number of stories matching the George Floyd query. The spikes in the chart reveal key events, like the appearance of the initial stories shortly after his death. There were peaks and valleys during the next month, but a plateau was achieved thereafter indicative of a more stable or "normal" level of attention.

The top ten themes were determined by the Media Cloud machine learning model. Figure 5.4 indicates that "demonstrations and riots" was the dominant theme, followed by mentions of "blacks," "police," "politics and government," and police brutality and misconduct.

Analysis of these themes (Fig. 5.5) provides greater insight, as, for example, the theme "demonstrations and riots" is linked with the most mentioned organization—the National Guard (9 percent). CNN (8 percent), the White House (7 percent), and Facebook (7 percent) were also mentioned.

Figure 5.6 depicts the top ten names of people mentioned in stories. Ninety-five percent of the stories mentioned George Floyd, followed by Derek Chauvin (18 percent), the police officer who is the subject of the controversy. Donald Trump (16 percent), and Breonna Taylor (13 percent) were also mentioned.

Fig. 5.3 Number of George Floyd stories over time

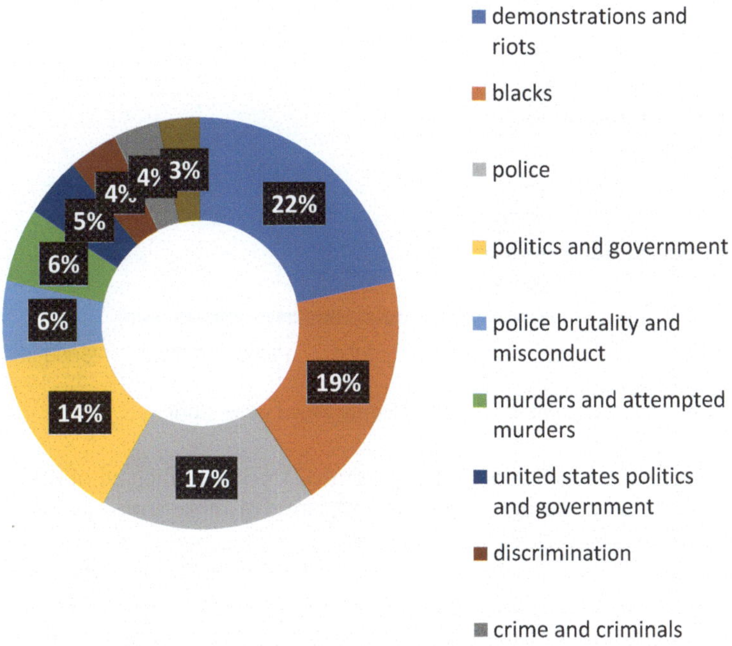

Fig. 5.4 Top 10 themes on George Floyd news stories

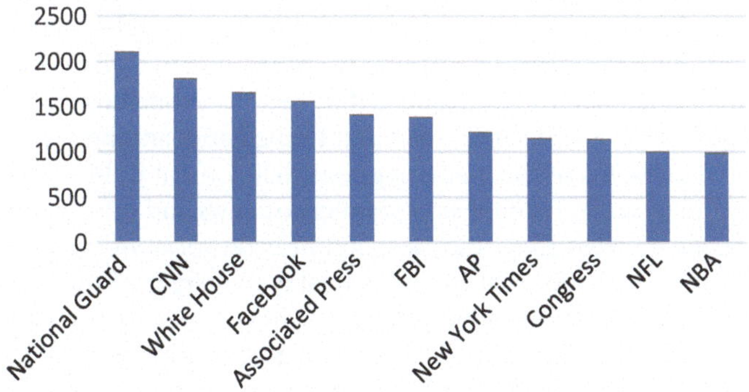

Fig. 5.5 Top ten organizations mentioned in George Floyd news network

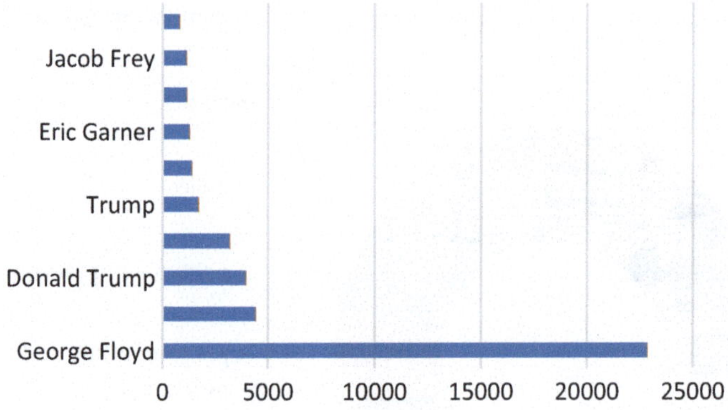

Fig. 5.6 Top names mentioned in George Floyd news stories

In Fig. 5.7 the network map is presented through which all of the linkages can be seen. Larger circles are indicative of more stories; colors are indicative of connections among media.

The digital media network in Part I of this case study indicates that those media outlets reporting on the death of George Floyd did not act so much as a set of independent actors publishing content. Rather, as depicted in Fig. 5.7, what can be seen is media as a multi-platform complex set of inter-webs between diverse media organizations, in particular mainstream content publishers whose ideas are conveyed through social media platforms. As the network map indicates by the larger circles, mainstream media including the *New York Times*, *Washington Post*, CNN, Fox News, NBC News dominate the messaging, thus serve as moderators of content regarding George Floyd's death and as intermediaries among other media outlets. This analysis of the media suggests that content publishers should be viewed in a similar manner as consumers of news and information who also disseminate what they read, see, and hear on social media platforms. In that manner, it is not that the individual is the target of the media but rather media should be viewed as an actor in the social network, a core mediator. The role that individuals play in this process is through their own social engagement sharing items of interest and reading or viewing stories shared by others in the network. By the turn of the twenty-first century, the new media system that integrates—perhaps not fully—newer digital media platforms with older mainstream news outlets has changed the ways in which civic-minded journalism conveys information with the

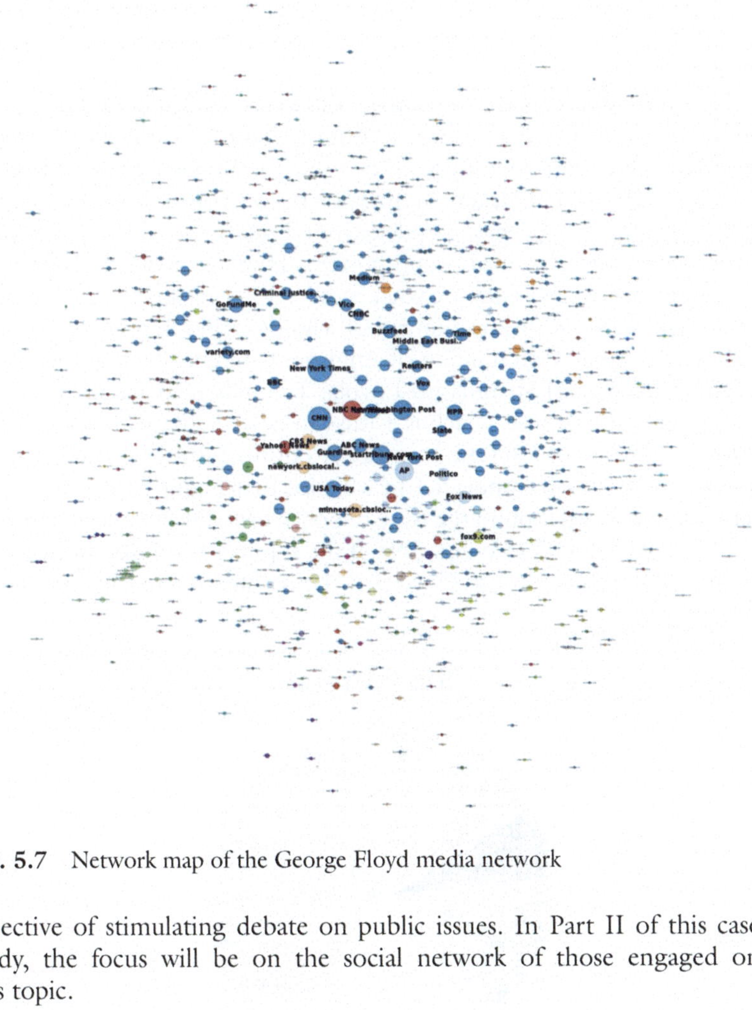

Fig. 5.7 Network map of the George Floyd media network

objective of stimulating debate on public issues. In Part II of this case study, the focus will be on the social network of those engaged on this topic.

#George Floyd on Twitter: Part II

Central to the idea of a multi-platform approach to activism is that modularity is a contributing factor to the development of digital communities. For this part of the case study, Netlytic, a cloud software, was utilized to collect 100,000 posts from 88,601 posters on Twitter that either utilized the hashtag #GeorgeFloyd or mentioned the name George Floyd in the tweet. The data was collected in the week following George Floyd's death.[48]

Figure 5.8 presents the percentage of tweets from the top ten posters on the network. The FatedLoves account is that of a fiction writer, who is responsible for almost one-third of the tweets in this George Floyd hashtag network. The second largest number of tweets comes from @steviepax, whose account has been suspended from Twitter for violating the platform's rules. And, the third largest poster is Hotpage News, with almost 9 percent of the tweets. They are what is called a "cheatsheet" news curator. That is followed by Bishop Lumanog, who describes himself as Anglican Bishop (Apostolic Communion of Anglican Churches) and leader of the Anglican Diocese of St. Ignatius Loyola. The only media among the top ten posters is CDNnow, which is a Russian news outlet with one Twitter follower. This list of top posters presents a distinct irony, as none of them appears to be closely connected by salience that might be expected of a network that forms around the issue of police brutality and racial injustice.

The word "cloud" (see Fig. 5.9) of the top words utilized in tweets at the top of which is George Floyd and the hashtag referencing his name.

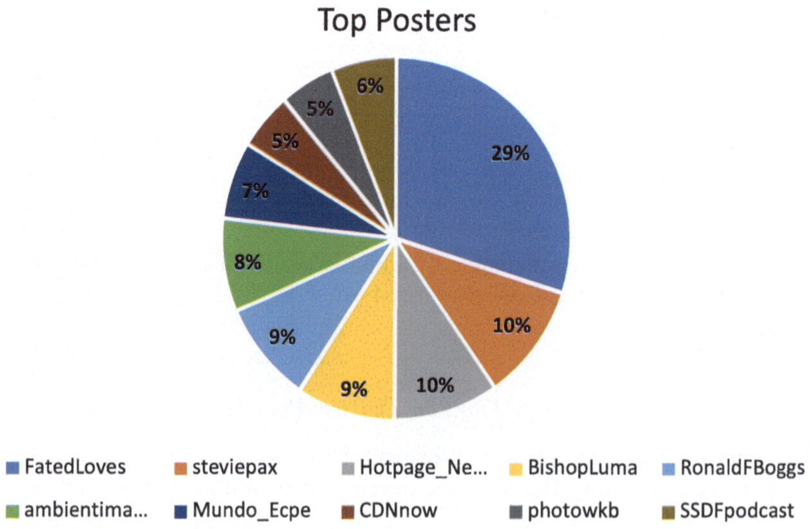

Fig. 5.8 Top ten posters on #GeorgeFloyd Twitter social network

Fig. 5.9 Most frequently used words in George Floyd network

Following are words like "police," "murder," "family," and the phrase "Black Lives Matter." In the course of the tweet storm, the name George Floyd and Black Lives Matter became synonymous.

In addition to words utilized in tweets, looking at those who are mentioned in tweets provides additional information about how the network is operating. Figure 5.10 identifies NBC Washington and the Chicago Tribune, both media companies as the most mentioned, most likely because their stories were the basis for retweets. Interestingly Mehdir Hasan, a British-American political journalist and broadcaster is the third most mentioned person in the social network.

In order to better understand the social network revolving around the death of George Floyd, a sentiment analysis was conducted to look at both positive and negative words that appear in tweets as identified by the Netlytic algorithm. There were 1760 terms that were expressions of good feelings and 1191 terms were expressions of bad feelings. Some of the positive emotions included great (375), good (282), proud (176), determined (231), gentle (112), and fantastic (103). Among the negative terms

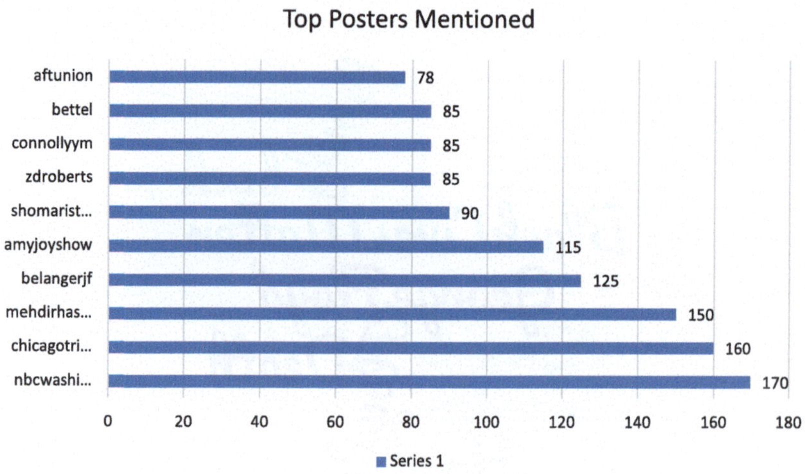

Fig. 5.10 Top ten posters mentioned in George Floyd social network

utilized in the tweets included angry (246), bad (224), hurt (137), grieving (109), tired (79), helpless (57), and evil (49).

A closer look at the data indicates the word "proud," for example, is used in 176 tweets. Language is, of course, contextual, as in one tweet proud was used in a celebratory manner in regard to peaceful protests in Houston, Texas, as in the following:

> **2020-05-31 12:47:32**:
> I'm so dang **proud** of Houston today. A day long of peaceful protesting, marching, and crying for #GeorgeFloyd—they were joined by @houstonpolice who guided them along their march and shut down all necessary roads. Love you Htown

On the other hand, in another example, the word "proud" is utilized in a political manner strongly contesting the presence of right-wing agitators at the protests honoring George Floyd.

> **2020-05-31 12:24:39**:
> @tedwheeler Can you please stuff the **proud** boys back into the cave they came from! You need to protect the protesters from the **proud** boys/antifa who are destroying the city. They are ruining our right to protest peacefully. This is about GEORGE FLOYD not the fucking white nazis. #georgefloyd

An example of how one of the negative terms was utilized, evil, is exemplified in the following tweet:

> **2020-05-31 10:15:12**:
> Peaceful protest is how you honor George Floyd.
> Looting is a disgrace to everything he stood for. It erases his message and changes the narrative.
> **Evil** will never overcome **evil**. | #GeorgeFloyd #GeorgeFloydProtests #BlackLiveMatter

And the term "helpless" is utilized in the following manner:

> **2020-05-31 14:09:30**:
> i feel so **helpless** in these moments, thank u to all the ones who are bravely protesting. the most important thank u goes to George Floyd who made us realize where we live. thank u thank u thank u so much, hope u're resting in peace. #BlackLivesMatter #GeorgeFloyd #protests2020

Figure 5.11 visualizes the name network in order to discover connections among the networked community. Clusters of a particular color represents the 'nodes' or groups of users communicating/sharing/reposting a tweet or tweets. The larger the group, indicated by a particular color, is composed of more users interacting around the issue. The lines connecting the users represent 'ties' between users who may mention another user in a tweet or retweet. A name network examines messages while connecting one person to another if they mention, reply, or repost another person's tweet. In the case of the hashtag #GeorgeFloyd, the resulting network generated by Netlytic included 21,773 nodes and 36,318 ties (including self-loops). There was a total of 91,452 names in the network. In the figure below clusters can be seen forming within the structure of the social network. In this name network, the clusters represent different name clusters built from mining personal names in the messages. The clusters represent subgroups of users who are more interconnected among themselves than with users in other clusters, although there is clearly spillover from one cluster to another.

The clusters are based on degree, which refers to both in and out communication. At the center of the blue network, for example, there are two media outlets, EastBay Times and MercNews, that were tweeting that a protester in San Jose was taking a knee in support of the Minneapolis

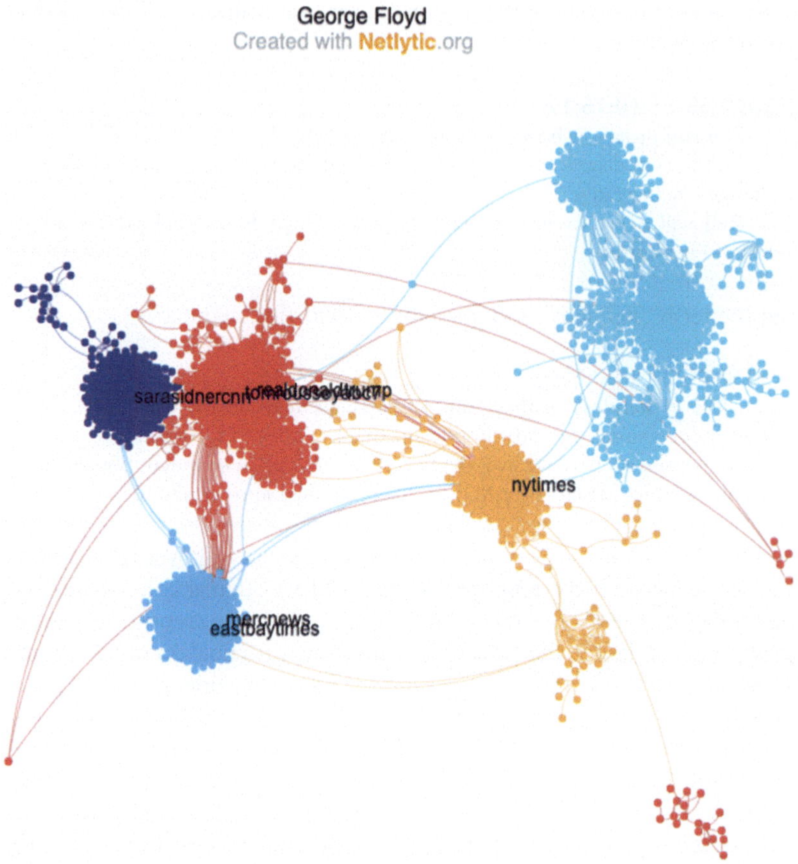

Fig. 5.11 #George Floyd name network visualization

protests. The red cluster is based on retweets of a video that related to the protests in Washington, DC, whereby people were being moved away from the White House by police. The tweets all used the tag @ realdonaldtrump.

Modularity is a measure of the communities within the network. In this case the modularity is high (0.89) indicating there are distinct communities operating within the network, as opposed to a core or central group of nodes. In other words, this is not a well-connected network but rather one made up of loosely connected clusters. Other network measures include network diameter (18), density (0.000057), reciprocity (0.003), and centrality (0.07).

Figure 5.12 represents the #GeorgeFloyd hashtag chain network, reflecting who is replying to whom. There were 1324 posters with ties in the network, and there were 3567 ties (including self-loops) in the network. There was minimal two-way, back-and-forth conversation ongoing, suggesting that much of what is happening in the network is retweeting. The reciprocity value was low (0.001). The relatively high modularity (0.86) suggests there are a number of independent clusters operating within the larger social network. A poster with the handle @FatedLoves is central to the "fuchsia"-colored cluster having tweeted to 143 others. Her

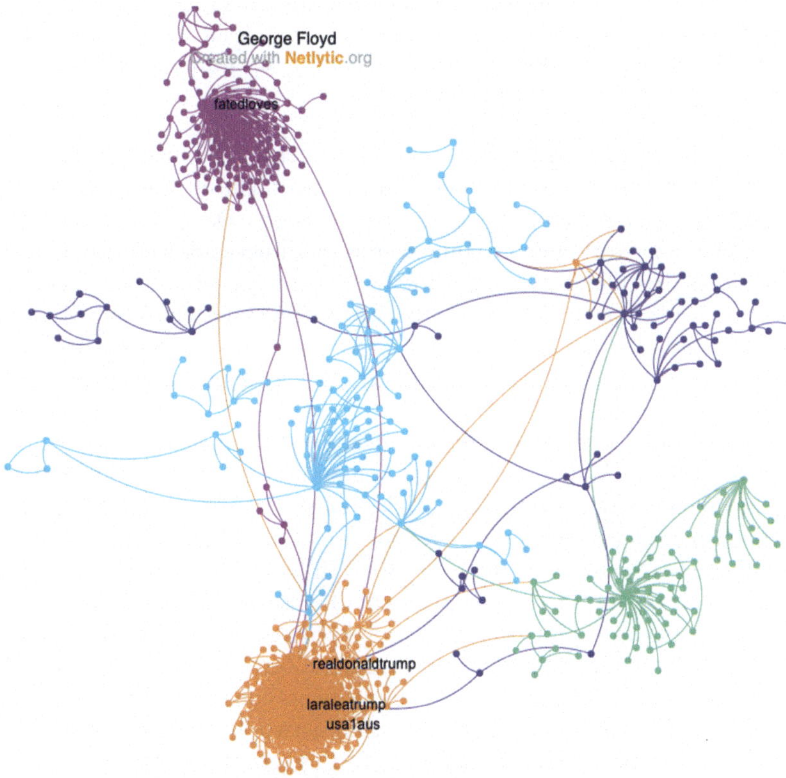

Fig. 5.12 #GeorgeFloyd chain network visualization

tweet was actually a retweet that encouraged people to go to the change.org website to sign a petition supporting the George Floyd Police Reform Act. CNN is the object in the "purple"-color cluster as people tweeted in reaction to the following:

> "If you look at this from 35,000 feet, this man died over $20. Really? … Why do you think people are so damn angry."
> @sarasidnerCNN
> reflects on the events that led to George Floyd's death. https://cnn.it/2BfG34t

One person reacted thusly:

> To say #GeorgeFloyd died over $20 is a gross insult to African Americans in this country. George Floyd was murdered because his life was not valued. Just like all the others that have died innocently at the hands of police brutality, it was disregard of life. Stay on issue!

Those in the orange cluster were reacting to @realdonaldtrump's insensitivity to the George Floyd murder, and the green cluster was made up of people who were recounting George Floyd Protest Days. As is indicative of this chain network, people come to the social network for varying reasons. Some to offer news and announce events or share their feelings about police brutality. Others may engage with greater emotion directed at public officials. In this way, we can see that social networks are not monolithic but may be made up of clusters that represent salient aspects of the social movement.

Sharing footage of George Floyd's death added onto an already enlivened Black Lives Matter movement. Sometimes the graphic videos that appear online of injustice toward Black people in particular are necessary to create media spectacle that drives the attention. Sharing those images even through "likes" or retweets are ways in which an online social network is built through the multi-platform interweaving of media content. The death of George Floyd certainly mobilized people who had previously been inactive on the issue of racial injustice. Zeynep Tufekci, author of *Twitter and Tear Gas*, suggests social movements consider "network internalities," which she describes as ties within networks that allow actors in the network to become more effective. In this case study, we can see the ways in which both media networks and social networks form and, at some point, intertwine. Tufekci warns in speaking about internet-enabled activism that some of the benefits of online activism have significant handicaps in which we see more movements and in that hashtag campaigns, but they are short lived and unable to sustain the movement. Clearly aware of the stages of development of social movements, the author looks to capacity building in order to move movements such as Black Lives Matter and the racial injustice brought upon George Floyd in a more strategic direction and a more sustaining manner.

Conclusion

This chapter began with a discussion regarding the overabundance of data in society and raised the question regarding what is being done with it. Focusing on AI and machine learning, ways in which technologies are being utilized to surveil and monitor protesters, as evidenced by the Hong Kong pro-democracy protests, represent just one of the ways in which data and activism collide. The chapter looks not only at government surveillance but also at the role that corporations play in collecting, packaging, and reselling data. Algorithms trained over time to impact marginalized people are created in a way that makes it difficult to even determine authorship, as machine learning increases the algorithm's power in the form of algorithmic bias. This bias spills over into data inequities affecting housing, for example. Stephania Milan offers up cloud protesting as a form of resistance. Hashtags play a role in generating enthusiasm among digital activists, and the #BlackLivesMatter movement is a prime example. But hashtags, as the chapter points out, are utilized in many parts of the world to support various social and political issues. The platforms themselves are considered in terms of their role in datafication, as Ruha Benjamin applies the "New Jim Code," to describe how discriminatory design impacts marginalized people. The case study for this chapter focused on George Floyd, a Black man killed by a police officer, who sparked outrage in many parts of the world as the video of his killing went viral across a multitude of platforms. The case study illustrated through an analysis of media—both mainstream and alternative—how they serve as mediators of a network that is to some extent solipsistic, feeding on itself. And a social network analysis of the George Floyd on Twitter highlighted the clusters that make up the social network based on varying interests of those engaged.

In the next chapter, some of the issues introduced here are extended to focus on social movement ethics, privacy, accessibility, and inclusiveness in mediated networks. Chapter 6 looks at, among other things, the algorithmic cloud, a subject written about by Louise Amoore, and introduced here, in which algorithms intended to reduce uncertainty are often created in anonymity, leading to questionable ethics. The case study in Chap. 6 will take up issues of accessibility and inclusiveness in social movements.

Notes

1. Schmidt, B. (October 23, 2019). Hong Kong police have AI facial recognition tech—are they using it against protesters? *The Japan Times*. Retrieved from: https://www.japantimes.co.jp/news/2019/10/23/asia-pacific/hong-kong-protests-ai-facial-recognition-tech/.
2. Zuboff, S. (2018). *The Age of Surveillance Capitalism. The fight for a human future at the new frontier of power.* New York: Public Affairs. P. 14.
3. Gurley, L.K. (November 23, 2020). Secret Amazon Reports Expose the Company's Surveillance of Labor and Environmental Groups. *Vice.com*. Retrieved from: https://www.vice.com/en/article/5dp3yn/amazon-leaked-reports-expose-spying-warehouse-workers-labor-union-environmental-groups-social-movements.
4. Siegler, M.G. (August 4, 2010). Eric Schmidt: Every 2 Days We Create As Much Information As We Did Up To 2003. Techcrunch.com. Retrieved from: https://techcrunch.com/2010/08/04/schmidt-data/.
5. Steinberger, M. (October 21, 2020). Does Palantir See Too Much? *The New York Times*. Retrieved from: https://www.nytimes.com/interactive/2020/10/21/magazine/palantir-alex-karp.html.
6. Waldman, P., Chapman, L., & Robertson, J. (April 19, 2018). Bloomberg.com. Retrieved from: https://www.bloomberg.com/features/2018-palantir-peter-thiel/.
7. Shead, S. (November 19, 2020). George Soros' fund is offloading Palantir shares because it 'does not approve' of its business practices. CNBC.com. Retrieved from: https://www.cnbc.com/2020/11/19/george-soros-is-offloading-palantir-shares-due-to-business-practices.html.
8. Waldman et al. ibid.
9. Simonite, T. (July 18, 2020). Meet the Secret Algorithm That's Keeping Students Out of College. *Wired.com*. Retrieved from: https://www.wired.com/story/algorithm-set-students-grades-altered-futures/.
10. Rockmore, D. (November 6, 2014). What's Missing from "The Imitation Game". *The New Yorker*. Retrieved from: https://www.newyorker.com/tech/annals-of-technology/imitation-game-alan-turing.

11. Dave, P. & Dastin, J. (December 2, 2020). Top AI ethics researcher says Google fired her; company denies it. *Reuters.com*. Retrieved from: https://www.reuters.com/article/us-alphabet-google-research/top-ai-ethics-researcher-says-google-fired-her-company-denies-it-idUSKBN28D3JN.
12. Ragipally, A. (June 3, 2020). A Quick Introduction to Algorithms. *Medium.com*. Retrieved from: https://medium.com/@alekya3/what-is-an-algorithm-everything-you-need-to-know-about-algorithms-79bb99cb0c11.
13. Kirchner, L., (September 24, 2020). Can Algorithms Violate Fair Housing Laws? The*MarkUp.com*. Retrieved from: https://themarkup.org/locked-out/2020/09/24/fair-housing-laws-algorithms-tenant-screenings.
14. Massarenti, M. (June 19, 2020). How Covid-19 led to a #Rentstrike and what it can teach us about online organizing. *Interface: a journal for and about social movements*. 12:1, pp. 339–346.
15. Ibid., p. 340.
16. Eubanks, V. (2018). *Automating Inequality*. New York: St. Martin's Press.
17. Abercrombie, N. & Longhust, B. (1998). Audiences: A Sociological Theory of Performance and Imagination. Washington, DC, Sage Publications, Inc.
18. Newton, C. (October 12, 2020). Twitter Adds Friction: Can you slow down the internet with quote-tweets? *Platformer.news*. Retrieved from: https://www.platformer.news/p/twitter-adds-friction.
19. Andrews, K. T., & Caren, N. (2010). Making the News: Movement Organizations, Media Attention, and the Public Agenda. *American Sociological Review*, *75*(6), 841–866. https://doi.org/10.1177/0003122410386689.
20. Ferreira, G. (July 4, 2017). *European Journalism Observatory*. Retrieved from: https://en.ejo.ch/digital-news/who-sets-the-agenda-in-the-internet-age.
21. Nobel, S. (2018). *Algorithms of Oppression: How Search Engines Reinforce Racism*. New York: NYU Press.
22. Milan, S. (October 11, 2011). Seen in I. Poetranto. Cloud protesting: Dissent in times of social media. *The Citizen Lab*. Retrieved from: https://citizenlab.ca/2011/10/cloud-protesting-dissent-in-times-of-social-media/.
23. Milan, S., ibid.
24. Golden, H. (October 7, 2020). In a Season of Protests, Some Stand Alone. Bloomberg.com. Retrieved from: https://www.bloomberg.com/news/articles/2020-10-07/how-solo-protesters-can-make-their-voices-heard.
25. Milan, S., (October 11, 2011).

26. Cobb, J. (March 6, 2016). The Matter of Black Lives. *The New Yorker*. https://www.newyorker.com/magazine/2016/03/14/where-is-black-lives-matter-headed.
27. Mcllwain, C. (2019). *Black Software: The Internet & Racial Justice, from the AfroNet to Black Lives Matte*. New York, NY: Oxford University Press 2019.
28. Pew Research Center (August 15, 2016). The hashtag #BlackLivesMatter emerges: Social activism on Twitter. Retrieved from: https://www.pewresearch.org/internet/2016/08/15/the-hashtag-blacklivesmatter-emerges-social-activism-on-twitter/.
29. Sayarath, M. (October 9, 2020). #BLM and Hashtag Activism. *FutureHindsight.com*. https://www.futurehindsight.com/blm-and-hashtag-activism/.
30. Kenechukwi, S. (October 4, 2020). VIDEO: How SARS officials 'killed man, fled with his car' in Delta. *Thecable.ng*. Retrieved from: https://lifestyle.thecable.ng/video-how-sars-officials-killed-man-fled-with-his-car-in-delta/.
31. Adebayo, S. (October 15, 2020). Young Nigerians rise up to demand a different kind of freedom. *TheConversation.com*. Retrieved from: https://theconversation.com/young-nigerians-rise-up-to-demand-a-different-kind-of-freedom-148105.
32. Thompson, A. & Heijes, C. (December 3, 2020). *The Conversation*. In a year of Black Lives Matter protests, Dutch wrestle (again) with the tradition of Black Pete. Retrieved from: https://theconversation.com/in-a-year-of-black-lives-matter-protests-dutch-wrestle-again-with-the-tradition-of-black-pete-150592.
33. Sorman, G. (September 10, 2020). Black Lives Matter in Paris: An American Movement in France. *France-Amerique.com*. Retrieved from: https://france-amerique.com/en/black-lives-matter-in-paris-an-american-movement-in-france/.
34. Oduah, C. (December 9, 2020). The revoluti9on will be hashtagged. RestOfTheWorld.com. Retrieved from: https://restofworld.org/2020/the-revolution-will-be-hashtagged/.
35. Blanke, T. & Pybus, J. (2020). The Material Conditions of Platforms: Monopolization Through Decentralization. *Social Media + Society*. October–December, pp. 1–13.
36. Helmond, A. (2015). The platformization of the web: Making web data platform ready. *Social Media+ Society*, 1:2, https://doi.org/10.1177/2056305115603080.
37. Kidd, D. (September 28, 2020). Predictive Futures: The Normalisation of Monitoring and Surveillance in Education. Medium.com. Retrieved from: https://medium.com/@Info_Activism/predictive-futures-the-

normalisation-of-monitoring-and-surveillance-in-education-c201e5a75f92.
38. Rieder, B. & Hofmann, J. (2020). Towards platform observability. *Internet Policy Review*. 9:4. https://doi.org/10.14763/2020.4.1535.
39. Manifest Destiny. (n.d.) Web-based app permissions tracker. Retrieved from: https://manifestdestiny.reveb.la/.
40. Benjamin, R. (2019). *Race After Technology: Abolitionist Tools for the New Jim Code*. Cambridge: Polity Press, p.1.
41. Benjamin, R., ibid., p. 11.
42. Benjamin, R., Op Cit., p. 5.
43. Vogel, M. (June 20, 2020). Biased AI perpetuates racial injustice. Techcrunch.com. Retrieved from: https://techcrunch.com/2020/06/24/biased-ai-perpetuates-racial-injustice/.
44. Associated Press. (June 20, 2020). In wake of George Floyd's death, IBM gets out of the facial recognition business. *Los Angeles Times*. Retrieved from: https://www.latimes.com/world-nation/story/2020-06-10/after-george-floyd-death-ibm-quits-facial-recognition.
45. YouTube.com. (May 28, 2020). Fox 9 News Account of George Floyd Murder. Retrieved from: https://www.youtube.com/watch?v=RGr6WOIkHyw.
46. Berreby, D. (November 22, 2020). Can We Make Our Robots Less Biased Than We Are? *The New York Times*. Retrieved from: https://www.nytimes.com/2020/11/22/science/artificial-intelligence-robots-racism-police.html.
47. Media Cloud. (n.d.). Mediacloud.org.
48. Gruzd, A. (2016). *Netlytic: Software for Automated Text and Social Network Analysis*. Available at http://Netlytic.org.

CHAPTER 6

Issues of Social Movement Ethics, Privacy, Accessibility, and Inclusiveness in Mediated Networks

In April 2019, a woman of Sri Lankan read-descent, living in the United States was accused by the Sri Lankan police of being a suspect in an Easter Sunday terrorist attack in which 283 people were killed.[1] The accused was Amara Majeed, a Muslim activist who, perhaps ironically, wrote a book titled *The Foreigners* to combat stereotypes about Islam. The Sri Lankan police released Majeed's photograph to the public accusing her of being a terrorist. It's important to point out that Ms. Majeed is not a terrorist, and she was falsely accused of this horrific crime. So how did it happen? As it turns out facial recognition software mistakenly identified the activist: once an image is released to the public and is spread throughout the world on digital media, there is little that one can do to correct the mistake, although the Sri Lankan government did apologize. But facial recognition, which has been around for some time, is no longer just about the face, but also about broader data contexts beyond the face that are merged together to form a decision. This is an example of machine learning algorithms that are increasingly invasive in all walks of life, including social movements.

As AI allows for deep learning beyond programming of the algorithm, it raises significant ethical implications, the subject of this chapter. The major question is when does it matter and when does it not matter. In other words, are all algorithms bad because they are involved in significant things, like facial or context recognition? Or as sometimes is the case, are algorithms inherently biased, although on the face of it seemingly benign, like the recommender algorithms that are utilized on a music platform like

N. Alperstein, *Performing Media Activism in the Digital Age*,
https://doi.org/10.1007/978-3-030-73804-4_6

Spotify? This chapter discusses socio-techno ethics as they relate to social movements from the end-user's point of view with a particular focus on the issues presented to researchers interested in studying performing activism in the digital age. Ethical issues extend beyond techno-ethics to consider, as in this chapter's case study, the capabilities of social media platforms to exclude participation as those platforms lack accessibility and in that inclusiveness for those people wishing to engage in social, political, and environmental issues.

According to the State of AI 2020 report, facial recognition technologies are in use in 50 percent of the world, with Belgium, Luxembourg, and Morocco being the only three countries that have partial bans on such technologies. Over the years, facial recognition technology has grown beyond merely recognizing faces to include broader contextual factors. Facial recognition is just one technology within the broader field of artificial intelligence (AI) that seeks to build machines that can meet or exceed the capabilities of humans. Machine learning is a subset of AI that is based on a set of instructions—algorithms—that can teach a machine to learn from data that is fed into the machine intended to improve its performance. And an algorithm is simply a mathematical method of solving a problem. In some instances, machine learning is unsupervised when an algorithm, for example, looks to distinguish positive, neutral, and negative comments in a data set of tweets. But one can train the model through supervised learning to provide more specificity or give the analysis direction. There also is an area within artificial intelligence where deep learning (DL) may take place in which case the model seeks to identify complex patterns in data; deep referring to the learning of rich representation of data. An algorithm is not merely math; rather algorithms need to be understood as culture and, in culture, going beyond big data to look more closely at individual algorithmic practices not only those of computer programmers but also those who use or are the subject of algorithms who employ their own tactics, hence the rise of ethical issues.

What to Prevent/What to Protect

The primary issue for those concerned about digital ethics regards what to prevent and what to protect, in other words, what is at stake is the place of machine learning models in society. Louise Amoore maintains in her book *Cloud Ethics* that what is at stake for democracy, border crossings, social movements, elections, or public protests are the predictive powers of algorithms to undermine all of these. Amoore develops three lines of argument regarding cloud ethics, which she refers to as apertures, opacity, and the unattributable. The unattributable, for instance, refers to an algorithm's ability to exceed its capacity to "show and tell" that opens up a different mode of being together that she labels ethicopolitical, all of which relates to the lack of transparency in algorithmic development.[2]

Social movements have not engaged adequately on the issue of cloud ethics, as there are tensions between the values of activists and values of technologies. Ethics in this sense should be seen not as a code or simply as a neutral algorithm; rather digital ethics should be viewed in relationship to others: in particular there is a need to create different types of relationships with those on the margins of society, to give voice to other ways of seeing social movements and empowering individuals in society that works toward inclusiveness, a topic that will be taken up in this chapter's case study. For example, there is tension between what is being referred to as cloud ethics and corporate power. Often times public data that is collected by governments enters into the private sphere as consulting firms, for one, offer their services to governments gratis in exchange for access to data. In one instance, the New York City Council wanted access to an algorithm with the idea, in an attempt to take an ethical stance, that they could trace back to the author of that code; however, based on the definition of machine learning, as the algorithm begins to train itself or is trained by others, one simply cannot trace the authorship. Under such circumstances a corporate value is generated that impacts not only algorithms but corporate influence.

Algorithms can produce racist results as was the case in the UK with what is described as their "streaming tool" that identified those migrants applying for a visa as non-white, in essence creating a discriminatory practice for which the government was sued. While the government scraped the tool before the courts could hear the case, this example nevertheless exemplifies one of the many types of ethical dilemmas that arise when machine learning begins, in this instance, to focus on person-centric attributes.[3] Also in the UK, there is ample evidence that Councils, 53 by one count, are using algorithmic systems to predict social issues. Such predictive systems can save time and money, at least so say the proponents, but on the other hand there is the ever-looming ethical issue of protecting people's privacy. The General Data Protection Regulation (GDPR) was introduced throughout the EU in 2018 to protect privacy. And because many multinational corporations operate both in the EU and elsewhere, they comply with the regulation. GDPR is intended to provide protection for people's data, but it has apparently failed to thwart data breaches in the UK.[4] As will be covered later in this chapter, rules and regulations regarding data privacy on the internet are different than those for apps, like those used on mobile devices.

Most people do not realize that when they engage online as activists that they leave a digital footprint, which raises the question as to where the boundaries are between public safety and privacy; hence, what to protect and what to prevent. When the government or a corporation harvests an individual's data, they are not necessarily doing so with informed consent. Therefore, if the US National Security Agency (NSA) collects phone and surveillance data, where do individuals that want to protest such intrusions into their rights go to determine if, indeed, they are being tracked? In such a situation, a group of individuals in the hybrid "Restore the Fourth" movement not only took to the streets to protest the National Security Agency's surveillance program, also as a grassroots, nonpartisan sub-Reddit they formed online in an effort to generate awareness and take action. As Amoore writes, "All algorithmic decisions contain within them the residue, or the sediment, of past political weightings."[5] She refers to antiapartheid, civil rights movements, and movements for LGBTQ rights that have been "impeded by state access to algorithms," as well she claims that it becomes more difficult for ethicopolitical claims to be made because of the "algorithmic forces of attribution." In other words, an algorithmic society is an unattributive society as machine learning trains the algorithm to take on a life of its own.[6]

Toward the end of 2020, Google Research fired its AI ethicist, Timnit Gebru, although the company maintains she resigned as a result of a research paper that was critical of large-scare AI systems. Gebru played a significant role in AI ethics in terms of inclusion for people of color in a field that is dominated by white males. The issue of inclusion goes beyond Google, as other tech companies are faced with the same workforce dilemma in terms of gender and race. In their editorial in *Wired* magazine, Alex Hanna and Meredith Whittaker state: "With the proliferation of AI into domains such as healthcare, criminal justice, and education, researchers and advocates are raising urgent concerns. These (AI) systems make determinations that directly shape lives, at the same time that they are embedded in organizations structured to reinforce histories of racial discrimination."[7]

One associated organized movement is Women in AI Ethics that describes itself as a "global initiative with a mission to increase recognition, representation, and empowerment of women in AI Ethics."[8] Most notably, the organization created the 100 Brilliant Women in AI Ethics list that identifies leaders in the field of AI. The organization notes: "The exponential growth of AI and potential for significant harm necessitates a comprehensive and inclusive approach. After an extensive evaluation of the AI ecosystem and implications of AI, we have developed a holistic framework for AI + Ethics with 6 key focus areas that consider all ethical implications of AI beyond just technology." Another organization working in this area is the Center for Human Technology. The organization is "dedicated to radically reimagining our digital infrastructure. Our mission is to drive a comprehensive shift toward humane technology that supports our well-being, democracy, and shared information environment."[9]

There are countersurveillance tools, like an iPhone shortcut that utilizes Siri, the Apple digital assistant, that can record an incident if someone is pulled over by the police. This use of corporate technology exemplifies a form of resistance to body cameras worn by some police officers and is just one of several apps, including the Legal Equalizer app that informs someone of their rights if while driving they are pulled over by the police. There is the Appolition app that allows users to contribute financially toward a bail fund for Black people who have been arrested. These uses of counter-technology come on the heels of the George Floyd killing and Sandra Bland arrest.[10] There are tools by community organizations like Survived and Punished, the Bay Area Transformative Justice Collective, AAPI Women Lead, and Stop Spying LAPD Coalition whose resources "work to produce the conditions for social transformation by stealthily disrupting anti-Black surveillance."[11] Amazon, the global retailer, shares doorbell camera footage from its Ring surveillance platform with policing agencies; the footage is not end-to-end encrypted, meaning that data breaches are easily accomplished.[12] As well, Amazon engages in corporate surveillance when it comes to monitoring social movements that may affect their business. In what might be called the Amazon paradox, the company and its founder make significant financial contributions to support climate groups but at the same time Amazon's Global Security Operations Center collects and analyzes data obtained from organizations and social movements it tracks that are considered a threat to the company. In what appears to be a David and Goliath situation, the company tracks Extinction Rebellion, Greenpeace, and the Fridays for Future movement started by environmental activist Greta Thunberg for fear that these movements could disrupt Amazon's operations.[13]

Cloud Ethics

Louise Amoore, in her book *Cloud Ethics*, points out how the cloud is a mystification, which she refers to as Cloud One because such a conceptualization refers to the cloud as machinery that is situated in places that make it more concrete than we would likely imagine. Rather, she thinks of the cloud as a diffuse system in which data collected in one setting might inform decisions in another. Those decisions accumulate and spread in ways that cannot be traced, as the cloud is neither a concrete nor vague idealization of the software industry. Amoore metaphorically describes the cloud as weighted in the history of decisions that contain the residue of past decisions; as she describes it, the cloud is a strange aperture, that can be both opened and closed, on the social world. From the socio-technical perspective, there is particular import for criminal justice systems and policing that rely more heavily on algorithmic decision making. But the outcome of an algorithm, she points out, is never the same as the decision. The implication she stresses is that models of machine learning are sites of profound ethical consequence.

The algorithmic cloud is a means to reduce uncertainty and as such the calculation ends in a flash moment of decision. We don't really know where the decision comes from. It would seem evident that what is needed is merely a fuller accounting of cloud decisions; transparency would be one solution. But that model, she argues is too simplistic. Rather, we don't need more algorithmic certainty but an ethics that works from doubt and partial knowledge. Cloud ethics, therefore, reflects the tension that exists between certainty and doubt. Moore raises the question: Who is best positioned to perform cloud ethics? Cloud ethics should be rooted in how algorithms are built, utilized, and trained. The tension, therefore, doesn't just exist between doubt and certainty but between computer software engineers and others engaged in a socio-technical world. Those others may offer resistance to the use of data, as data becomes instantiated upon others, and that resistance becomes a form of empowerment. Therefore, ethics should not be seen as code but code in relationship to others. Importantly, a cloud ethic needs to consider types of relationships as digital practices affect cultures all around the world, but particular concern needs to be focused on those at the margins so to give voice, that is, empower them to be able to see the elements of coding. Digital practices impact much of everyday life concerning the interplay between the private and public sectors in AI and machine learning, as well as predictive policing and predictive politics that need constant attention. The problem is that once the proverbial genie is out of the bottle, the algorithm is let loose so to speak; there are few ways to correct mistakes. Consider the plight of Amara Majeed who was introduced at the beginning of this chapter. The question that societies have to grapple with is what to prevent and what to protect.

Cloud Protesting

The topic of cloud protesting was taken up in Chap. 5 of this book; however, in this chapter the concept can be reconsidered in light of cloud ethics. If we begin with the concept of cloud computing as we understand it to refer to the centralized storage of digital data, then cloud protesting is a way to, as Stephania Milan puts it "to conceptualize the type of collective interaction fashioned by social media and a strategic solution for its empirical investigation."[14] Cloud protesting is a metaphor for the "imagined space" where collective action takes place, and it refers to the ways in which individuals connect to one another as a form of collective action. Important to this conceptualization is the connection of cloud protesting to performance, a central theme of this book.

Milan contends that social movements have not elaborated adequately on cloud ethics, pointing out the tensions between values of activists and values of technologies. One rationale is that social movements are many and diverse not only in terms of their issues but diverse in the people that engage in a movement. It might be that the diffused nature of movements as a whole provides a partial explanation as to why the issue of cloud ethics has not by and large been taken up by organizers or participants in most social movements; however, exceptions do exist. A counter-cloud resistance, however, did take form when Hong Kong activists took down lampposts that supported cameras capable of facial recognition. In another example, a grassroots approach referred to as "care work" in Mexico helps people as a way of working within a community reclaim their data from the state. During the 2020 COVID-19 pandemic, people in Wuhan, China, used GitHub to bypass the state mechanism as a means of expressing solidarity. And there are movements that create mechanisms to track pollution in the Amazon, a form of "citizen sensing." The COVID-19 pandemic has only served to highlight gaps in inequality, ranging from poverty in the Global South to sex workers in Amsterdam. The ethical issues surround not just issues related to data colonialism but also the ways in which humans demonstrate aspects of everyday life like survival and caring. The pandemic has only served to exacerbate differences and make even more evident the digital divide. Milan argues for a critical computer science that might look like critical studies in the humanities. In that sense, ethics would not be seen as merely related to a "code" but in relationship to others with particular concern for relationships with those on the margins, giving voice to other ways of seeing these elements and empowering people.[15]

While media have always served in the formation of a collective identity, as a social movement defines "who we are," in the digital age, the platforms themselves have become, as Milan describes them, "actors in their own right," intervening in the meaning making process of social actors by means of their algorithmic power. That power exhibited through the use of hashtags, for example, serves as a visible form of performance that leads to collective action, contributing to individual and collective identity on social media. Milan supports the contention that visibility on social media is a practice that constitutes a performance through posts, videos among other material manifestations embodied in digital platforms that become the building blocks of collective identity. Performance in this sense takes place in multiple stages, meaning multiple digital platforms that constitutes a virtual "expression of action."[16] Furthermore, such dramatized expressions, like hashtagging, serve to build not only a collective identity but also individual identity. In this way, cloud protesting takes on two meanings: "firstly, it designates a digital imagined space where soft resources vital to collective action are stowed and experienced by participants; secondly, it stays as a metaphor for a way of connecting individuals in an instance of collective action which is specific to the age of social media."[17] All of that data—collective and individual—is collected and stored and ultimately utilized by others whose intentions may not be in line with those to whom the data belongs. This act on the part of algorithms might be referred to as a "stolen performance."

Social Movement Research: Ethics of Engagement

An issue that arises for those interested in researching social movements is the treatment of movements as a form of abstract objects of knowledge rather than real-world issues that are marked by contention. The various research methods, like data science, used to study social movements have an impact on the knowledge the research produces. This can be said for any social science research, but for those interested in studying social movements in the digital age, the implications are greater, as the relationship between the researcher and the research object is greater.[18] Stephania Milan posits four reasons why the implications are greater for those researchers studying social movements. First, social movement research operates on the plane of knowledge produced by social movements and their political imaginaries that require a sense of awareness; as is often the case, research is participatory in nature. Second, there is risk associated with studying social movements in authoritarian and democratic countries where surveillance is a possibility. In other words, the researcher has an obligation not to put the subjects in jeopardy. Third, because subjects under study are activists, meaning they are fully invested and engaged in their movement, they might demand that the researcher be aligned with their beliefs or positions on a social, political, or environmental issue. Fourth, researchers in a sense are "using" activists as the object of their research, which may impinge on the energy that the activist might otherwise devote to the movement. For all of these reasons approaching social movement research ethically requires a reflexive process that requires the critical explorations of these implications.

To that end, Milan (see Fig. 6.1) developed four main questions for social movement researchers, each as she describes them presents a challenge: "the question of relevance of the research to the activist community; the risks for the research that result from the study of their dissenting practices; the question of power, in recognition of the unbalanced relationship that research establishes between the investigator and the research object; and, the issue of accountability towards research objects."[19] Milan suggests that each question can be applied to various stages of a research project with regard to methodology, theory, and results. This process is one of continual self-reflection, which she claims is central to ethical engagement with social movements.

As social movements in modern industrial democratic society have become quite commonplace as a means of democratic participation,

Fig. 6.1 Four ethics questions for social movement researchers

Grame Chesters argues that social movements are "largely perceived as objects of knowledge … rather than as knowledge-producers in their own right."[20] He suggests this normative framework is ethically problematic. What is called for is an "ethics of engagement" that he says "emphasises relationality, reciprocity and an openness to causal mechanisms of 'becoming' that are outside liberal democratic strictures."[21] Cordner and colleagues argue for a reflexive approach to studying social movements in an ethical manner including "ethical guidelines and decision-making principles that depend on continual reflexivity concerning the relationships between researches and participants," thus providing protection for the researchers and those being researched.[22] To that end Dawson and Sinwell call for a separation of theory and action, which is consistent with the reflexive approach advocated by these social movement researchers, in that way, researchers become scholar-activists.[23] Anne de Jong demonstrates the application of this approach, as a social movement researcher she joined the Gaza Freedom Flotilla suggesting that her theoretical orientation led her to become more of an activist on the issue related to Israeli-Palestinian struggles.[24] What these social movement researchers are working toward is the development of a critical framework for understanding the role of the researcher in an ethical approach to studying social movements.

Social Movements and Corporate Responsibility

It's not only AI developers and social science researchers that have to approach their subject within ethical guidelines, but also there is the ancillary issue of the role of corporations in the ethical use of data regarding employees, competitors, and the communities in which they operate. There has been a long-growing effort on the part of corporate capitalism to shift from a shareholder orientation toward a stakeholder orientation. Shareholder capitalism is long-held position proffered by economist and free-market capitalist Milton Freidman based on the proposition that the purpose of a corporation is to serve only the interests of its shareholders, including owners, employees, and customers. For example, under shareholder capitalism, climate change would not be a priority for manufacturers who may contribute to carbon in the air we breathe. It is the standard by which many corporations operated until relatively recently. Shareholder capitalism is also one of the motivators—profit coming before anything else—behind the Occupy Wall Street movement that calls for an alternative, somehow serving both shareholders and society at the same time. Corporate social responsibility is primarily a twentieth-century phenomenon, the approach seeing much growth in the 1970s with the development of a "social contract" between corporations and society, founded on the idea that corporations exist based on public consent and therefore they should contribute to the needs of society. This idea was developed by the Committee for Economic Development and was extended in the 1990s and beyond. Stakeholder capitalism, a movement within itself, is supported by another Nobel Prize–winning economist Joseph Stiglitz. Stakeholder capitalism is a perspective that is more inclusive in that all a corporation's stakeholders need to be considered with the goal of maximizing societal welfare. Such a position is consistent with modern approaches to corporate social responsibility, as corporations have a significant role to play on issues of climate change, income inequality, among other issues with the idea that if corporations act responsibly, they will deliver long-term value to their shareholders.[25]

Whether shareholder capitalism is just a newer way of co-opting social movements or whether this ushers in an era of partnership between corporation and society remains over the long-term to be seen. Having said that, Just Capital represents one example of stakeholder capitalism, as they describe themselves as the "only independent nonprofit that tracks, analyzes, and engages with large corporations and their investors on how they perform on the public's priorities."[26] To that end, the organization polls tens of thousands of Americans on their attitudes toward "just" business behavior, analyzes almost 1000 companies on a variety of issues, and engages with hundreds of US companies on how to improve business practices, among other activities. As examples of their impact, the organization cites a large hotel company that updated their human rights policy, a retailer that improved policies regarding wages for low-wage earners, and a restaurant company that improved their data privacy policy as regards online sales. But interest in stakeholder capitalism seems to ebb and flow with the state of capitalist economies. For example, the imbalance in corporate greed that led to the 2008 economic meltdown spurred renewed interest among some corporate leaders to invoke a more shareholder-oriented model. In this way stakeholder capitalism or rather its emergence works in response to social movements like the 2011 Occupy Wall Street movement. There is an associated phenomenon of CEO activists, in which corporate leaders are called upon to speak out on social and political issues, representing a major shift in the role of corporate managers who get involved in issues like immigration, racial injustice, among others that may have little or nothing to do with the immediate concerns of their businesses. However, stakeholder capitalism calls for not only a bottom-up call to action but a top-down one as well.

In this chapter, issues related to cloud ethics have been presented questioning the role of algorithms in everyday life with a focus on who is creating them and concerned is raised regarding machine learning as algorithms grow beyond their original authorship to become something else, going beyond what they were originally intended to do. There are implications for social movements, as monitoring activists is being done by governments and private companies. The chapter also presented issues for researchers interested in studying social movements and the ethics of participant-observation methods that may embed the researcher within the movement. And the chapter has alluded to the role that corporations play as socially responsible for of their role beyond serving the interests of shareholders. In the case study that follows, a different way to look at social movement ethics is presented, as it considers who gets to participate online and offline, based on issues related to accessibility and inclusion.

Case Study: Accessibility and Inclusion in Mediated Social Movements

In 1989 when Sir Tim Berners Lee invented the internet, he said "We can build a web that is accessible to all, one that empowers all of us to achieve our dignity, rights, and potential as humans."[27] However, the internet populated by hundreds of millions of websites is anything but accessible and, in most instances, lacks inclusion for people with disabilities. Under such conditions, when it comes to inclusion and accessibility, performing activism becomes problematic, as social media platforms including Facebook and Twitter do not meet international accessibility standards. Youtube.com is moderately accessible, as videos may be closed captioned for hearing impaired viewers. These platforms by their very nature may never become fully accessible, and to that end there have been thousands of lawsuits aimed at educational institutions, banks, sports franchises, among others regarding their lack of accessibility. As social movements like Black Lives Matter, for example, "scale-up" the movement, through building new connections and mobilizing people to become activist on the issues of racial and social injustice, this means that those individuals with disabilities who may want to become digital activists may be prevented or inhibited from doing so. The deterrence of a segment of the population to participate in social movements in the digital age is both an ethical dilemma and moral problem, especially when it comes to inclusivity; there are legal implications as well. From a research point of view, while social media data is hardly random, measures of engagement are complicated and perhaps spurious when considering the exclusion of people with particular disabilities that inhibit their access to social media platforms.

The hundreds of millions of active websites are legally required to provide equal access to all people based on Title III of the Americans with Disabilities Act (ADA). In order to be compliant with ADA regulations, a website must be free of barriers that would make it difficult or impossible for some people with disabilities to use it. The US Centers for Disease Control (CDC) estimates there are 61 million people, or a quarter of the adult US population, who have a disability. And, in 2019 there were over 11,000 lawsuits filed in the US federal courts over accessibility issues.[28] Internationally, the World Wide Web Consortium (W3C) develops Web standards including the Web Content Accessibility Guidelines (WCAG) for both creators and users of the web.

Disability Influencers on YouTube

This case study begins by looking at the ways in which disability is presented on YouTube.com. Using YouTube Data Tools, Video Network Module,[29] related videos were analyzed among five of the top disability influencers using that platform: Lucy Edwards, Oliver Lam-Watson, Daniel M. Jones, Hannah Witton, and Jessica Kellgren-Fozard.[30] Based on the channel id's, the cloud-based software searches for and then generates a network of channels based on their relationship to one another. The channels serve as nodes and the edges are calculated based on the weight of the connection. A graph file is created that is then uploaded to Gephi to create a map of the video network.

Figure 6.2 is a visualization of the interlaced network of these five channels. Each channel is represented by a different color. And the lines (edges) depict the connections among the channels and within the clusters. One question raised by disability influencers on YouTube is whether their influence extends beyond the disability community. In this case, there are 182 nodes in this network with 1139 edges. The average degree, referring to the average number of edges connected to a node, is 6.25. The network

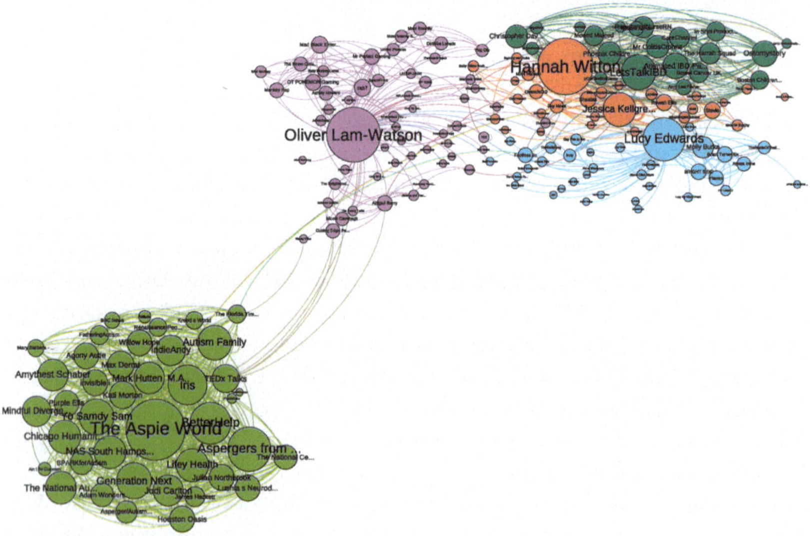

Fig. 6.2 YouTube disability influencers network

diameter, which refers to the length of the longest of all paths between pairs of nodes, is 7. The graph *density* is 0.035 which suggests a sparse graph, while the average path length is 3.122 suggesting an average of information flow.

And modularity is 0.60, indicating there are 5 distinct communities within the network as indicated by the visualization. Beyond the structure of the social network are the characteristics of these clusters, focusing on the dominant actors and the coalition of comments leading to a discussion of the issue each cluster represents.

The communities can be seen through the color-coding of each. As these vloggers have themselves expressed, there is concern that they may only be reaching like-minded people and not extending their reach in a way that raises awareness of their disability to others. Each cluster is represented by the individually named influencer; each is depicted as prominent within their cluster, based on a measure of in- and out-degree. In order to look more closely at one of the clusters, the Video Info and Comments Module was utilized in order to extract comments and network information from one of the communities.[31] In this case the Aspie World, a public YouTube channel, was selected; the particular video under study was titled ASPERGERS Meltdowns: What YOU need to know about OVERLOAD. For this particular video there were 4769 likes and 178 dislikes with 1952 comments. And, there were 156,000 views of this video. The network is made up of 1134 nodes and 783 edges. The graph file associated with the comment network was uploaded to Gephi and a network map was created (Fig. 6.3). At the center of the large fuchsia cluster is the video comprising approximately 40 percent of the comment network. Among the concerns disabled creators cite is the line between sharing and oversharing. In studies of micro-celebrity, oversharing, representing disclosure of aspects of one's personal life, is one of the ways in which to establish authenticity and create intimacy within an audience, and the high level of disclosure among micro-celebrities is one of the elements that distinguishes micro-celebrity from bonafide celebrity. To an extent, these influencers are talking about self-acceptance and creating a comfortable space for others to share their experiences and disclosing aspects of their personal life is one way to accomplish that task. Along the way, these influencers are serving as advocates and motivators and providing inspiration for others with a disability.

Fig. 6.3 Aspie World comment network map

Looking at the Aspie World video channel, that vlogs about Asperger syndrome, the creator seeks a reciprocal relationship; he is about community building and creating camaraderie among his followers.

The most prominent category of comments is that of sharing personal experiences. Many of the comments have to do with the commenter's diagnosis, and as this particular video is about "meltdowns," many of the comments relate to sharing personal experiences and how to deal with this issue. The network of commenters is also represented by mothers advocating for their children and speaking about themselves and other members of their families, children who express concerns about issues related to Asperger's, and others including males and females sharing their experiences. Table 6.1 provides a list of categories of YouTube comments and sample comments from each category.

The relationship between the number of people with disabilities and the depiction of people with a disability in mainstream media is dismal.

Table 6.1 Categories of YouTube video comments

Category	*Comment*
Self-Acceptance	I am a girl with autism and I have not been diagnosed and I don't know what to tell people when I am flapping my hands and/or rocking back and forth. What do I do. On top of that I am a kid so I can't do anything about but keep talking about it and showing videos to my mom.
Sharing Experience	I have autism and have meltdowns when I don't want to go somewhere or if I got my routine changed and it sucks
Advocate	Thank you Dan! I've been experiencing meltdowns more recently due to all kinds of stress factors in my life. Just listening to this video was like a peer support situation. Helps with generating a self—compassionate attitude. Self—compassion by the way is a topic I recommend to everyone dealing with these kinds of challenges in their lives.
Motivate	Thank you! All of this helps immensely. I really appreciate all of the help you give.
Inspire	Thank you so much for these videos! I'm dating someone who has two kids. One is a average 10 year old. The other is a 13 year old boy with aspergers syndrome. Your videos help so much!! Keep up the amazing work!! Hey dude, thank you for being so awesome. I have had a feeling for quite some time now that there's something about me that's not just "different" and after doing hours and hours of digging, reading, watching and thinking (though it could be confirmation bias) I realise now that Aspergers is the closest thing to how I feel constantly. I'll be looking into it professionally. Much love

For example, both in the UK and in the United States about 20 percent of the population have a disability but only about 3 percent of characters with disabilities are represented in entertainment media.[32] One of the goals of these influencers is to represent their disability in a way that they hope leads to normalization. Their presence on a platform like YouTube opens up that possibility but only if followers extend beyond their bubble so as not to create an echo chamber effect. On the one hand disability itself constitutes a social movement, and as will be seen in this case study, participation in social movements by disabled people represent issues for both offline and online engagement.

Homophily, which is the tendency of individuals to associate and bond with those of similar interests, those that are similar to themselves, is presented in clear terms through the distinctive clusters in the disability video network. Lucy Edwards, for example, vlogs about blindness, and in her videos, she takes a measured approach between sharing enough information about herself and oversharing. Daniel Jones whose Aspie World network is analyzed above has 143,000 subscribers. And Jessica Kellgren-Fozard has 793,000 subscribers to her YouTube channel, where she vlogs about being hearing impaired.

Disability Facebook Groups: ADAPT

For this analysis, posts by Facebook groups were extracted using CrowdTangle (a public insights tool owned by Facebook). The terms and hashtags ADAPTandResist, #ADAPTandResist, #DIAToday, disability freedom, #DisabilityFreedom, Community for All, #CommunityForAll, and #Community4All were utilized in the search from January to December 2020. There were 1992 interactions noted on Facebook and 2,136 on Instagram. After de-duplicating the posts and creating node and edge tables the data was visualized and analyzed utilizing Gephi (Fig. 6.4).

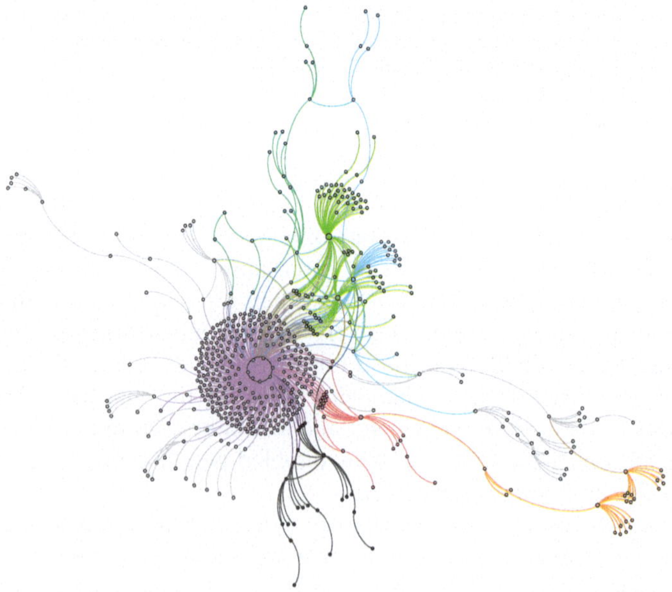

Fig. 6.4 Facebook disability network

The social network on Facebook is made up of 700 nodes and 770 edges. The partitioned colors are indicative of various clusters that make up the larger social network. The modularity of this network is 0.627 indicating the partition detected distinct communities within the network; some nodes in the network are more densely connected with each other than with the rest of the network. The largest cluster in the network, fuchsia in color, is the ADAPT Facebook group. ADAPT is an acronym for Americans Disabled for Attendance Programs Today, self-described as a disability rights grassroots collective that seeks to create awareness of institutional discrimination by disabled people and ultimately to change the system.[33]

According to the ADAPT website, the organization utilizes various protest tactics ranging from marches, hostage-taking, civil disobedience, destruction of property, arrest, legislation, and social media campaigns. The organization has a long history but more recently has been active in trying to stop the repeal of the Affordable Care Act (ACA) by the US Congress. Besides occupying Senate hallways during the 2017 attempt by Congress to repeal the bill, the group utilized the hashtag #ADAPTandRESIST on social media to spread their message. Table 6.2 represents the top ten Facebook groups engaged in the disability network.

Hashtags like #ADAPTandRESIST are a content form that becomes an agent of those spreading the hashtag. The value of those hashtags is dependent upon those actors who spread the messaging. What's important here is that those actors are circulators of meaning whose actions help

Table 6.2 Disability network Facebook groups—total interactions

Id	*Appearance*	*Total interactions*	*Type*
ADAPT—American Disabled for Attendant Programs Today	604	13,062	FBGroup
Lydia X. Z. Brown—Autistic Hoya	4	1667	FBGroup
ADAPT of Texas	86	460	FBGroup
Center for Disability Rights	14	348	FBGroup
Access Living	17	341	FBGroup
Third Wave Feminism	1	268	FBGroup
Colorado Cross-Disability Coalition	13	191	FBGroup
Jason's Connection	3	176	FBGroup
Thomas Oh for Congress	1	78	FBGroup
Side with Love	1	69	FBGroup

to spread and amplify the messaging as it circulates within and builds out the network. The intent, therefore, is to use hashtags to not only build the community but also to reach across to other clusters that form the larger social network, in essence becoming boundary breakers. Spreading a hashtag across a network generates a larger network, although this may result in a less dense network that refers to the proportion of existing ties to the total number of possible ties in the network. In other words, the larger the network, the greater possibility that it will be less dense.

Disability Rights on Twitter

Often overlooked are the disability communities who may be prevented from utilizing social media to its fullest due to the lack of accessibility of platforms denying them inclusion on disability issues and other social movements in which they would like to engage. This part of the case study focuses on the disability rights social network on Twitter. The Twitter application programming interface (API; http://apiwiki.twitter.com) was utilized to retrieve 5557 tweets from August to December 2020. To process, analyze, and visualize the data, the research relied on Netlytic software (Netlytic.org). The data set was comprised of 4503 unique posters; the search included terms—"disabled," "disability," "disabilities." Figure 6.5 charts the number of posts over time with peak periods at the end of August, September, and December.

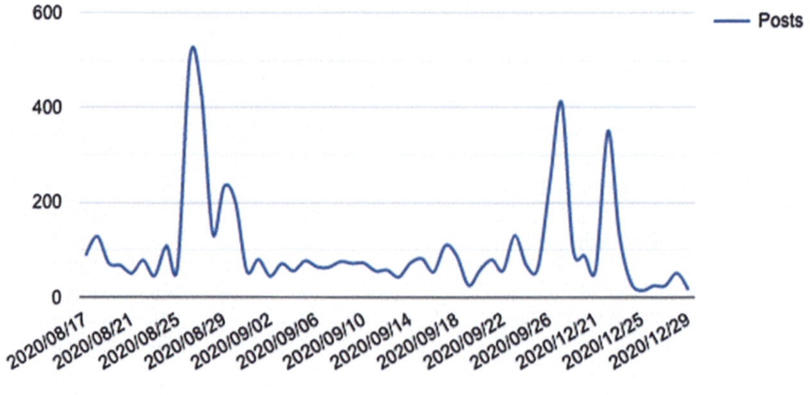

Fig. 6.5 Disability rights Twitter posts over time

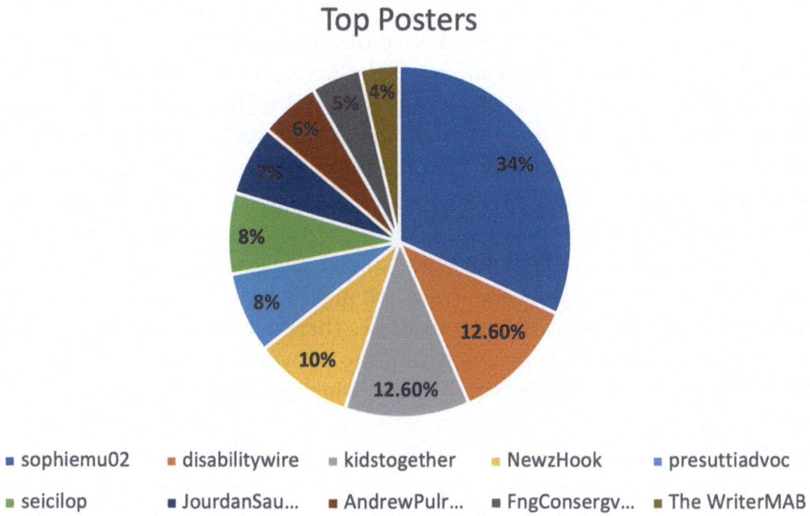

Fig. 6.6 Top ten disability rights posters

The top ten posters in the network are indicated below with their respective percentages (Fig. 6.6). Poster @sophiemu02 was responsible for 34 percent of the interactions on the disability network. This poster's cluster can be seen in the visualizations below (Fig. 6.8) reflecting interest in cerebral palsy.

The name network (Fig. 6.7) refers to a social network of who mentions whom. Netlytic mines personal names in the messages in order to build the network. This network is comprised of 1241 posters with ties, with 3355 ties (including self-loops). The total number of names found in the network is 5685.

Himelboim and colleagues studied topic networks on Twitter looking for information flow characteristics as measured by network density, modularity, centralization, and isolated users.[34] These researchers developed a classification system based on centralization, which refers to the ways in which users are connected to a few actors in the network, hence a hierarchy forms regarding the flow of information. They identify six social network structures: Polarized Crowds (divided), In-Group (unified), Brand (fragmented), Communities (clustered), Broadcast, and Support (inward and outward hub and spoke). Those network structures come into play as measures of density and modularity are applied to the network. Using the LGL layout in Netlytic, a network map of the disability topic network on Twitter is visualized. The diameter of the network is 14, which refers to the maximum number of connections required to traverse the graph. In other words, network diameter is the number of steps it takes for the two most distant nodes to reach one another. Graph density is 0.002, which is a measure of the level of connected edges. As well, this measures the interconnectedness of individuals within the network. A density measure closer to one is considered a dense network, conversely a number closer to zero, as is the case here, suggests a sparse graph in which the users are not highly interlinked. As the network map indicates there are holes within the network. The separation of clusters within the network can also be measured through the modularity statistic (0.83), which is a common indicator of the number of clusters within the network. As the network grows, users (subsets of nodes) form clusters. However, as those clusters form, it is possible that network may become less dense. When users follow one another on Twitter or friend one another on Facebook, they begin to develop pathways regarding the flow (edges) of information. As pathways develop and the clusters form, information flows freely within a given cluster; however, information flow across clusters may be restricted because of the lack of connectivity between the clusters. As modularity in the disability topic network is closer to 1, the network is considered divided as opposed to unified, although different clusters may in and of themselves be dense. Reciprocity at 0.03 is low suggesting there is little back and forth but more retweeting than commenting or replying to others.

In addition to the ways in which like-minded people engage on a topic within a social network, so too do social networks tend to have a hierarchical structure (Fig. 6.7). Oftentimes when we think of hierarchy in a social network, reference is being made to a news medium, media figure, or opinion leader of some sort. And sometimes social networks are more egalitarian with many actors extending the flow of information and sharing. However, because an actant can be an ordinary person who for various reasons may share more information than others, a non-elite influencer, for example, in essence amplifying the topic. Therefore, hierarchy in this sense is not necessarily a top-down affair but rather can be a bottom up. In the disability topic network, at the center of the fuchsia-colored cluster is @sophiemu02, who tweets about cerebral palsy. In this cluster, she has an out-degree centrality of 180 connections. Each of the clusters depicted

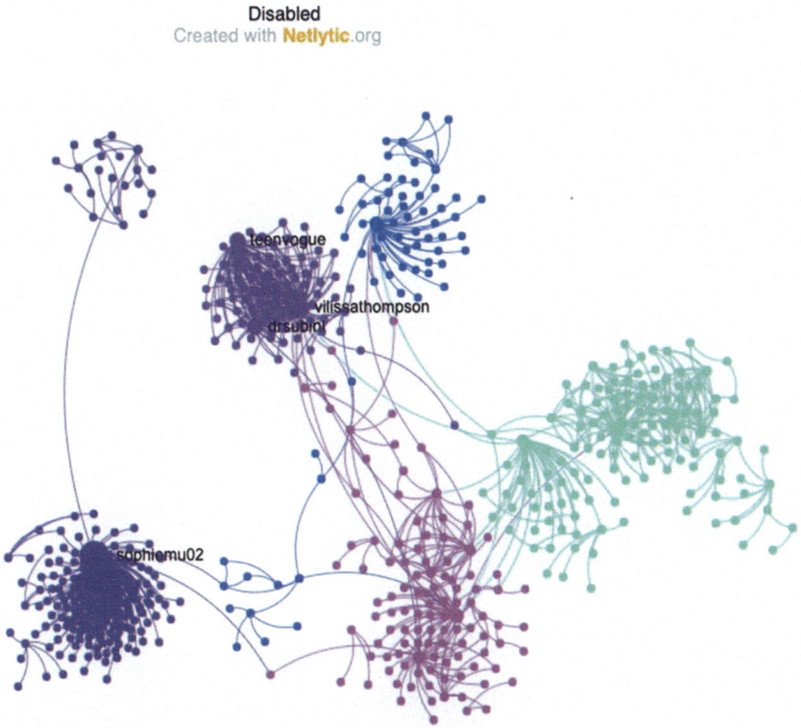

Fig. 6.7 Disability rights Twitter name network

below reflect an interest in a particular aspect of disability. The blue and yellow clusters, for example, reference news articles about disabilities.

The chain network (Fig. 6.8), which refers to the network of who replies to whom reflects posting behavior among those engaged in the social network. In this disability chain network, there are 574 posters with ties and 1872 ties (including self-loops). As the network map below indicates, there is one dominant cluster within the broader social network. The overall network statistics are as follows:

Diameter: 7
Density: 0.004
Centralization: 0.35
Modularity: 0.48

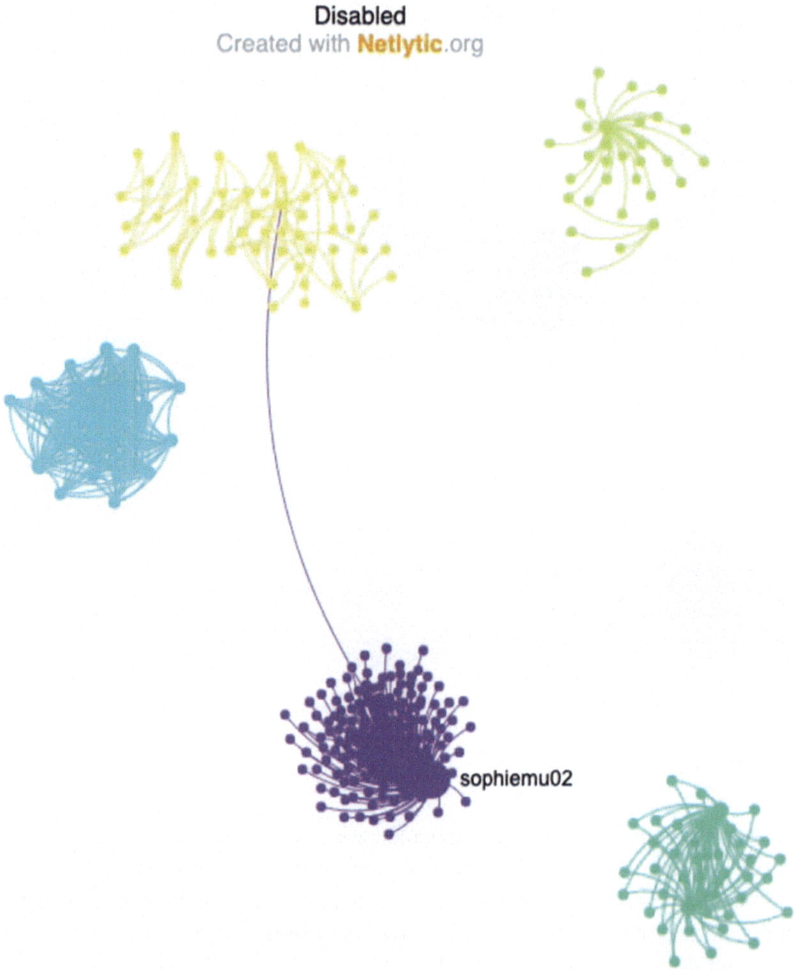

Fig. 6.8 Disability rights Twitter chain network

The largest cluster, a typical hub and spoke, in the chain network is based on 180 replies to a Tweet regarding preexisting condition for those afflicted by cerebral palsy. This is noted in the visualization below (Fig. 6.8) by the large red cluster. The yellow cluster, it is noted, is a reply to US Representative Tony Coelho regarding the lack of opportunity afforded by the government regarding employment of disabled people. The green cluster represents replies regarding a video that went viral in which a young man with a pronounced stutter who attributed his ability to speak publicly to then presidential candidate Joe Biden. What makes this disability network interesting is the varied aspects of disability that are represented in the different clusters. We can also see in the visualization how messages spread outward within the cluster, but with few instances of breaking boundaries reaching other clusters within the network.

This is not a highly centralized network, reflective of a hub and spoke structure. This can be seen most distinctly in the cluster surrounding @ sophiemu02. Applying the network typology, the disability network based on various measures can be categorized as Broadcast and Support, as these represent "hub and spoke" typologies.

Disability Influencers on Twitter

Similar to the ways in which clusters are segmented in the disability network, reflecting different disabilities or aspects of disabilities, so too does the disability influencer network on Twitter. That is to say, each of the influencers is supporting a community serving as an advocate and inspiring others on various disability issues. In order to round out this case study, an analysis of disability influencers on Twitter was conducted. The following Twitter handles were identified as being active in supporting disability issues: @dbrodey, @RebeccaCokley, @GlobalDisabilit, @gettinghired, @AndrewPulrang, @jonhassell, @DisabilityIN, @MSFTEnable, @ TheArcUS, and @DHorizons. Similar to the analysis above, the Twitter application programming interface (API; http://apiwiki.twitter.com) was utilized to retrieve 2605 tweets from December 26, 2020, to January 1, 2021 (Fig. 6.9). To process, analyze, and visualize the data, the research relied on Netlytic software (Netlytic.org). The data set was comprised of 1427 unique posters, using the Twitter handles of the influencers identified above.

Among the influencers is Denise Brodey, a journalist writing for several major news and feature publications. Global Disability Inclusion is a company that builds disability inclusion programs on a global basis. Their interest is inclusion in the workplace and marketplace. Andrew Pulrang is a disability rights advocate who focuses on disability issues with a unique angle. Microsoft also Tweets about accessibility touting their accessible hardware and training. The Arc is a US national community rights

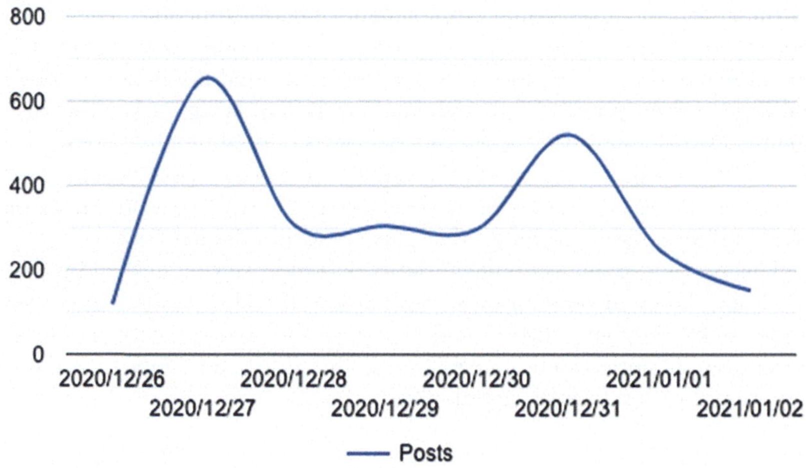

Fig. 6.9 Disability influencers posts over time

advocate on behalf of people with disabilities. Disability Horizons is an online magazine publishing stories about disability and education for an inclusive world. Disability: IN is a nonprofit organization serving businesses worldwide promoting inclusion of people with disabilities. Jonathan Hassell is thought leader and consultant in the area of usability and accessibility. Getting Hired is a recruitment service for employers seeking to hire people with disabilities. And Rebecca Cokley is a disability rights advocate working for the Center for American Progress.

Figure 6.10 maps the disability influencers name network. The network diameter refers to the maximum number of connections required to traverse the graph. The diameter for this network is 30, which suggests there are that many steps for the two most distant nodes to reach one another. This disability influencers network is not very dense, as the density measure is 0.003. The closer the value is to one, the network is considered to be dense; this network, however, is sparse. This suggests there are gaps or holes within the network.

Each of these influencers represents a distinct area of interest regarding disability, and each offers a unique approach to accessibility and inclusion. Reciprocity refers to ties that show two-way communication. It is a measure of the reciprocal ties in relation to the total number of ties in the network. Reciprocity, in this instance, is 0.176, which is a low value

Fig. 6.10 Disability influencers Twitter name network

suggesting that conversations are one-sided, perhaps reflective of retweeting a message. This is significant as retweeting a message is one way to build out the cluster and perhaps reach across boundaries to other clusters within the broader social network. The next network measure, centralization is 0.241, which is a low measurement, indicating this is a decentralized network where information flows more freely between participants in the network. Finally, modularity is a way to determine distinct communities within the broader social network. In this instance, modularity is 0.40. Netlytic calculates low modularity, less than 0.5, which suggests that clusters will overlap more and that the network will be made up of a core

Fig. 6.11 Disability influencers Twitter name network (number of times name is mentioned)

group of nodes. This is apparent in the colors of clusters within the visualization that indicate various clusters that make up the network.

As this is a network of influencers, Fig. 6.11 is a representation of top 30 names most mentioned in the flow of network information. For example, civil rights activist Rebecca Cokley is mentioned 1122 times and Andrew Pulrang, who tweets from the perspective of a person with a disability, is mentioned 516 times. Tony Martinez, a former Obama White House official, was mentioned 489 times. As their stories, experiences, and ideas, along with those of their followers circulate on Twitter, person to person, everyone is not connected to everyone else. However, key actors within the network—influencers—serve as connectors.

Conclusion

In this chapter ethical considerations were applied to the use of technologies that may impact those engaged in social movements. The chapter applied the concepts of accessibility as exemplars of how technology may impact inclusion. The chapter began with a discussion of the ethics of artificial intelligence in facial recognition and in newer more advanced uses context recognition that through deep learning such technologies may result in discriminatory practices. It was pointed out that both governments and private enterprises are utilizing this technology. The question raised in the chapter regards how far such technologies intrude into everyday life. Working toward cloud ethics, the chapter further questioned the issue of authorship when it comes to algorithmic development, as it was point out that through machine learning, there is little or no transparency as an algorithm may take on a life of its own. There are tensions that arise between activists who may be engaged in cloud protesting and those values of technologists who create algorithms in a vacuum not knowing or understanding the full implications of their work.

Ethical issues, it was pointed out, extend beyond technologies and the technologists who are responsible for creating them to consider those who are engaged in social movement research. It was pointed out that social movement research is unique because of the potentially involving relationship between the object of research, a social movement, and the researcher. Direct participation in a movement was one consideration, and the "outing" of those engaged in a movement in the process of researching a movement is another ethical issue. The chapter concluded that it is essential that researchers studying social movements remain aware of their role as observer-participants and the implications for "outing" those engaged in the movement. Additionally, there are issues regarding the objective/subjective role that researchers may play when studying social movements. The chapter moved on to consider the socially responsible role that corporations play as they shift from a shareholder to stakeholder orientation. In the latter, stakeholder capitalism was pointed out to be a movement itself as corporations play a role in contemporary society to go beyond mere profit making to consider issues related to societal welfare.

As social movement ethics is such a broad topic, the case study presented in this chapter goes back to issues related to the development of technologies, but instead of looking at algorithmic bias, the case study focuses on another form of bias, accessibility both with regard to the ability of disabled people to utilize social media platforms to engage on issues related to particular disabilities and their ability to engage directly in social movements. For example, the Disability March was part of the Women's March on Washington (https://disabilitymarch.com/).

Chapter 7 takes a forward look at performing media activism as social media platforms continue to evolve and splinter into newer platforms. The Twitter of 2007 or the Facebook of 2004 are quite different today then their humble beginnings. But in addition to the larger networks utilized by activists—Facebook, Twitter, and YouTube, there continues to evolve newer platforms like Parler, Gab, Rumble, and MeWe whose focus is more narrowly directed toward right-wing politics. The chapter concludes with a description of the software that was utilized in this book to describe performing media activism and analyze the social networks.

Notes

1. BBC.com (April 26, 2019). Sri Lanka attacks: Death toll revised down by 'about 100'. Retrieved from: https://www.bbc.com/news/world-asia-48059328.
2. Amoore, L. (2020). *Cloud Ethics: Algorithms and the Attributes of Ourselves and Others*. Durham, NC: Duke University Press. p. 4.
3. Jennings, R. (August 6, 2020) Government Scraps Immigration "Streaming Tool" before Judicial Review. UK Human Rights Blog. Retrieved from: https://ukhumanrightsblog.com/2020/08/06/government-scraps-immigration-streaming-tool-before-judicial-review/.
4. John, B. (n.d.) Governed by Numbers. Retrieved from: https://www.doc.gold.ac.uk/~bjohn002/councilwatch/index.html.
5. Amoore, L. *Cloud Ethics*. p. 164.
6. Amoore, L. Ibid., p. 170.
7. Hanna, A. & Whittake, M. (December 31, 2020). Timnit Gebru's Exit from Google Exposes a Crisis in AI. *Wired.com*. Retrieved from: https://www.wired.com/story/timnit-gebru-exit-google-exposes-crisis-in-ai/amp.
8. Women in AI Ethics. (n.d.). https://lighthouse3.com/womeninaiethics/about.html.
9. Center for Human Technology. (n.d.). https://www.humanetech.com/who-we-are.
10. Boswell, L. (n.d.). Getting Pulled Over? Siri Can Secretly Record It. Medium.Com. Retrieved from: https://medium.com/@lilalilaboswell/getting-pulled-over-siri-can-secretly-record-it-2f58b02d63e0.
11. Browne, Ibid.
12. Browne, S. (2020). The Feds Are Watching: A History of Resisting Anti-Black Surveillance. *Level.Medium.Com*. Retrieved from: https://level.medium.com/the-feds-are-watching-a-history-of-resisting-anti-black-surveillance-b2242d6ceaad.

13. Hamilton, I.A. (November 24, 2020). While Jeff Bezos spends billions on his 'Earth Fund,' Amazon is reportedly monitoring climate change groups including Greta Thunberg's as potential threats. *BusinessInsider.com*. Retrieved from: https://www.businessinsider.com/amazon-jeff-bezos-climate-change-groups-greta-thunberg-2020-11.
14. Milan, S. (2015). From Social Movements to Cloud Protesting: The evolution of collective identity. *Information, Communication & Society*, 18:8, pp. 887–900
15. Datactive. (n.d.). Covid19 from the margins. *Data-activism.net*. Retrieved from: https://data-activism.net/blog-covid-19-from-the-margins/.
16. Milan, S. (2015). Ibid., p. 11.
17. Milan, S. (2015). Ibid., p. 8.
18. Milan, S. (2014). The Ethics of Social Movement Research. In Methodological Practices in Social Movement Research. Oxford University Press. Retrieved from: https://oxford.universitypressscholarship.com/view/10.1093/acprof:oso/9780198719571.001.0001/acprof-9780198719571-chapter-18.
19. Milan, S. (2014). Ibid.
20. Chesters, G. (2012). Social Movements and the Ethics of Knowledge Production. *Social Movement Studies*. iFirst, pp. 1–16. https://doi.org/10.1080/14742837.2012.664894.
21. Chester, G. (2012). Ibid., p. 2.
22. Cordner, A., Ciplet, D., Brown, P. & Morello-Frosch, R. (2012). Reflexive Research Ethics for Environmental Health and Justice: Academics and Movement Building. *Social Movement Studies*. 11:2, pp. 161–176, DOI: https://doi.org/10.1080/14742837.2012.664898.
23. Dawson, M.C. & Sinwell, L. (2012). Ethical and Political Challenges of Participatory Action Research in the Academy: Reflections on Social Movements and Knowledge Production in South Africa. *Social Movement Studies*, 11:2, pp. 177–191, DOI: https://doi.org/10.1080/14742837.2012.664900.
24. de Jong, A. (2012). The Gaza Freedom Flotilla: Human Rights, Activism and Academic Neutrality. *Social Movement Studies* 11:2, pp. 193–209, DOI: https://doi.org/10.1080/14742837.2012.664901.
25. Detrixhe, J. (October 7, 2020). The difference between shareholder and stakeholder capitalism. *Quartz.com*. Retrieved from: https://qz.com/1909715/the-difference-between-stakeholder-and-shareholder-capitalism/.
26. Just Capital. (n.d.). https://justcapital.com/mission-impact/.
27. McFadden, C. (May 23, 2020). How Did Tim Berners-Lee Change the World With the World Wide Web? *Interesting*

Engineering. Retrieved from: https://interestingengineering.com/how-did-tim-berners-lee-change-the-world-with-the-world-wide-web.
28. Essential Accessibility. (May 6, 2020). Web Accessibility Lawsuits: What's the Current Landscape. Retrieved from: https://www.essentialaccessibility.com/blog/web-accessibility-lawsuits.
29. YouTube Data Tools. (n.d.). *Digital Methods.com*. https://tools.digitalmethods.net/netvizz/youtube/mod_videos_net.php.
30. Leak, B. (May 30, 2020). Disability on YouTube: Growing Representation Within the Digital Sphere. *Teneighty magazine*. Retrieved from: https://teneightymagazine.com/2020/05/30/disability-on-youtube-growing-representation-within-the-digital-sphere/.
31. YouTube Data Tools. (n.d.) Digital Methods.com. https://tools.digitalmethods.net/netvizz/youtube/mod_video_info.php.
32. Smith, G. (August 28, 2020). Hollywood's Diversity Push Has Left Out One Important Group. *Bloomberg.com*. Retrieved from: https://www.bloomberg.com/news/articles/2020-08-28/hollywood-s-diversity-push-has-left-out-one-important-group.
33. ADAPT—Americans Disabled for Attendance Programs Today (n.d.). https://adapt.org/.
34. Himelboim, I., Smith, M., Rainie, L, Shneiderman, B. & Espina, C. (2017). Classifying Twitter Topic-Networks Using Social Network Analysis. *Social Media & Society*. January-March, pp. 1–13.

CHAPTER 7

The Present and Future of Performing Media Activism

It was over 400 years ago that William Shakespeare, in his play *The Tempest*, used the phrase, "What's past is prologue." Could that same quote apply to today's performance space we commonly refer to as digital media? Or to put it in more practical terms, as Melina Abdullah, co-founder of Black Lives Matter, states about the future of the movement: "While there is still plenty of work to be done to achieve lasting social justice, one of the … main goals seems to be coming to fruition as thousands around the globe have taken to the streets to support the movement's message. 'People all over the country and the world are recognizing that they have to plug in. We have all got to be engaged in the transformative work that's taking place. One of my greatest hopes when we first initiated Black Lives Matter, [is] that we become a mass movement. As we become a mass movement, we have the capacity to again fundamentally transform the world that we live in.' "[1] This final chapter takes a critical look at performing media activism as the role of technology continues to impact the everyday lives of citizens all around the world and the social movements that reflect their desire for a better world. The chapter will conclude with a description of the social network analysis (SNA) tools utilized in researching case studies presented in this book.

Concerns related to communicating about political, social, economic, and environmental issues did not start with the digital media revolution but rather had their beginnings decades before during the "print" era. Some would argue that the polarization that is experienced today at least

N. Alperstein, *Performing Media Activism in the Digital Age*,
https://doi.org/10.1007/978-3-030-73804-4_7

in the United States is rooted in the dissolution of the US Fairness Doctrine during Ronald Reagan's presidential administration in the 1980s. It was then that partisanship emerged as a feature of what we might characterize as left- and right-wing media. Of course, there was a partisan press in the eighteenth century. But partisanship of today is a key feature of the 24-7 cable news cycle, as news media disseminate news not only on mainstream channels but also utilize digital channels as well. However, platforms like Facebook or Twitter claim they are not news media, because as private corporations they are not subject to the "free speech" requirements of the US First Amendment. Into this multi-platform and multipurpose mix comes autonomous individuals who operate within this seemingly democratized media system in which anyone with a digital device and internet access can become a digital activist. Looking at the present with an eye toward the future, where does this polarized mix of media and actors position us as performers of media activism?

Cyberconflict and Performance

In terms of a theoretical framework, this book began by considering cyberconflict theory and what conflict might look like on various digital media platforms. The book defined conflict as a performance with the accoutrement of dramatic conventions that play out as posts or comments, tweets or retweets, videos, and still images, among other forms evident in social network content. When considering something "playing out," what came to mind is the idea of performance, social media being the stage where acts of complicity or resistance can take place. The stage most certainly can be the actual streets of Minneapolis or Paris. But the stage could traverse the offline world to play out on social media platforms where text and image perform the task of disseminating news and information; but moreover, they serve to align one's self with an issue or cause and help shape one's identity as a requirement for membership in a movement. What makes this performance orientation apropos of media activism is the unique characteristics of social media—connectivity and spreadability. Connectivity, in the form of engagement, can also be a way of distancing one's self from a political orientation, as in right- or left-wing politics. Performance also requires actors whose social roles could be those that might be considered lead actors—politicians, entertainers, sports figures, or other media or authority figures—or news media that perform their role within the social network, serving as intermediaries in disseminating news and information about a topic or issue. But performance extends to ordinary people who can serve as influencers in a movement, sometimes by virtue of some self-appointed status conferred on themselves or conferred by others and at other times status is a function of the individual tweeting or posting a lot of content, their own content, or that which is curated from others. As social networks that form around all of these actants, there inevitably is an associated hierarchy within an online social movement in which one person or organization may serve at the center as a hub and others within the network becoming like spokes in a wheel or actors serving as bridges to other clusters within the broader social network.

When conflict is an expression of the collective consciousness, textually or visually in online discourse, the network tends to form connected clusters, as well there may be isolates who circle around the network but don't connect to spokes within any of the clusters that make up the network. The polarization that we sometimes see in online discourse around social issues can be demonstrated and measured through the use of, among other attention-grabbing devices, toxic language by those engaged on an issue who may utilize language as well as images to amplify a particular position. And conflict is always going to involve drama, and by that, I mean a heightened sense of emotions associated with a social, economic, political, or environmental issue. In such cases sentiment—positive, neutral, or negative—can serve as a response to conflict. Considering those factors, the combination of a platform, actors, and heightened emotion provides an understanding that those are the key variables of performing media activism. Such a conceptualization of performance is a product of the digital age in which we live, and it manifests not only online, performance manifests in hybrid form and offline as well as people jockey for their own position in a protest for a selfie or to snap an image they plan to post declaring their presence and connection within a spectacle, in which case the action is more likely to be performative. Performing media activism, therefore, becomes a framework for understanding social movements in the digital age.

Changing Media Ecosystem

The digital media ecosystem changes as new platforms come online and others go by the wayside. There have been a plethora of new apps and messaging services, nascent one's like Parler, Gab, Rumble, or Telegraph growing their narrowly focused audiences as more established platforms like Facebook, Google, Apple, and Twitter come under the eye of regulators both in the United States and in Europe. The Facebook of 2004 is not the same as Facebook circa 2021. Twitter has changed too when it moved from 140 to 280 characters per tweet. While Facebook and other platforms continue to evolve, their user base is not likely to go away anytime soon; the mediaverse, however, continues to fracture into smaller and smaller pieces, appealing to more narrow interests of smaller audiences. Whether such niche platforms can exist within an advertising supported system remains to be seen. If Twitter, as it has been accused, has a liberal bias, then platforms like Parler, Gab, Rumble, and MeWe, along with messaging apps Signal and Telegram, take up the mantle for conservative causes. It is as if the ecosystem is turning into an echo chamber where the only voices heard are those with similar opinions; the implications for social movements are obvious. Even within contemporary social issues like those written about this book, the clusters that form within the broader network reflect not the general cause or hashtag campaign but are made up of attractors, those aligned with a movement, and detractors, those who operate within the same network sometimes with toxicity, amplifying their voices in an attempt to be heard above the din. Actors in the network may serve as hub and others within the cluster may serve as bridges to other clusters; that is the nature of an online social network that has taken up a cause or issue whether it be on the political right or left.

Social media platforms are not only splintering, but they are also evolving, like the short form video site TikTok or gaming site Twitch, which have both been utilized on behalf of social movements. Figure 7.1 provides a list of the most popular social media networks worldwide as of October 2020. Facebook Live, too, has demonstrated the successful use of livestreaming social movements. Signal is yet another messaging app whose subscribers doubled to 40 million monthly subscribers when Facebook changed the subscriber rules to WhatsApp. The platform has drawn the attention of right-wing political idealogues based on its "no holds barred" policy regarding content publishing. The attraction at present is those who don't feel comfortable on what they might call the liberal leaning Twitter or Facebook (whether that's true or not is another story). Even though their users may be narrow in ideology and small in number, it remains to be seen how such platforms might be a useful adjunct to digitally based social movements. In the world of digital technology, the only thing constant is change, so those organizing and participating in social

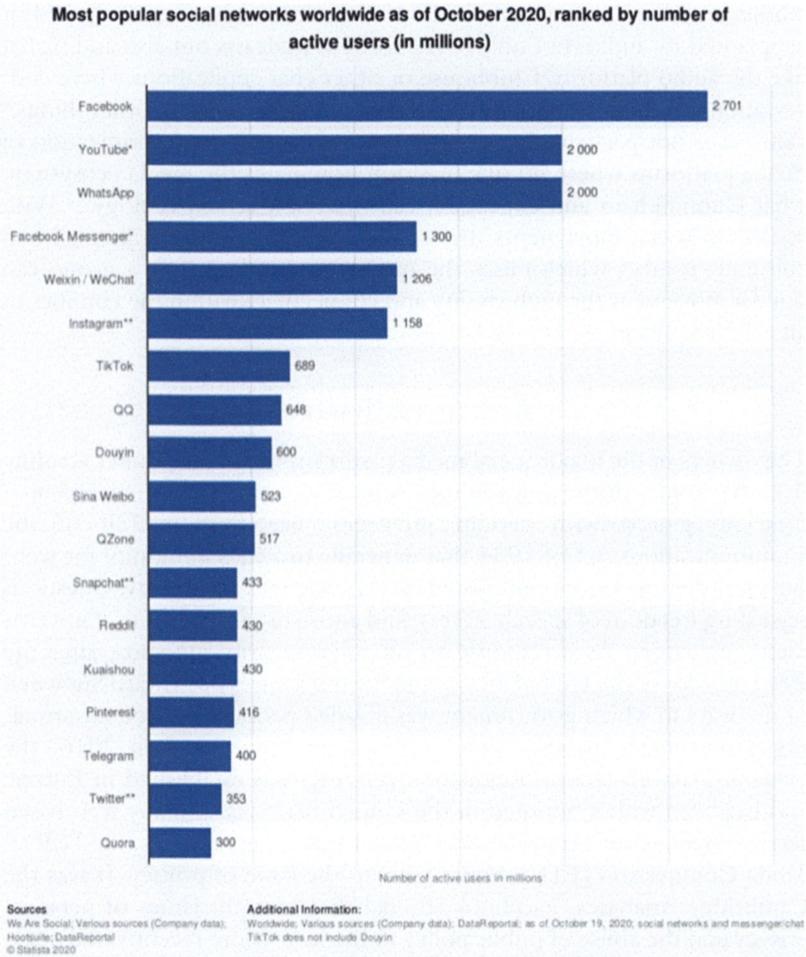

Fig. 7.1 Most popular social media networks. (Statistica.com (n.d.). Global Social Media Users 2020. Retrieved from: https://www.statista.com/statistics/272014/global-social-networks-ranked-by-number-of-users/)

movements need to maintain awareness of the social media platforms on which their audience or publics live. As well as platform evolution there is also a change in the types of content that is presented on social media platforms. From text—long and short forms—to image—still, including emojis or video—or any combination of those has been supplemented or supplanted by audio, not only in the form of podcasts but also audio chat like the audio platform, Clubhouse or other chat applications where conversation can focus on various topics or social issues, among other things.[2] While it is not particularly new, what we are seeing is a hybridization of media platforms where no one platform dominates the media ecosystem, what Cunningham and colleagues call the "new screen ecology."[3] With regard to social movements, these nascent platforms are still small and culturally insular, which raises the question regarding how a group can build a movement through virality and connectivity within the confines of an echo chamber?

Algorithm Barons

The owners of the major social media platforms have come under scrutiny from both sides of the political spectrum. And while social media companies are graced with certain privileges, like Section 230 of the Communications Act of 1934 that generally provides immunity for website publishers from content posted on their site by a third party. Questions regarding freedom of speech, access, and anti-trust are the focus if government regulators. As a response to intrusive security measures after the 9/11 attacks on the United States, and the disclosures by Edward Snowden of the ways in which government was invaded people's privacy, a transnational movement arose to force regulations. Established in 2016, the General Data Protection Regulation (GDPR) was established in Europe and has been widely adopted in the United States as so many web-based services operate on a transnational basis. In the United States, the Federal Trade Commission (FTC) would take up the issue of privacy. It was the Cambridge Analytica/Facebook scandal that brought issues of personal privacy and the abuse of public policy to the fore. More recently, the question as to whether social media companies like Facebook or Twitter are in actuality news media, which they contend they are not, has come under discussion, especially with regard to First Amendment, Freedom of the Press, rights afforded by the US Constitution. There are discussions regarding whether some of the internet behemoths should be broken up. Facebook, in particular, as the owner of Facebook, Facebook Messenger, Instagram, and WhatsApp is considered by some to a violation of antitrust regulations.[4] Over concerns about data privacy, Tim Berners Lee has called for more data privacy but not in the same way that regulators in the

US and Europe are calling for legislation. Rather, he has started two companies that provide individuals with more power regarding their data. "Too much power and too much personal data, he says, reside with the tech giants like Google and Facebook—'silos' is the generic term he favors, instead of referring to the companies by name." He says they have become "surveillance platforms and gatekeepers of innovation."[5]

Erica Chenoweth, best known perhaps for the 3.5 percent rule, that posits nonviolent protests are more likely to succeed if 3.5 percent of the population are engaged, suggests that looking forward, the COVID-19 pandemic may have driven social movements to focus on "relationship-building, grassroots organizing, strategy, and planning."[6] She makes reference to new information technologies that enable people in various parts of the world with internet access to learn about and perhaps be inspired by what is happening in countries other than their own. Also, civil resistance, a hot button issue, is drawing attention from global news media, and as digital media afford people with the opportunity to bypass traditional gatekeepers, they can communicate on a one-to-one basis. Additionally, she claims, in the digital age large numbers of people can engage in a movement without the need for a structured organization to plan and coordinate activities. She also points to the darker side of communication technologies in that it is easier for governments to monitor or surveil online activity. Among the ways she sees the future of nonviolent resistance is through the establishment of strengthened communication networks.

Truth vs. Misinformation

The digital age is one where it is difficult to discern truth from falsity. To that point, the late-night talk show host Steven Colbert coined the term "truthiness" in reference to the space between truth, and well, not so true. Many who grew up in the digital age or adapted to its foibles have experienced the tension between truth and alternative facts. It is perhaps simplistic to say that digital technologies have caused a society of misinformation or disinformation. But during the COVID-19 pandemic, the World Health Organization began to utilize the term "infodemic," referring to both the overload of information about the disease and the associated misinformation and disinformation that accompanies that overload. Because 70 percent of people in the United States obtain their news and information from the internet, we can attribute the tensions that people experience to the role that technology plays in everyday life with regard to misinformation and the significance of the role of misinformation is no less important for people engaged in the struggle for social justice or environmental change.

Writing in the 1640s, John Milton in his speech, *Areopagitica*, said "Let truth and falsehood grapple," as he believed that truth would always come out on top. Milton, like other moral philosophers of the Enlightenment, believed that people were reasoning, rational, individuals, deliberate in their thinking, and as such could judge an argument based on its merits. Simply put: a bad argument is best corrected by a good one. That was then, but in the digital age the issue has become so complex that the argument is no longer about the distinction between truth and misinformation or disinformation but rather about the doubt that emerges as people are called upon to work through what Milton would have called a rational judgment process. Perhaps what Milton wrote needs to be updated to fit the environment of the digital age: let truth and error grapple, doubt will out. If the net product of misinformation and disinformation stems from the inability of people to make rational judgments, especially in the context of an online environment, then we are left with the performance or worse the performative activism that has been written about in this book. Doubt is not a friend of social movements, as it is often fueled by misinformation or disinformation. The ability to damage or inhibit the development of a social movement may be rooted in, among other things, seeds of doubt. For example, Chap. 4, Conflict and Contentiousness, explored the anti-vaccine movement that predates issues related to a COVID-19 vaccine. Anti-vaxxers, in that case, planted seeds of doubt some of which were derived by a now debunked article claiming that vaccines cause autism. Out of that issue a movement grew and extends on the negative side to the treatment of people of color when it comes to vaccines and associated medical care. And, the anti-vaccine movement is fueled by conspiracy theories, including one that the vaccine has a micro-chip in it that allows the government to track anyone who has been vaccinated. Not true, but we live in an age where the QAnon movement has cornered the proverbial market on conspiracies and adherents use digital media to spread misinformation. Is the motivation for some digital activism to create a lack of certainty? People certainly prefer certainty in their lives, something echoed by both Descartes, the seventeenth-century French philosopher, and Wittgenstein, the twentieth-century Austrian philosophy. A relative to uncertainty is polarization, not knowing who or what to trust. All of this leads to attempts at amplification on various sides of an issue, not only manifested in words and sometimes action but also emotionally charged messaging on social media and the additional effect of having something repeated or rather circulated among a social network many times over. All of which potentially leads to information exhaustion. How to get back to the truth is anyone's guess.

Youth Culture and Social Movements

The deceased grunge rocker Kurt Cobain once said, "The duty of youth is to challenge corruption." If younger generations like Millennials and GenZ have lost faith in institutions, then it is likely that social movements will in the future take a different form, as institutionalization, the end of the four stages of social movement development no longer provides a likely outcome. As autonomous individuals replace institutions with self-reliance, significant shifts take place in the ways or means by which social movements develop. In his book *A Power and Governments Cannot Suppress*, historian and social thinker Howard Zinn states: "We don't have to engage in grand, heroic actions to participate in the process of change. Small acts, when multiplied by millions of people, can quietly become a power no government can suppress, a power that can transform the world."[7] However, many of those engaged in social movements operate outside the system. For example, leaders of the March for Our Lives movement bypassing government pressured retailers to change their approach to gun sales.

The likelihood therefore is that there will be more social movements, shorter-term social movements, less "sticky" social ideas tied to newer forms of mediated civic engagement. Digital media in the new age of social movements provide a platform by which individuals can engage in various ways without commitment and in that without getting their proverbial hands dirty in physically present protests, as social movements become more virtual, the actual only serving as spectacle to be transmitted perhaps as a livestream. As a result, the spectacle of real-life protest becomes mere fodder for online entertainment. The distrust of institutions is fueled by the proliferation of technologies that allow operatives to "game" the system, including algorithms that push content to the top of search or the more than 40 million bots operating on Twitter. According to a report by the Ford Foundation, "In fact, 62 percent of all Internet traffic is made up of programs acting on their own to analyze information, find vulnerabilities, or spread messages. Up to 48 million of Twitter's 320 million users are bots, or applications that perform automated tasks."[8] On the one hand, an automated system using bots to register voters might be a good thing, but they can also be utilized to spread misinformation. If we start from the present state of slacktivism, what can we expect from a future in which my bot is talking to your bot? Of course, not all bots are bad, as they can be a useful means to elevate stories, for example. But bots are just the tip of the proverbial iceberg, as newer forms like deep fakes become more prevalent, societies will continue to grapple with issues concerning privacy as they are related to the datafication of society. When considering the failure of institutions to solve many of today's problems, like climate change, Greta Thunberg has been described in the following way: "She's evidence of a changing culture of digital activism, one that's skewing younger and younger every time adult-run institutions get stuck in political gridlock."[9] However, young people are not necessarily rejecting all institutions but rather they are using them in a means-ends schema. As individuals usurp the traditional power and place of institutions replacing them with self-reliance, significant shifts take place in the development of social movements.

TikTok Generation

In Chap. 2, a discussion of the #NeverAgain hashtag associated with the March for Our Lives movement was presented. The teenagers who survived that shooting at the Marjory Stoneman Douglas school in Parkland, Florida, in 2018 grew up aware of past mass shootings from Columbine High School to the Sandy Hook Elementary School tragedy. In other words, members of GenZ have grown up with gun violence.[10] Because the Stoneman Douglas students were approaching voting age, they decided to use some of their energy at the voting polls to register younger voters in order to affect change not only in regard to gun violence but climate change, racial injustice, and immigration as well. GenZ is the most diverse generation in history. What makes this generation different than Millennials or GenXers is their use of social media and related technologies. But technology is never the cause of a social movement, as these are young people whose understanding and empathy for others drives them toward collective action, and as such social media is a means to an end. I think it's important not to refer to this as a social media revolution; rather it is an engaged generation that has grown up media savvy, and as a result they know how to utilize the tools that have been given to them.

TikTok has become one of the go-to platforms where young people perform media activism, perhaps because its short form is easily digested and has opened up creative opportunities for engagement. It is the "performativity" of visual platforms, like TikTok but also YouTube and Instagram that allow individuals to express their personalities as well as their personal beliefs within their peer subcultures. These platforms have lowered the barriers of entry and expanded the possibilities of what it means to be politically engaged. Creative value is placed on social media skillsets that young people feel confident in, and normalized the idea that being politically involved is not a niche but can be an everyday staple in one's social media diet. "As a result, posts that engage with some degree of social justice on TikTok tend to be favoured, and many TikTokers engage in viral duets and replies that publicly shame other TikTokers as a route to internet celebrity."[11] TikTok has been utilized on behalf of the global climate change movement to spark political action on the platform through, for example, time-lapse videos and other artistic endeavors. So too were the Australian bushfires of 2020 highlighted on TikTok through "informative updates, peer teaching and using humour to cope." The platform has been utilized to raise awareness of the Muslim Uyghurs in China.[12] And, there is an associated transmedia phenomenon whereby TikTok videos show up in Instagram Reels and YouTube Shorts, which could be seen as a form of cross posting or pilfering of content.

In one now-infamous instance, TikTokers and fans of K-Pop used the platform in a countermovement to disrupt a political rally of then presidential candidate Donald Trump. In that instance, as a result of the posts there were more than a million ticket requests, but the would-be attendees of the rally never showed up. It was all a ruse as this group of TikTokers registered for tickets but never had any intention of showing up.[13] Reflective of the diversity of youth culture, in what at first may seem like an ironic twist, it was K-pop fans of groups like BTS and Blackpink that used their social media prowess to use TikTok to engage in issues of race and social justice. They are strange bedfellows or at least seemingly so—TikTok, K-Pop fans, and social activism—and while most of the adherents are US based, these social issues have strong social resonance globally.[14] Henry Jenkins and colleagues in their book *By Any Media Necessary* see the use of new media among youth culture as a natural progression. The world of new platforms, like TikTok, memes, videos, and remixing pop culture are also being applied to political and social change. The authors cite the Harry Potter Alliance that fights for human rights, as an example. These newer forms of protest are dynamic practices of participatory culture.

Virtual Protesting

Whether it is a long-term trend or an effect of the COVID-19 pandemic, organizations are launching virtual protests to replace or supplement in-person protests. These include virtual walkouts, video conferencing protests, and video-game rallies.[15] Some examples include a virtual Black Lives Matter Protest by the Scottish Trades Union Congress (STUC), a London-based BLM virtual protest, in Mexico a virtual feminist protest against the death of a young woman thought to be murdered because of her feminist beliefs, and even Facebook employees staged a virtual "walk-out" to protest inflammatory language used on the site by Donald Trump. It might be that in the future social movements will take a multiplex approach to include in-person (offline) protests, virtual protests using apps, gaming, and video conferencing, all taking place simultaneously.

As most movements center their focus around an episodic event, like a march, organizers may believe that in order to gain the attention of mainstream media they have to utilize such tactics. However, in the digital age, temporality can be extended beyond the episode to consider the use of digital technologies before, during, and after an action, as a way to sustain the movement to further and perhaps more deeply engage with activists. Poell studied the connections between social media, temporality, and social protest. He concludes that despite the rise of social media and its use, it has not become easier to sustain attention to issues.[16] This dilemma is an outgrowth of the temporality of media—24-hour news cycle—in which attention is short-lived, and because a protest is "episodic," journalists are likely to move on as the news agenda dictates. Even the use of social media to extend beyond real-time reporting may not be enough to sustain interest. The question remains: how to sustain interest and in that engagement in the social movement? While the shift toward virtual protesting may be limited at this point and it may be short lived, however, because of the changing nature of much of global digital culture, there is reason to believe that virtual protesting will become a normal way to engage in a social movement, and it would behoove those who organize social movements to include those people who would rather opt for the virtual form of engagement.

As social movements have already taken to TikTok and Twitch to post commentary or live stream, protests also take place in the virtual worlds of gaming. To some people, whether it's the inability to attend a public protest or just the desire to participate virtually, engagement can take the form of a virtual protest within a game. In one instance, Hong Kong protesters used the game Grand Theft Auto V online, dressing up (in game) like riot police with water cannon trucks, players even dressed in riot gear, including gas masks. The players use a Reddit-like social site, LIHKG, to organize. Players "in game" trash subway stations, attack police, and throw bombs. The game which depicts a fictitious city based on Los Angeles, California, serves as virtual space where Hong Kong protesters can overlay their experience onto the "stage" without actually being on the streets of Hong Kong—a hyperreal form of performing media activism.[17] Grand Theft auto is not the only game utilized to simulate protests, as players of Animal Crossing, now banned in China, used the platform to stage virtual protests to fight for democracy (Fig. 7.1).[18] While some would say shifting to virtual protesting is a product of COVID-19 and the fear of catching or spreading the virus during actual protests, it remains to be seen whether this is a form of protest will be added to the repertoire of dissenters or is an effect of the pandemic moment.

Another virtual form of activism comes in the form of Public_Public_Address: A Nationwide Virtual Protest site (http://www.publicpublicaddress.com). The site is geared toward making participation in social movements accessible. In one instance, a teenager who wanted to protest the killing of George Floyd by a Minneapolis police officer but couldn't because she for health reasons uses a walker, submitted a video to the site from her home expressing her views. The website gathers all of the videos, an example of connective action, and broadcasts a live online feed 24 hours a day.[19] In another instance of virtual activism that spans multiple platforms, including Zoom, Instagram, and Facebook Live, 22,000 people from various parts of the world got together in an anti-racism protest to support the Black Lives Matter movement. The virtual protest, announced via an Instagram invitation (Fig. 7.2) in this case, took place at the same time as an in-person protest in London.[20] All of these examples portend a future of media activism that is virtual and continuous (Fig. 7.3).

Fig. 7.2 Animal Crossing Video Game Used to Protest Hong Kong Government

Influence of Influencers

Evgeny Morozov, author of *The Net Delusion: The Dark Side of Internet Freedom*, believes that technology makes digital activism affordable and accessible. While that is not always or universally true, as was pointed out in Chap. 6 of this book. Based on those two points, the author believes that digital activism could eventually displace the older type of in-person activism.[21] Morozov argues that social movements are in most instances hierarchical in their organizational structure, but the internet opens up digital activism to a "leaderless, decentralized, and not bound by any organizational structures." This view of digital activism, even as a leaderless and decentralized movement does not hold up to scrutiny, as influencers

Fig. 7.3 Instagram Invite to Virtual BLM Protest

serve in lieu of the kinds of opinion leaders we might historically have seen as driving a movement. Influencers come in many forms from digital media, who are actors in a social network in much the same way as individuals, political figures, and other media figures, like celebrities or microcelebrities. And although the digitally based social networks may at first appear monolithic, based on images of past experiences with in-person protests, in the digital age, anyone with a hashtag that triggers discourse or the ability to post, tweet, or retweet a lot can impact the network. When the digital network of a social movement is visualized, what we generally see, are clusters or communities—big and small—that form within the larger network. And, while some clusters may be tightly knit, others become less dense as the network over time begins to enlarge. While the Arab Spring may have turned into the Arab Winter, there is ample evidence that digitally based social movements or hybrid movements are alive and well, they just look different than they used to look. In Chap. 1 of this book the stages of social movement development were discussed, and at one stage the expectation is that the movement will become organized and perhaps more bureaucratic. But I think we need to in the digital age alter the model of what a social movement looks like as it moves through its stages of growth and development, and how its organization may not fit the mold of a pre-internet era. Yes, as Morozov contends, mobilizing is not organizing, but maybe what it means to be organized needs a new model; social movements in the digital age are messy. After all, the key elements of digitally based social movements are connectivity and spreadability. Based on those two characteristics, the virtual social movement, along with an in-person component, as Tere' calls them hybrid social movements, may be more inclusive than an in-person movement alone. But inclusivity implies there will be contentiousness at work as those engaged in the online network grapple with issues of truth and misinformation as individuals find their place at the hub, bridge or spoke of a social network.

Derek Thompson who writes about the results of an American values survey states, "it looks like something bigger is going on. Millennials and Gen Z are not only unlikely to call themselves Protestants and patriots, but also less likely to call themselves Democrats or Republicans. They seem most comfortable with being unaffiliated, even anti-affiliated. They are less likely than preceding generations to identify as 'environmentalists,' less likely to be loyal to specific brands, and less likely to trust authorities, or companies, or institutions. Less than one-third of them say they have 'a lot of confidence' in unions, or Silicon Valley, or the federal government, or the news, or the justice system. And don't even get them started on the banks."[22] One could assume that such widespread distrust in institutions would lead to greater activism especially on the part of younger generations. It may be, however, that they are "voting" with their thumbs not their feet when it comes to social activism. These findings echo a 2014 study of Millennials that characterized them as "detached from institutions, networked with friends."[23] Young people are tired of waiting, as evidenced by the very quick growth of the March for Our Lives movement that launched shortly after the killing of Parkland, Florida, high school students. And the Fridays4Future and Climate Strike movements led by young people like Greta Thunberg, whose unyielding persistence keeps her and the issue of climate change in the global spotlight.

Collective Action to Connective Action to Collective Consciousness

The concept of collective action is an extension of cyberconflict theory that fits squarely within the patterns of networked social movements. In a networked society collective action is tied to the concept of connective action as connectivity and spreadability are hallmarks of social media that are important to the present and future of media activism. Therefore, collective action leads to connective action which is a product of the collective consciousness of social networks. As such the networked social movement is transformed into a conscious, connected actor. The idea of collective consciousness is derived from Jung's theory of collective unconscious, which he describes as the "collection of knowledge and imagery that every person is born with and is shared by all human beings due to ancestral experience. Though humans may not know what thoughts and images are in their collective unconscious, it is thought that in moments of crisis the psyche can tap into the collective unconscious."[24] Through their expressions on digital platforms, autonomous individuals engaged in social movements are making their shared beliefs and ideas that they hold true and personal transparent for all to see, hence, the collective consciousness is the expression of shared beliefs and ideas that are common to a group engaged in a social movement. It is the collective that ultimately is important as it is the sum total of beliefs and ideas that do not require formal leadership or coordinated organization. As Castells points out, a "decentered structure maximizes changes of participation in the movement, given these are open-ended networks without defined boundaries, always reconfiguring themselves according to the level of involvement of the population at large."[25] The dynamic nature of a networked social movement allows the stage where media activism is performed to be both local and global, perhaps at the same time. The Black Lives Matter, Climate Strike, and MeToo movements stand as examples of the local/global nature of social movements.

Digital technologies serve as a conduit not a cause of social movements. As a conduit, they play a critical role as expressions of beliefs and ideas serve in the formation of attitudes and perhaps action. But in a digital world action takes on newer meaning as social practices may be limited to sharing thoughts and feelings and perhaps outrage, as issues become "amped-up" within the networked movement. As such collective action gives way to connected action that manifests as the collective consciousness of the movement. Interaction is the sum total of tweets, posts, or videos or through some other simulation. Having said that, digital media are not mere instruments of social movements; rather they are the foundation of a cultural practice that is based on the theory of performance explored in this book and the individual and connected actors—news media and media figures as well as ordinary people—that extend beyond traditional institutions to establish a new social compact among those actants. Such an arrangement is messy, uncontrolled, subject to the vagaries of polarized positions and conspiracy theories. Whether this is the World Wide Web societies initially bargained for or merely the Wild West remains to be seen. Regardless, people will always, as they have in the past, seek new means of expression and ways to engage with one another, as digital media are not static but are evolving and transformative as people find new ways to utilize existing media and shift to newer platforms in a quest to present their story and challenge the political and social order.

Social Network Analysis Techniques and Tools

There has been a shift over the past 50 years toward the recognition of the importance of structures of social networks including their hierarchies, but it has only been in the past 20 years that the use of communication technologies, and interactions among those engaged in innumerable social issues has required scholars to study activism on online social networks. Historically, such investigations might have been the domain of computer scientists, it has become the responsibility of humanities and social science researchers to gain access to digital date for critical analysis. The tools utilized in this book to study social movements, in essence, mediate the research by framing the kinds of questions that those tools are capable of answering, and scrutiny of social media platforms requires the use of digitally based research tools. In addition to presenting "hard numbers," the goal of this research has been to describe and interpret what is going on in the social networks under study. Fortunately, there are scholars who have the requisite background in computer science to build the tools needed to study online social networks. In this book, you have seen the use of not just one tool, but multiple social network analysis tools, sometimes used in combination. Research based on the social network analysis approach is always going to be impacted by the limits placed on access to APIs by the companies that own the platforms. It's also important, as this book has stressed, to keep in mind that there are ethics that need to be applied to the study of social networks with particular regard to privacy. And finally, not only have the tools available for social network analysis changed over the years, but the web also itself has changed with some platforms and their data going away and at the same time newer platforms emerge. This book represents a step forward in elucidating how social movements in the digital age are structured and measured with an eye toward better understanding their formation and growth as movements work through established stages of development.

The approach taken in this book represents a reconciliation of the fields of media studies and digital humanities with computer science as newer techniques allow researchers to study the complex interactions and relationships that people have as they perform media activism. John Turkey, who coined the term "software," wrote in *Exploring Data Analysis* that a philosophy was needed that went beyond computational science to consider what underlies those numbers. Such thinking led to critical media studies approach, media systems approach, or culture of connectivity approach applied to the study of digital platforms. There was a time when there were few television channels, and limited number of daily newspapers, but the media landscape has exploded which calls for newer ways of accessing data and considering the multiple platforms both mainstream and alternative that operate as a multiplex media system. Bernard Reider maintains that the difference between "digital" or "computation" methods in media studies and the digital humanities is the research object: rather than digitized sources, we study "natively digital objects."[26]

The theories used in this book that serve as a framework for understanding social movements in the digital age were supported by novel research methods including social network analysis software to study social media platforms and their users. The analytic approach taken in this book, based on the study of social networks, required the use of research tools and computational methods that allowed for thematic analysis, sentiment analysis, and visual mapping of the social structures that make up online social networks. The book concentrated on major platforms like Twitter, Facebook, Reddit, and YouTube to examine key social movements including the March for Our Lives, Climate Strike, Vaxxhappens, George Floyd, and Disability Network. The section that follows provides a description of particular social media analysis techniques and tools utilized in conducting research on social movements. Sometimes the research tools are utilized on their own because they are comprehensive, while others are utilized in combination. For example, YouTube data tools yielded data regarding the structure of disability video networks described in Chap. 6. The tool provides a data file in graph ml format that can then be exported to Gephi for additional analysis. A description of each tool, including Gephi, Netlytic, Communalytic, CrowdTangle, Media Cloud, Stanford Cable TV News Analyzer, and YouTube Data Tools, as well as Google Trends and nGram follows, along with a discussion of the applicability of each to studying performing media activism in the digital age.

Netlytic (https://netlytic.org/home/)

Netlytic is a community-supported text and social networks analyzer that can automatically summarize and visualize public online conversations on social media sites. Netlytic also conducts textual analysis that provides a sense of sentiment regarding an online discussion. The software was developed at the Social Media Lab at Ryerson University in Canada. The research tool collects publicly available data from several social media platforms, although as of December 2018, Facebook disabled the Instagram API, which makes it impossible as of this writing for researchers to use this tool for such purposes. Presently, Twitter, YouTube, Reddit data, RSS feeds, and text/csv files (which can be uploaded for processing) can be analyzed. In addition, there is an ancillary tool Communalytic (description below) that allows researchers to analyze Twitter and Reddit posts and comments. With Netlytic researchers can examine conversations taking place online and look for patterns through various data visualizations. Netlytic was utilized in Chap. 2 to analyze the #NeverAgain hashtag movement of the March for Our Lives. The software was also utilized to analyze the social movement associated with #GeorgeFloyd and Black Lives Matter.

Communalytic (https://communalytic.com)

Communalytic is a newer research tool designed to collect, analyze, and visualize publicly available data from Reddit or Twitter. One of the unique qualities of this tool is its ability to investigate patterns of anti-social behavior, defined as toxicity. For example, users can identify a subreddit, which are online forums on specific topics, and Communalytic utilizing the Perspective API produces an analysis based on seven categories of toxicity. Currently there are over two million subreddits. Users subscribe to a subreddit and can post and comment according to rules set forth by the moderators. Communalytic allows researchers to specify a particular subreddit and to control the data collection within a seven-day period. Users can export an XML file for additional analysis and a graph file, the data of which may be upload to Gephi to create network visualizations. Communalytic was utilized in Chap. 4, Conflict and Contentiousness, to analyze the Vaxxhappens subreddit as an example of resistance movements. The focus on this analysis was to gauge the toxicity of the messaging on the Vaxxhappens subreddit.

CrowdTangle (https://help.crowdtangle.com/en/articles/4558716-understanding-and-citing-crowdtangle-data)

CrowdTangle tracks public content on Facebook Pages and Groups. It also tracks data on Instagram and popular subreddits. While the software does not track typical metrics like reach or impressions, it does track interaction and provides some data on sentiment. The service is clear to point out that they do not track private content, as in private Facebook Groups. But public content is discoverable through search and engagement data, also known as interactions, including shares, video views, comments, and reactions are available for sorting and additional analysis. CrowdTangle data can be cleaned and organized into node and edge files that can be exported to Gephi in order to create visualizations of social networks. CrowdTangle was used in Chap. 6 to study the Disability Network on Facebook, and it was utilized in Chap. 3 to study the climate strike influencer network.

YouTube Data Tools (https://tools.digitalmethods.net/netvizz/youtube/)

YouTube Data Tools (YTDT) were developed out of the University of Amsterdam by Bernhard Rieder. There are several modules that extract data using the YouTube API v3. These modules include Channel Search, Channel Network, Video List, Video Network, and Video Info. In addition to providing the data in tabular format for additional processing and analysis, graph files are produced that may be exported to Gephi in order to create visualizations of the various YouTube-related networks. In Chap. 6, YouTube Data Tools was utilized in order to analyze and visualize the disability video vloggers network.

Gephi (https://gephi.org/)

Gephi is an open-source graph visualization program that runs on Windows, Mac OS X, and Linux. It has a number of features of value to social network analysis. The software creates network maps of community organizations and small-world networks. It provides calculations important to understanding network connections including the following: network centrality, density, path length, diameter, modularity, and clustering coefficient. There are plug-ins with additional measures and a spigot Twitter Streaming Importer to extract data directly from Twitter and analyze networks in real time. Gephi was utilized in the case study in Chap. 3 to analyze and visualize the influence of Greta Thunberg, and it was utilized in Chap. 6 in the case study of the Disability Network.

Media Cloud (https://mediacloud.org/)

Media Cloud is another open-source platform that analyzes the news media ecosystem. It tracks millions of stories published online and provides data to researchers to analyze and visualize how stories traverse the news media network. There are three tools available to researchers: Explorer, Topic Mapper, and Source Manager. Media Cloud was utilized in the Chap. 5 case to study the stories related to the murder of George Floyd. The platform was also utilized in the Chap. 3 case study of stories related to climate activist Greta Thunberg.

Stanford Cable TV News Analyzer (https://tvnews.stanford.edu/)

The Stanford Cable TV News Analyzer was created by the Computer Graphics Lab at Stanford University in collaboration with the John S. Knight Fellowship Program. The analyzer is based on the Internet Archive's TV News Archive that includes 24-7 recordings of CNN, Fox News, and MSNBC between January 1, 2010, and January 20, 2021. The data set is updated regularly and includes 280,000 hours of video. Search can be for a number of variables including a name, network, date, or topic. In addition to producing a graph including a timeline denoting coverage, the analyzer provides clips of the actual news segment for further analysis of content.

Google Trends (https://trends.google.com/trends/?geo=US)

Google Trends is tool that allows researchers to monitor search behavior of those users of Google search on a regional, national, or worldwide basis over time. Trends allows you to view web search data back to 2004. It can also be utilized for comparative keyword search as was the case in Chap. 5 to explore search for several hashtags related to Black Lives Matter. The graphs produced by Google Trends indicate event-triggered spikes in search which is of value to those studying social movements, as they can mark periods when topics or issues are trending. Trends does not provide search volume; rather, it provides a scale of 1–100 indicating degree of relevance to a search term or terms. Trends data comes from five sources: web search, image search, news, shopping, and YouTube, and data can be location based.

Google Books nGram Viewer (https://books.google.com/ngrams/info)

In addition to Google Trends, Google also offers nGram book viewer that provides insights into the use of words and phrases in books dating back to the 1800s. nGram was utilized in Chap. 1 to look at the use of terms "activism" and "social movements" over an extended period of time. Users can specify years and trends based on a large number of criteria. Data can be extracted for further analysis as well as graphs that may be published.

Notes

1. Scheer, R. (June 19, 2020). The Powerful Past, Present and Future of Black Lives Matter. KCRW.com. Retrieved from: https://www.kcrw.com/culture/shows/scheer-intelligence/the-powerful-past-present-and-future-of-black-lives-matter.
2. Pardes, A. (May 22, 2020). What is Clubhouse, and Why Does Silicon Valley Care? *Wired.com*. Retrieved from: https://www.wired.com/story/what-is-clubhouse-why-does-silicon-valley-care/.
3. Cunningham, S., Craig, D. & Silver, J. (April 2016). YouTube, multichannel networks and the accelerated evolution of the new screen ecology, *Convergence*. 22:4. DOI: https://doi.org/10.1177/1354856516641620.

4. Hughes, C. (May 9, 2019). It's Time to Break Up Facebook. *The New York Times.* Retrieved from: https://www.nytimes.com/2019/05/09/opinion/sunday/chris-hughes-facebook-zuckerberg.html.
5. Lohr, S. (January 10, 2021). He Created the Web. Now He's Out tok Remake the Digital World." The New York Times. Retrieved from: https://www.nytimes.com/2021/01/10/technology/tim-berners-lee-privacy-internet.html.
6. Chenoweth, E. (2020). The Future of Nonviolent Resistance. *Journal of Democracy.* 31:3, pp. 69–84.
7. Zinn, H. (2006). *A Power Governments Cannot Suppress.* CA: City Lights Publishers.
8. Negrón, W. & Hargrave, M. (May 30, 2017). Why you should care about bots if you care about social justice. FordFoundation.org. Retrieved from: https://www.fordfoundation.org/just-matters/equals-change-blog/posts/why-you-should-care-about-bots-if-you-care-about-social-justice/.
9. Ellis, E. (September 28, 2019). Greta Thunberg's Digital Rise Calls Back to a Pre-Digital Era. *Wired.com.* Retrieved from: https://www.wired.com/story/greta-thunberg-social-media/.
10. Janfaza, R. (June 22, 2020). 'We're tired of waiting': GenZ is ready for a revolution. *Cnn.com.* Retrieved from: https://www.cnn.com/2020/06/16/politics/genz-voters-2020-election/index.html.
11. Abidin, C. (2021). Mapping Internet Celebrity on TikTok: Exploring Attention Economies and Visibility Labours. *Cultural Science Journal*, 12:1, pp.77–103. DOI: https://doi.org/10.5334/csci.140.
12. Abidin, C, (2021). Ibid.
13. Lorenz, T, Browning, J. & Frenkel, Sheera. (June 21, 2020). TikTok Teens and K-Pop Stans Say They Sank Trump Rally. *The New York Times.* Retrieved from: www.nytimes.com/2020/06/21/style/tiktok-trump.
14. Coscarelli, J. (June 22, 2020). Why Obsessive K-Pop Fans Are Turning Toward Political Activism. *The New York Times.* Retrieved from: https://www.nytimes.com/2020/06/22/arts/music/k-pop-fans-trump-politics.html.
15. Trendhunter.com. (n.d.). Organizations are launching online protests to fight injustices. Retrieved from: https://www.trendhunter.com/pro-trends/virtual-protesting.
16. Poell, T. (2020). Social media, temporality, and the legitimacy of protest. *Social Movement Studies.* 19:5–6, pp. 609–624. Retrieved from: https://doi.org/10.1080/14742837.2019.1605287.
17. BBC News (December 23, 2019). Hong Kong and mainland China gamers clash on GTA V. *BBCnews.com.* Retrieved from: https://www.bbc.com/news/technology-50894769.

18. BBCnews. (April 13, 2020). Animal Crossing removed from sale in China amid Hong Kong protests. *BBCnews.com*. Retrieved from: https://www.bbc.com/news/technology-52269671.
19. Wm. Moyer, J. (September 22, 2020). An around-the-clock virtual protest lifts voices of those unable to take to the streets. *The Washington Post*. Retrieved from: https://www.washingtonpost.com/lifestyle/2020/09/22/public-public-address/.
20. Manch, L., (July 6, 2020). Black Lives Matter Virtual Protest: 22,000 People Join Online. *Londonist.com*. Retrieved from: https://londonist.com/london/politics/black-lives-matter-virtual-protest-22-000-people-join-online.
21. Morozov, E. (December 9, 2010). Virtual vs. Real Protests. *The New York Times*. Retrieved from: https://www.nytimes.com/roomfordebate/2010/09/29/can-twitter-lead-people-to-the-streets/virtual-vs-real-protests.
22. Thompson, D. (September 5, 2019). Elite Failure Has Brought Americans to the Edge of an Existential Crisis. *The Atlantic*. Retrieved from: https://www.theatlantic.com/ideas/archive/2019/09/america-without-family-god-or-patriotism/597382/.
23. Pew Social Trends. (2014). Millennials in Adulthood: Detached from Institutions, Networked with Friends. *PewSocialTrends.org*. Retrieved from: https://www.pewsocialtrends.org/2014/03/07/millennials-in-adulthood/.
24. Fritscher, L., (May 15, 2020). Understanding the Collective Unconscious. Verywellmind.com. Retrieved from: https://www.verywellmind.com/what-is-the-collective-unconscious-2671571.
25. Castells, M. (2012) *Networks of Outrage and Hope*. Cambridge: UK. Polity Press.
26. Rogers, R. (2015). *Digital Methods for Web Research*. Wiley Online Library. https://doi.org/10.1002/9781118900772.etrds0076.

Index

A

Accessibility, xi, 174, 179–208
Actor Network Theory (ANT), 12, 52–53, 57, 70
#ADAPTandResist, 196, 197
AI, *see* Artificial intelligence
Algorithms, xi, xii, 3, 19, 45, 55, 61, 96, 144, 146–148, 152, 157–160, 167, 173, 174, 179–182, 184–186, 190, 207, 216–217, 219
Amplification, xiii, 18, 25, 52, 53, 55, 85–86, 94, 111, 117–120, 123, 138, 219
Anti-austerity movement, 107
Anti-establishment movement, 107
Anti-European Union movement, 107
Anti-Eurozone movement, 107
Anti-government movement, 107
Anti-immigration movement, 107
Anti-Islam movement, 107
Anti-mask League of San Francisco, 113
Anti-mask movement, 111–113, 137
Anti-vaccine movement, 108, 112, 127, 128, 218
Arab Spring, vi, 4, 9, 16, 17, 25, 54, 152, 225
Artificial intelligence (AI), xi, xii, 144, 147, 148, 160, 161, 173, 179, 180, 182, 183, 185, 189, 207
Audiences, v, ix, xii, xiii, 2, 10, 16, 17, 20, 22, 23, 29, 34, 44, 47, 54, 60, 77, 78, 83–85, 92, 114–116, 120–122, 126, 150, 151, 153, 193, 214, 215
  diffused, 20, 21, 53, 114, 150, 152
Authenticating self, 19, 77, 82, 85, 86
Authenticity, 4, 19, 82, 193

B

Black Lives Matter, vi, xi, 1, 48, 85, 119, 155–158, 161, 167, 172, 173, 191, 211, 223, 227, 230, 233

N. Alperstein, *Performing Media Activism in the Digital Age*,
https://doi.org/10.1007/978-3-030-73804-4

C

Celebrities–bonafide, x, 76, 81, 83–85, 100, 113, 193
Centrality, 23, 42, 55, 57, 70, 96–98, 134, 171, 200, 232
Centralization, 55, 97, 199, 205
Clicktivism, 2, 3, 33
#ClimateStrike, vii, 9, 56, 70, 76, 85, 87, 90, 153
Cloud ethics, 181, 184–185, 190, 207
Cloud protesting, 152–154, 157, 173, 185–186, 207
Clusters, vi, viii, ix, 2, 4, 23, 30, 32, 34, 42, 45, 48–51, 56, 57, 65–67, 69, 84, 89, 94, 96, 98–100, 109, 121–123, 133–135, 153, 169–173, 192, 193, 195, 197, 198, 200–203, 205, 206, 213, 214, 225
Collective action, 6, 10, 11, 27, 33, 84, 123, 125, 126, 149, 185, 186, 220, 227–228
Collective consciousness, 10, 33, 34, 45, 49, 213, 227–228
Communalytic, xii, 129–133, 138, 230, 231
Communities, vi–ix, xi, 2, 21, 25–27, 30, 32, 34, 41–45, 48–50, 54–56, 58, 65, 67, 70, 79, 94, 97, 109, 111, 113, 117, 120, 127–130, 134, 135, 137, 138, 143, 147, 149, 151, 153, 161, 165, 169, 170, 183, 185, 187, 189, 192–194, 197–199, 203, 205, 225, 230, 232
  virtual, x, 42–45, 70
Connective action, viii, ix, 2, 10, 11, 16, 20, 23, 27, 33, 34, 126, 223, 227–228
Connectivity, 12, 24, 30, 77, 84, 200, 212, 216, 226, 227, 229
Contentious politics, x, 20, 101, 106, 108–109, 126, 128, 137
Context collapse, 44, 76–77, 80, 120–123, 138
Counter-surveillance, 183
CrowdTangle, 90, 97, 196, 230, 231
Cyberconflict theory, ix, 2, 9–13, 30, 33, 109, 212, 227

D

Data activism, xi, 138, 143–174
Datafication, xi, xii, 144, 159, 173, 220
Data inequities, xi, 144, 149–150, 173
Data resistance, 144
Density, 55, 56, 97, 171, 193, 199, 200, 204, 232
Digital activism, 3, 9, 10, 53, 84, 109, 119, 120, 135, 137, 138, 150, 153, 218, 220, 224
Digital ethics, 147, 180, 181
Digital media, vi, vii, ix–xi, xiii, 1–4, 10, 12, 15–18, 20, 21, 23, 25, 28, 31–34, 41–43, 52–54, 76, 82, 83, 114, 117, 126, 127, 149–151, 154, 155, 161, 164, 179, 211–213, 217–219, 225, 228
Digital platforms, vi–viii, xiii, 2, 4, 13, 24, 26, 33, 53, 70, 84, 154, 186, 227, 229
Disability rights, xi, 197–204
Disinformation, 18, 123, 150, 151, 217, 218

E

#ENDSARS, 156
Engineering of consent, ix, 2, 15, 25, 33
Ethics–AI, 182, 183
Ethics of engagement, 187–188

F

Facebook, vii, ix, x, 5, 20, 21, 24, 25, 27, 32, 41, 44, 47, 48, 53, 87, 90–97, 114, 116, 117, 121, 122, 124, 128, 145, 149, 151, 153–155, 159, 162, 191, 196–198, 200, 208, 212, 214, 216, 217, 222, 229–231
Facial recognition, 143, 144, 147, 159, 161, 179, 180, 185, 207
Ferguson, Missouri, 1, 18, 19, 154
Floyd, George, vi, 111, 119, 138, 155, 157, 161–168, 170, 172, 173, 183, 223, 229, 232
#Fridays4Future, 24, 28, 87

G

Gab, 116, 208, 213, 214
General Data Protection Regulation (GDPR), xi, 159, 181, 182, 216
GenZ, xii, 219, 220, 226
Gephi, xii, 97, 133, 192, 193, 196, 230–232
Gilet jaunes, 145
Google Books nGram, 233
Google Trends, 115, 154, 230, 233

H

Hashtag activism, 149, 154–157
Homophily, 79, 121, 195
Hubs, 53, 96, 199, 202, 203, 213, 214, 226
Hybrid media activism, 3

I

Imagined communities, 2, 21–22, 42, 70
Inclusiveness, xi, 150, 174, 179–208
In-degree, 23, 46, 51, 55, 57, 96, 97
Influencers, x, 35, 42, 45, 51, 55, 70, 75–101, 110, 111, 113, 114, 118, 120, 122, 137, 151, 156, 193, 195, 200, 203, 204, 206, 213, 224–226
Influencers–disability, 192–196, 203–206
Infodemic, 18, 19, 217
Instagram, ix, 5, 41, 47, 48, 82, 83, 85, 113, 114, 117, 196, 221, 223, 225, 230, 231
Institutions, xii, 8, 9, 28, 108, 149, 150, 191, 219, 220, 226, 228
Institutions–distrust, xii, 219, 226

L

Lincoln Project, 108

M

Machine learning, xi, 144, 146–148, 162, 173, 179–182, 184, 185, 190, 207
Mainstream media, xiii, 2, 3, 14, 31, 34, 52, 53, 57, 82, 85, 88, 151, 153, 158, 164, 194, 222
March for Our Lives, ix, x, 7, 41, 42, 55–58, 60, 108, 219, 220, 226, 229, 230
Marjory Stoneman Douglas High School, 7, 57, 220
Media activism, vii, xiii, 3, 15, 23, 27, 75, 84, 211–213, 221, 223, 227, 229
Media Cloud, 87, 88, 98, 100, 161, 162, 230, 232
Media ecosystem, xiii, 161, 213, 216, 232
Mediated networks, viii, 1–35, 174, 179–208

Mediators, vii–x, 4, 10, 12, 17, 18, 23, 28, 30, 34, 42, 45, 48, 52–55, 57–61, 65–67, 69, 70, 75–101, 110, 112, 113, 149, 150, 164, 173
#MeToo, xiii, 9, 22
MeWe, 116, 208, 214
Microcelebrities, x, 70, 76, 81–83, 87, 90, 97, 100, 121, 193, 225
Micro-influencer, 83
Millennials, xii, 219, 220, 226
Misinformation, 18, 110, 122, 123, 127, 128, 138, 150, 151, 217–220, 226
Modularity, 42, 56, 65, 67, 97, 134, 165, 170, 171, 193, 197, 199, 200, 205, 232
Moveon.org, 1, 4, 24, 33
Multi-step flow, x, 70, 76

N
Netlytic, xii, 48, 58, 61, 65, 165, 167, 169, 198–200, 203, 205, 230
Networked individualism, 8, 26–29
Networked social movements, ix, 41, 42, 227
Network structures, 48–51, 134, 161, 199
#NeverAgain, vii, 7, 9, 16, 28, 42, 54–70, 220, 230
New Jim Code, 160, 173
New Social Movement Theory, 8–9, 34
Niches, vi, viii, ix, 2, 4, 30, 32, 34, 42, 45, 48, 51, 56, 69, 83, 214, 221
Norms
  descriptive, 109–111, 116, 137, 153
  injunctive, 109, 110, 116, 137, 153

O
Occupy Wall Street, 1, 4, 22, 25, 27, 189, 190
Opinion leader, 76–79, 84, 96, 110, 112, 200, 225
Opinion leadership, x, 70, 76–79
Out-degree, 46, 51, 55, 56, 97, 193, 200

P
Parler, 117, 208, 213, 214
Participatory culture, 17, 20, 22–24, 222
Performance, vii, viii, xiii, 3, 17–20, 33, 47, 77, 82–85, 114, 115, 122, 137, 153, 180, 185, 186, 211–213, 218, 228
Performative, xii, xiii, 3, 18, 19, 27, 47, 75, 77, 115–117, 119–122, 213
  activism, 84–85, 218
Performing, vi–viii, xiii, 1–35, 52, 85, 108, 109, 114–117, 119, 135, 138, 146, 153, 161, 180, 191, 211, 213, 223
Performing media activism, vii, x, xii, xiii, 4, 44, 45, 52–53, 81–83, 109, 117, 126, 208, 211–233
Planatir, 146
Platformitization, 157–160
Pluralistic ignorance, 111
Populism
  common man movement, 105
  plutocratic, 105
Predictive analytics, 148
Privacy, xi, xii, 10, 122, 143, 144, 159, 174, 179–208, 216, 220, 229
Publics, vii, ix, xi, 2, 4, 7, 8, 10, 12–16, 19, 20, 23, 27, 29–34, 47, 53, 54, 65, 67, 81, 84, 87,

90, 96, 99, 100, 121, 123, 129, 146, 149, 150, 156, 157, 159, 161, 165, 172, 179–182, 185, 189, 190, 193, 196, 215, 216, 223, 230, 231

Q

QAnon, 110, 114–118, 137, 218

R

Reciprocity, 56, 65–67, 97, 171, 188, 200, 204
Reddit, vii, viii, 5, 17, 31, 47, 87, 101, 108, 117, 127–130, 133, 135, 138, 223, 229, 230
Rumble, 208, 213, 214

S

Sentiment analysis, 32, 56, 58, 167, 229
Situational theory, ix, 2, 23, 29–33
Slacktivism, xii, 3, 28, 33, 220
Social actors, 21, 46, 53, 70, 94, 96, 186
Social capital, x, 24, 26, 42, 45, 51, 70, 76, 79, 85, 94, 96, 110
Social comparison theory, 110, 137
Social justice, vii, xi, 18, 23, 47, 80, 138, 143–174, 211, 218, 221
Social media platforms, v, vii, viii, x, 3, 4, 10–13, 16, 20, 21, 26, 42, 48, 70, 84–87, 110, 116, 119, 122, 127, 128, 157, 158, 164, 180, 191, 207, 208, 212, 214–216, 228–230
Social movements, v–xii, 1–13, 15–18, 20–28, 30, 32–35, 41–70, 75–101, 105–138, 144, 147, 149, 150, 152–154, 157, 158, 160, 172–174, 179–208, 211, 213–220, 222–230, 233
  four stages, xii, 2, 5–7, 30, 219
Social network, vii–x, xii, 4, 10–12, 16–20, 22, 23, 26–28, 30, 32–34, 41–70, 76, 79, 82–84, 87, 89, 90, 92, 94, 96–100, 109–111, 120–123, 133, 135–137, 149, 152, 161, 164–169, 171–173, 193, 197–201, 205, 208, 212–214, 219, 225–231
Social network analysis (SNA), vii, viii, x, xii, 10, 34, 42, 45, 47, 48, 53, 55, 96–100, 108, 127, 133–138, 173, 211, 228–233
Socio-centered approach, 49
Spectacle, xii, 15, 24, 25, 34, 53, 76, 80, 81, 83, 85, 86, 114, 118, 122, 136, 138, 161, 172, 213, 219
Spokes, 199, 202, 203, 213, 226
Spreadability, 16, 212, 226, 227
Stakeholder capitalism, 189, 190, 207
Stanford Cable TV News Analyzer, 106, 107, 230, 232
Strategic amplification, xiii, 53, 85, 117, 118, 121, 122
Strength of weak ties theory, 12, 54, 70, 79, 111
Surveillance capitalism, 144, 145

T

Techno-chauvinism, 147, 160
Telegram, 116, 214
Theory of normative social behavior (TNSB), 109–111, 114, 137
3.5 percent rule, 125–127, 217

Thunberg, Greta, x, xiii, 24, 25, 70, 76, 83, 86–92, 94, 98–100, 145, 153, 184, 220, 226, 232
TikTok, vii, 47, 109, 119, 126, 151, 158, 214, 221, 223
Torches of Freedom, viii, 2, 13–15, 24, 33
Twitch, 214, 223
Twitter, vii, ix, xii, 3, 5, 17, 20, 21, 32, 41, 42, 47–49, 56–58, 65, 87, 94, 114, 115, 117, 123, 124, 126, 128, 149, 151, 153, 155, 159, 165, 166, 173, 191, 198–206, 208, 212, 214, 216, 219, 220, 229, 230, 232

W

Web Content Accessibility Guidelines (WCAG), 191
WhatsApp, 29, 150, 214, 216
Women in AI Ethics, 183

Y

Yellow jacket movement (France), 27
YouTube, vii, viii, 5, 12, 47, 83, 87, 90, 112, 113, 115, 151, 153, 155, 191–196, 208, 221, 229–231, 233
YouTube Data Tools (YTDT), xii, 229, 231

The manufacturer's authorised representative in the EU is Springer Nature Customer Service Centre GmbH, Europaplatz 3, 69115 Heidelberg, Germany. If you have any concerns regarding our products, please contact ProductSafety@springernature.com

Printed and bound by CPI Group (UK) Ltd, Croydon, CR0 4YY

30/09/2026

02225456-0005